CHARACTER

CHARACTER

JOEL J. KUPPERMAN

New York   Oxford
OXFORD UNIVERSITY PRESS
1991

Oxford University Press

Oxford   New York   Toronto
Delhi   Bombay   Calcutta   Madras   Karachi
Petaling Jaya   Singapore   Hong Kong   Toyko
Nairobi   Dar es Salaam   Cape Town
Melbourne   Auckland

and associated companies in
Berlin   Ibadan

Copyright © 1991 by Joel J. Kupperman

First published in 1991 by Oxford University Press, Inc.,
200 Madison Avenue, New York, NY 10016

First issued as an Oxford University Press paperback, 1995

Oxford is a registered trademark of Oxford University Press

Library of Congress Cataloging-in-Publication Data
Kupperman, Joel.
Character / Joel J. Kupperman.
p. cm.   Includes bibliographical references and index.
ISBN 0–19–506870–X; 0–19–509651 (pbk)
1. Character.   2. Ethics.   I. Title.
BJ1521.K87   1991
170—dc20   90–26463

1 3 5 7 9 8 6 4 2

Printed in the United States of America
on acid-free paper

PREFACE

Politicians, preachers, and ordinary people speak often of character; psychologists study *personality,* used as a term of art with meanings close to *character*. Most ethical philosophers in the last two hundred years, on the other hand, have not had much to say about character. This book will be an attempt to understand character and to refocus ethical philosophy so that character is taken as central.

Character approximates what a person is, so that there are respects in which an ethics that centers on character will be less impersonal than one that does not. An ethics of character also must take account of the ways in which projects and decisions are integrated through time. One running quarrel in the book is with what is called the snapshot view of ethical decision. Another is with virtue-ethics, the nearest rival of what is proposed.

My topic is in one respect highly specific, in that the entire book centers on one concept, and also highly general, in that we must explore how all of ethics looks different when character is taken seriously. Throughout this work I have been very conscious that the issues considered are of great importance to thoughtful people, whether they have been trained in philosophy or not. If philosophy is not to be an arcane discipline confined to academic circles, books on subjects such as these should be accessible to readers who are not teachers or students of philosophy. With this in mind, I have tried to keep the main line of argument as clear and untechnical as possible; references are concise and parenthetical within the text. At a dozen points at which it seemed helpful to examine the structure of the argument or to pursue its intricacies in ways that might seem too technical for nonspecialists, I have done this in notes at the end of chapters. This is all a matter of meeting the intelligent nonspecialist reader halfway, but such a reader may find that she or he also must meet the book halfway. There has been no attempt to make the issues simpler or solutions more catchy than they can possibly be.

This book is indebted to more philosophers than I can mention, including those whose work influenced me, many from whom I learned in discussion, and some who read portions of this manuscript at an early stage. Diana Meyers, Lynn Paine, and Philip Pettit should be thanked under all three headings. Reuben Baron, Celia Kitzinger, Jim Russell, and Nigel Walker were kind enough to orient me in portions of the psychological literature. An anonymous reader for Oxford University Press and Cynthia Read as editor made suggestions which were valuable in preparing the final version.

My serious thought about the concept of character began in the spring and summer of 1985 while I was a visiting fellow at Corpus Christi College, Oxford; I wish to thank the president and the fellows for their hospitality. The first draft of the manuscript was largely written during the latter part of 1988, first in the admirable working conditions afforded to a fellow in residence at the Rockefeller Foundation's Study Center at Bellagio, Italy, and then during a term as visiting fellow at Clare Hall, Cambridge. I wish to thank the Rockefeller Foundation and the president and fellows of Clare Hall for their hospitality.

Storrs, Conn.　　　　　　　　　　　　　　　　　　　　　　　J. J. K.
December 1990

CONTENTS

I

CHARACTER IN HUMAN LIFE

1

What Is Character?

The theses of this book are that character is of central importance to ethics and that ethical philosophy will have to be restructured once this is understood. This will require a complicated series of arguments, and the story of what character is will also not be simple. It may be helpful, therefore, to begin as close as possible to the level of unreflective common sense. We may begin by looking at the origin and ordinary use of the word *character* and of the word that is most easily confused with it, *personality*.

The *Oxford English Dictionary* (*OED*) derives *character* from the Greek for an "instrument for marking and graving, impress, stamp, distinctive mark, distinctive nature." The first literal sense is "a distinctive mark impressed, engraved, or otherwise formed." In Samuel Johnson's *Dictionary* the first meaning is "a mark; a stamp; a representation."

We may pause here, even though we have not reached the senses of *character* that will be the central concern of this book. These come later: The eleventh meaning in the *OED,* second edition, is "the sum of the moral and mental qualities which distinguish an individual or a race"; and the seventh meaning in Johnson's *Dictionary* is "personal qualities; particular constitution of the mind." The origin and literal meanings of *character,* however, are suggestive and help to shed light on what may be subtly implicit in the later, originally figurative and ethically important, meanings.

Suppose that we think of character as lines engraved in a surface as a metaphor for character in the ethically relevant sense. This suggests that character involves habits and tendencies of thought and action that are not, or at least need not have been, original to a person.

The image suggested is that of a mind, which may have been blank at birth (John Locke's tabula rasa) or may have had the beginnings of character engraved in it, but which in any case becomes incised with a developed character. Suppose the owner of this mind were to ask: "Who am I?" Would the answer consist of the mind that originally (on a view like Locke's) had no character at all and was as like another mind as two blank tablets in the tablet storeroom? Or, would it consist of the developed character that arguably can change in ways that seemingly have no limit?

Neither answer is entirely comfortable. The difficulties multiply if we consider aspects of our psychic life that seemingly are no part of character and do not stem from character. Recall Wolfgang Amadeus Mozart's famous remark about his musical ideas: "Whence and how do they come? I do not know and I have nothing to do with it." What springs into our heads may not be as illustrious as what popped into Mozart's, and it may be wildly variable. Harry Frankfurt has remarked, "A person is no more to be identified with everything that goes on in his mind . . . than he is to be identified with everything that goes on in his body" (1976, pp. 240–42). But if identifying oneself with stray and uncharacteristic thoughts seems foolish, as Frankfurt suggests, to treat them as totally separate from oneself would smack of schizophrenia. These issues of identity will be pursued in chapters 2 and 3.

Let us return to the metaphor of character as lines engraved in something like a tablet. One of the ways in which this is suggestive is as follows: When a surface with lines cut in it comes into contact with material outside of itself (e.g., sand or water), this material will tend to follow the paths engraved into the surface, although this may be a likelihood and not a certainty. In a comparable way someone's character may be the engraving of ways of thinking and acting which have become predictable but which do not preclude a person's acting out of character. If someone acts out of character, there still may be a cause of this behavior within her or his character, that is, the character may be such that certain forms of behavior that are uncharacteristic of that person become less unlikely in circumstances X, Y, and Z. David Hume suggests that we do not hold people responsible for acts which are uncaused by their characters (1739, p. 411).

How predictable do our characters make us? This is related to issues of freedom and determinism. Determinism is the view that our thoughts and actions could be predicted with entire certainty by someone who knew enough about us and the state of the world at present and who also knew the laws of the universe (including psychological laws). This position is sometimes confused with fatalism, the view that certain things will happen to us or will be done by us whatever we happen to want. But it has been pointed out that if determinism is true, one of the major causes of our thoughts and actions is our own character. Determinism, thus, does not conflict with the evident truth that we can have considerable control over our lives (see Dennett 1985, chap. 3). This, of course, does not show that determinism is correct, merely that it is not counterintuitive in a way that some people have supposed. We will have more to say in chapter 3 about the role of character in the causation and predictability of our thoughts and actions.

The word *personality* is sometimes treated as interchangeable with *character,* although its connotations are often very different. Anthony Quinton has suggested that we tend to speak of personality when our concern is with how a person presents herself or himself to the world (1982, pp. 21–26). One might be tempted to contrast character to personality as the inner to the outer, as what a person really is to her or his self-presentation. But to view the two words as simply, in a variety of contexts, fitting the pattern of this contrast would be as oversimple as to view them as generally interchangeable. In some contexts, it should be said, the words are virtually interchangeable. The subject of personality theory in psychology comes very close to what is normally meant by character, including as it does a person's characteristic ways of thinking and acting. One might wonder, indeed, why psychologists had not chosen to speak of character theory. Part of the answer, surely, is that the word *character* has moral overtones the word *personality* lacks. We will come to these shortly.

The second meaning of *personality* given in the *OED,* 2nd edition, is "that quality or assemblage of qualities which makes a person what he is, as distinct from other persons." The emphasis is on distinctiveness, although the first use in this sense that is listed, from 1795, seems to involve the idea of control of self-presentation: "A French girl of sixteen, if she has but a little personality, is a Machiavel." Personality, according to Dr. Johnson, is "the existence or individuality of any one." The one passage cited is from John Locke's discussion of personal identity.

Personality, then, in at least some of its uses, has to do with how one is different from other people, or (as Quinton's remarks would suggest) how one establishes oneself as different from other people. In a small group in which there are some (friends or psychologists) who take the trouble to know one well, personality verges on character. In a very large group or in mass society, in which it is not so easy to establish oneself as different from other people, personality can stand for little more than distinctive mannerisms or social gestures. At the extreme of this spectrum one might think of the show business personality.

There are uses of the word *character,* also, that have to do with distinctiveness and its public exhibition. Think of expressions such as "She's a character." There is a suggestion here of a distinctiveness that is very noticeable. It may be, too, that there is a theatrical association, that to be a character is like being a character in a play. One might think that any of us is like what could be a character in a play, but this is to ignore the conventions that make theater so different from the reality it mimes. The playwright and the actor have to create a strong sense of character by means of only a small number of words and gestures, so that the medium lends itself to characters of a few lines strongly etched rather than to characters that are far more intricate and less strongly etched. Even a great playwright such as William Shakespeare cannot deviate entirely from this: think of minor characters such as the nurse in *Romeo and Juliet* and Justice Shallow in *The Merry Wives of Windsor.* To be like a character in a play, thus, is usually to have a small number of distinctive and readily noticeable characteristics.

In some of its uses, however, the word *character* is less concerned with distinctiveness and individuality than the word *personality.* The differences between the two look most sharp when we consider contexts in which we speak negatively. To say that someone has a bad character has a clear and familiar meaning, whereas to say "bad personality" would normally be considered a misuse of language or a category mistake. We do often speak of someone as having no personality. This might be interpreted as attributing a lack of distinctiveness, as suggesting that the person in question is to a number of others as peas in a pod. People, however, who are exceptionally morose or taciturn are spoken of as having no personality if they are morose or taciturn in a way that is not interesting. Here, no personality means something like no charm. If personality is, in many contexts, a projection of oneself into other people's consciousness in a distinctive and possibly appealing way, then any failure to project can count as no personality.

What is it to have no character? This might conjure up the image of a mental tablet still largely blank after many years. Perhaps a better image would be of a tablet in which a large number of lines are engraved in such a way that none is deeper and more prominent than the others. Sand or water poured on such a tablet could go every which way.

The central idea seems to be something like this: All of us will find ourselves repeatedly placed in situations that we cannot entirely control and acted upon by forces that we cannot control. Character has a vital role in how we act. That is, to have a character is to act in such a way that the person one is plays a major role in any explanation of one's behavior. To have no character is to act in such a way that one's behavior might be viewed as (at least approximately) the product of forces acting on one. Thus, the person who always yields to temptation quickly, without a struggle, would be spoken of as having no character, as would the extreme conformist who always does what is expected of him or her.

To have no character, therefore, is to be morally unreliable, a state not as bad as being wicked. The wicked can be relied on in a negative way. It is sometimes observed that true wickedness is much rarer than many people would like to think: There are so few people we can really count on to behave badly in a variety of circumstances. People with no (or very little) character, on the other hand, may be quite common, as the notorious Stanley Milgram experiments (discussed in app. A) as well as studies of life in various dictatorships and in a simulated prison indicate (see Milgram 1974; Zimbardo 1973).

Plainly, it is the moral overtones of the word *character* that make it of such great interest to ethical philosophers and to practitioners of moral education. If *character*, in most of its uses, has to do with the ways in which we most commonly tend to think and act, then the thoughts and actions that are related to moral choice loom the largest. A person's habit of stuttering or of wearing unusually bright-colored clothes might have, at most, a marginal place in an account of that person's character; but his or her tendency to break promises or, conversely, to help people who badly need help would play a much larger role.

It would be a mistake to link the concept of character too closely to morality. For one thing, there are other kinds of choice that we make that greatly affect other people's, or our own, happiness; and these also loom large in our account of someone's character. We tend to exclude from the realm of morality subtle patterns in human relationships that do much to affect the happiness of friends and loved ones: even a controllable tendency to make family members feel depressed and unhappy with themselves is not commonly judged to be immoral, although it may be severely criticized in other ways. Such a pattern of behavior would certainly loom large in an account of someone's character. We also tend to exclude from the realm of morality most of the thought and action that primarily affects our own happiness. A tendency to rebound or not to rebound from failure, for example, is not normally judged as morally virtuous or the reverse. Yet something of this sort can play a major role in our account of a character. The frequently made claim that adversity builds character, for instance, does not have as its primary meaning that adversity makes people more moral.

Part of the point here is that what we praise and admire in someone's character often will include a broader range of excellences than those that would commonly be placed within the domain of morality; conversely, what we condemn and scorn can include unattractive qualities that would have no direct connection with what we would consider morally wrong behavior. Someone can be a weak and depressing oaf without ever behaving immorally. To realize this is to see how specialized and narrowly focused morality is in relation to the variety of evaluative judgments of people we take seriously (for an extended discussion of this point, see Kupperman 1983, chap. 1).[1]

Nevertheless, there is no doubt that we take morality especially seriously. No one would be spoken of as having a good character who did not, on the whole, make moral choices in a way that we considered correct. The divergence between character and personality looks sharpest when the word *good* is introduced. Occasionally, people are spoken of as having a good personality; usually this means something like the claim that they are charming. Attila the Hun may have had a good personality for all one knows, although this is not recorded. We know, however, that his character was not good: Cruelty and destructiveness count very heavily in that department.

To have a good character suggests the presence of virtues and the absence of major vices. An ambiguity in the word *virtues* needs to be noted. Usually virtues refer to good moral qualities such as being truthful or habitually refusing to steal, torture, commit murder, and so on. But, as we have already seen, morality concerns a narrow subset of our other-regarding choices. The boundary between moral and nonmoral choices or between moral good qualities and good qualities of other sorts is not at all sharp. Is being considerate a good moral quality? The most usual ways of being inconsiderate do not involve anything that we would judge to be morally wrong, and this might incline us not to classify considerateness as a moral virtue; but all the same, it is a virtue. We might be inclined also to speak of strength and self-reliance as virtues, even if they would not normally be classified as good *moral* qualities. They certainly matter to our assessment of someone's character, as does considerateness. But if Attila the Hun turns out to have been considerate of those close to him (as good leaders often are) as well as strong and self-reliant, this would not lead us to judge that he had a good character. Nonmoral virtues, if we are willing to speak of such, count in the assessment of character; but moral virtues count most heavily.

From the point of view of someone who is moralistic, that is, a person who wishes to treat moral categories as broadly as possible and to give moral terms the most frequent possible use, character will appear to lie entirely within the domain of morality. The education of character, then, will seem coextensive with moral education, and to have a good character equivalent to being morally virtuous to a high degree. Most of us in the latter part of the twentieth century are not moralistic and, thus, will have a less simple and reductive view of what good character is. We still will have to investigate, though, the nature of the connection between character and the elements of morality. Is having a good character mainly the possession of acceptable moral principles? I will argue otherwise in chapter 4. A further question is this: To the extent that moral virtues count in our assessment of someone's character, can talk of character be replaced by talk of virtues? Part of the argument of chapter 5 will be that there are inherent inadequacies in an ethics of virtues that can be remedied by an ethics that centers on character.

One fact that suggests that we cannot simply identify character with an assortment of virtues and vices is this: Virtues and vices have an especially close link to performances. To ascribe a moral virtue to someone is to suggest (among other things) that she or he tends to perform very well on occasions of a certain sort; to have a vice is to tend to perform badly. One might have an image of the virtues and vices waiting, inert, for the appropriate test of their presence to come up. Now we certainly do speak in much the same way of tests of character. But the role we ascribe to character in a person's life extends well beyond performance on tests. Character has much to do, we might say, with the particularity of a person's life, with making it the possibly distinctive life of *this* person. This suggests a more continuous and less impersonal role for character than that of, say, the virtue of being honest. What matters in the virtue of honesty will be pretty much shared by all honest people, and its importance will be largely limited to those special moments when we are offered a chance to be dishonest. What matters in your character may well be important continuously, as shaping your life and the way you experience it, and it also will set you apart from at least some other people of good character.[2]

One way in which the active, continuous, and particularizing role of character manifests itself is in a person's responsibilities. When morality is cast in the impersonal mold of adherence to a set of valid rules, it is easy to think of responsibilities as shared, at least latently, by everyone (although, if a man is drowning and should be saved, one of us may be much closer to him, etc.). Many of our responsibilities, though, are ones we take on. The responsibility to save a life when we can is hardly one that we could have declined or avoided, that for the well-being of this particular child has a slightly different character as does that for the business health of the Acme Bolt Company and its fifty employees or that to do one's best to see that the local Democratic party does not do too badly in next Tuesday's elections.

These responsibilities can be continuous. Drowning men pop up only once in a while; in between, one can have a nice swim with no worries. It may be that there is no time when one could not be doing something for a child or the well-being of the Acme Bolt Company or the local Democratic party; although a wise person will not be overindustrious. (The child may not like it or may fail to develop the proper independence; and in both business and politics, excessive activity can be counterproductive and can degenerate into fussiness.) The point in any case is that the responsibilities one takes on may well engage one's life more deeply (and reveal character more thoroughly) than will the responsibilities embodied in traditional moral laws, which (it may seem) can be fulfilled with less thought and attentiveness.

In the light of what has just been said, it might be tempting to equate having a character with having projects and categorical desires, as Bernard Williams seems to suggest (1976, p. 210). Are someone's projects and categorical desires a large part of her or his character? They certainly reveal character; nevertheless, our ordinary conception of character is independent of *what* someone's projects and commitments (apart from specifically moral commitments) happen to be. If Bludgeon, who has been a dogmatic and unreflective Communist, suddenly becomes a dogmatic and unreflective extreme right-wing conservative, we might well say that Bludgeon's character has not changed at all. If the next time we see O'Reilly she is married to a different man, this is not normally grounds for attributing a change of character. On the other hand, if Bludgeon or O'Reilly has a new policy with regard to taking other people's money, this counts as change of an element of character.

One possible source of confusion is this: There is a close connection between one's character and what one is (to be explored in chap. 2). On the other hand, virtually everyone goes about with a strong sense of who she or he is, which might be termed sense of self and which for most people includes, but also goes far beyond, what is contained in character. This is marked by the fact that many people when asked ''Who are you?'' will reply by mentioning their occupations and also by the fact of disorientation (a loss of a sense of place in the world) that many people experience as a result of divorce, expatriation, or retirement, which can lead to what some psychologists call an identity crisis. Someone's sense of who she or he is may include such matters as occupation, family connections, ethnic identity, nationality, and even aspects of physical appearance (see Rorty and Wong, forthcoming). If Bloggs, in an extreme case, takes on a new occupation, nationality, and political allegiances as well as acquires a new family and comes to look very different, we could, after observing him awhile, decide that his character had not changed. ''Same old Bloggs,'' we might say; ''He's the same person he was.'' But Bloggs's sense of self, as displayed in how he orients himself in the world and in his answers to questions like ''Who are you?'' might well have changed dramatically.

Williams's misleading view of the relation between projects and categorical desires, on the one hand, and character, on the other, may be connected with the notion that it is a loss of integrity if one has to abandon or suspend a commitment in order, say, to save lives. There are three grains of truth in this. One is that someone whose character is to take projects very seriously will not abandon them lightly. By definition a commitment is something that one does not abandon or suspend lightly. A second is that there are some projects or commitments that are so closely related to sense of self that to suspend or compromise them could be severely disorienting. The other grain is that there are certain specifically moral commitments which arguably can be embedded in someone's character so that they could not, and should not, be breached. We can hope that none of us would torture a child to death, whatever justifications might be offered. But it is worth bearing in mind that the moral commitment involved here has a special relation to character, which no nonmoral commitment can parallel. Integrity does not require that ordinary projects and commitments, however serious, be entrenched in the same way. Mark Halfron is surely correct when he points out that compromise of specifically moral commitments has a different relation to integrity than compromise of personal, social, economic, religious, or political commitments (Halfron 1989, pp. 61, 83–84; see also Williams in Smart and Williams 1973, pp. 116–17). Integrity is not at stake when someone is asked to abandon or suspend a commitment that is not a specifically moral one in order to attain something of moral urgency.

Whatever one's projects and commitments are (apart from specifically moral ones), they cannot be identified with character, but *how* someone maintains or fails to maintain commitments and responsibilities normally counts heavily toward character, as do the sorts of commitments and responsibilities someone takes on. Character also is displayed in the day-to-day quality of relationships with people to whom we have responsibilities or who have responsibilities to us. British and American ethical philosophers in this century have tended to focus on choices such as whether to break a promise when it is especially inconvenient to keep it or whether to kill an innocent man so that twenty others will be saved. The image is that the subject matter of ethics consists of dramatic choices under pressure which, fortunately, most of us do not have to make all that often; and the agent who makes these choices is presented in an impersonal role, in that essentially the same possibilities, with the same justificatory reasons, could occur for anyone else. If the concerns of ethics include, however, the development and evaluation of character, then its subject matter begins to look less impersonal as we examine how people take on and handle various kinds of responsibility—and what matters begins to look less intermittent in its display.

These topics will be examined in chapters 4, 5, and 7 of this book. Another way in which the concept of character takes on ethical significance will be looked at in chapter 6. Character can provide the threads that bind together the various episodes and commitments of a person's life. Thus, the topic of character is relevant not only to assessment of people's choices, but also to the values for which they should aim.

Recent ethical philosophy has fallen badly short in giving an account of values. The impersonality of the agent it presents is paralleled by the impersonality of the person who seeks and enjoys values, so that the good life becomes a matter of faceless consumers in search of preference-satisfaction. Because preferences have been treated as essentially isolated from one another, there has not been much serious treatment of how a lucky run of preference-satisfactions might add up to a good life. This is one topic on which nonphilosophers sometimes have shown more wisdom than philosophers by insisting that, apart from satisfactions, one might legitimately ask about the meaning of life. Meaning in this context implies structural connections, so that satisfactions and frustrations must be looked at in the context of a structure provided by a character that colors the incidents of life or by goals and commitments: It becomes easier, then, to see that the whole is not the sum of the parts. Character has a great deal to do with how we are prepared to maintain, modify, or abandon a structure of goals and commitments. In this respect, also, a close study of the topic of character changes the face of ethics.

The image of character that has emerged is that it is what a person is, especially in the areas of her or his life that concern major choices. Many of the contrasts between character and personality have to do with the difference between someone's nature and that person's self-presentation. Character has something to do with the particular quality of a person's life. The emphasis is not heavily on distinctiveness: One can have a strong character without being an especially distinctive person. But we normally assume that there will be at least subtle differences among characters; to describe someone's character is not to go down a checklist of qualities that that person either simply has or simply lacks.

It would be wrong to assume that the word *character* has a single, unified meaning in all of its uses. It also would be foolish not to assign it one for the purposes of the philosophical investigation that follows. The assigned meaning should capture features of important ordinary uses of the word and should help us grasp the implications and importance of these features.

A preliminary definition of *character* is:

> X's character is X's normal pattern of thought and action, especially in relation to matters affecting the happiness of others and of X, most especially in relation to moral choice.

This connects most of the dots found in common uses of *character* and mirrors these uses in assigning a special weight to what is related to the happiness of others or oneself and in giving greatest weight to what is related to moral choice. Some uses of *character,* such as "She's a character," are not subsumed; however, these drop out in any case when we come to speak of good character. It may be objected that if character is a normal pattern of thought and action, then it is hard to account for the frequently made judgment that many people have no character. Everyone, it will be said, has some characteristic pattern of thought and action. However, the phrase *no character* can be regarded as a hyperbolic way of saying that someone has a weak character, one that is not resistant to great pressures, temptations, difficulties, or to the insistent expectations of others. (As I think the Milgram experiments showed, insistent expectations can be a more difficult test of character than are direct pressures; most people like to do what is expected.) Our definition of strong character is:

> X has a strong character if and only if X's normal pattern of thought and action, especially in relation to matters affecting the happiness of others or of X (and most especially in relation to moral choices), is strongly resistant to pressures, temptations, difficulties, and to the insistent expectations of others.

Strength of character is independent of goodness of character, in that deeply wicked people have strong characters. Indeed, a strong character is required to be either extremely good or deeply wicked.

It is possible to have a strong character and yet to be fickle or unreliable in relation to what most people would have taken as serious commitments. Don Juan is the classic representation of this. However it is not possible to have what we would call a strong character and to have no ongoing concerns or commitments whatsoever. Don Juan's seriousness in maintaining his sole project is instructive in relation to this; many will think also of the monumental refusal to repent at the conclusion of Mozart's *Don Giovanni.* This tenacity is extreme, but it is not possible to have a strong character and to be in a state of readiness to abandon commitments or projects simply because of community pressure, difficulties, or other people's expectations. In this respect, there is a link between character, on one hand, and loyalty to commitments and projects on the other. I have already suggested that one can change commitments (other than specifically moral commitments) and projects without changing character, but someone of strong character will do this only for her or his own reasons; and if such a person has taken a commitment seriously, she or he will not change it lightly.

Two complications in the nature of character have not been clearly mirrored in the definitions just given. One is this: There are some traits of character that are part of a normal pattern of thought and action, in that they tend to show up predictably in appropriate circumstances. If, however, "normal pattern of thought and action" were taken to refer to what occurs repeatedly in everyday life, they might not be part of this picture. A good example is cruelty. It is unlikely that a cruel person will be cruel to most people in most circumstances: We call a man cruel if he predictably tends to be cruel in certain sorts of circumstances; and this can be the case even if these circumstances occur only rarely. In much the same way, a man can be dishonest if, given certain temptations of a standard sort, he will behave dishonestly; and this can be true even if these have not come his way for years. Because of this, "normal pattern of thought and action" should not be read merely as a summary of everyday thought and behavior but rather as an account of how someone normally tends to think and behave in various circumstances, some of them unusual ones that, however, we count heavily in our assessment of character. Another way to put this point is to say that character traits are propensities to behave in certain ways and that a person can have a propensity to behave in a certain way if given suitable opportunity, even if suitable opportunities hardly ever arise.

To qualify still further: Part of someone's character may be that in some unusual circumstances, certain kinds of behavior become not altogether unlikely for that person, although they would be for most people. Someone can be capable of great cruelty even if there is no specifiable situation in which it is more likely than not that that person will behave cruelly. Thus "*X*'s normal pattern of thought and action" should be taken as shorthand for what is normal, or at least not distinctly abnormal, for *X* in various circumstances, especially highly unusual circumstances that we might regard as moral test cases.

We also have not dwelt on a crucial aspect of character: the way in which it unifies a person's life through time. There is a sense in which, if it is true that newborn infants are not all alike, everyone has some degree of character even as a baby. But the normal patterns of thought and action of infants and small children are not highly developed and articulated. If we associate character with a certain degree of development, people typically have what we would unhesitatingly call characters only when they are past the years of early childhood. On the other hand, we normally assume that people do have developed characters by the time they are morally reflective adults, and at least from that point on, a person's character will provide some of the continuity in her or his life.

If X's character is X's normal pattern of thought and action (this being understood in the way just indicated), especially in relation to matters of importance, then there is an implication of stability. We are not looking for what is normal for X today or this month or while she is in this mood, but for what is normal for X, period. This is reflected in our concept of self-knowledge, which I have argued cannot be sharply separated from decisions about one's future (see Kupperman 1984–1985).

In fact, we do usually assume considerable stability in the characters of mature people. We assume that characters can change but that change is usually not at all rapid. Occasionally, we encounter someone whose character has been drastically transformed, and we say that so-and-so "hardly is the same person." It is tempting to say that remarks of this sort are not meant literally, except that it turns out to be exceptionally difficult to explain what a literal sense would be.

In any case, drastic changes are exceptions that prove the rule: The ways we hold people responsible for their actions and the ways in which we expect their lives to maintain some continuity are keyed to the assumption that people's characters normally are highly stable. A good example of a similar expectation about attitudes is to be found by examining the concept of sincerity. To be sincere has to be more than to speak and behave in accordance with one's thoughts and feelings of the moment. If the nature of someone's thoughts and feelings were in constant flux, then what he or she said and did might fit those of the present moment but be sharply at variance with those of the next day or the next week; we normally would not consider this sincerity. The concept implies that actions and words can accord with thoughts and feelings over a period of time; this implies a stability that parallels stability of character and may require some degree of strength of character.

If it is true that character normally is fairly stable and if it is true also that it is not easily changed, this presents great difficulties: both with regard to judgments of moral responsibility and with regard to the practice of moral education. If we hold someone responsible for an action that flows from his or her character, we might want to think that this character is itself the result of mature decision, an unwarranted assumption if virtually everyone comes to adult consciousness with a character that is very difficult to change. If character is formed along with, or somewhat in advance of, the ability for rational reflection, then moral education cannot merely be a series of rational appeals. It must affect the formation of character in children who are not yet in a position to go very far in making rational choices about the people they want to be.

The linkage through time that is implicit in what we call someone's character means that some thoughts and feelings will normally be taken to engage the person beyond the moment in which they occur. This aspect of character is captured if we speak of the kinds of concerns and commitments and the way in which these are taken on and treated as a large part of what we look at in assessing someone's character. Concerns and commitments provide temporal bridges. It is true that we speak sometimes of momentary feelings of concern; but, when we say "X is concerned about Y," the normal implication is that more than a momentary feeling is involved. Unless the situation involving Y has changed in some relevant respect, the fact that X is unconcerned about Y today counts against the claim that X was genuinely concerned yesterday. The word *commitment* has an even stronger implication of temporal continuity. If X has a commitment to a set of ideals or values, to a political cause, or to a person, this implies something not only about X's behavior today but also about what we can expect from X in the future. Concerns and commitments not only bridge the present and other parts of a person's life, but they also bridge thought and action. We normally would not speak of X as concerned with Y if X never thinks of Y, even when Y's success or security is at stake; on the other hand, we also would not speak of X as concerned with Y if X does nothing to protect or help Y when actions on X's part are needed. A similar point applies to commitments.

Accordingly, a definition of character that is somewhat more probing than the one previously given is:

> X's character is X's normal pattern of thought and action, especially with respect to concerns and commitments in matters affecting the happiness of others or of X, and most especially in relation to moral choices.

"Normal pattern," as explained earlier, is to be taken as shorthand for what is normal (or at least not distinctly abnormal) for X in various circumstances, especially including highly unusual circumstances that we might regard as moral test cases.

In what follows we will explore the role of character in a person's life and in ethics.

Notes

1. We should spell out the terminology of this book as regards morality and what lies beyond morality. Those choices, all or almost all of them other-regarding, which are such that a very poor choice would be commonly termed *immoral,* will be referred to as matters of morality or as moral choices. Similar terminology will be used in connection with the associated excellences of character, such as honesty. That a choice or excellence of character lies outside of morality or in a border area does not mean that it is not important. Ethical philosophy will be spoken of as the study of, or a study that can include, both moral and nonmoral choices and excellences.

The boundary between morality and the rest of life has been a major topic in modern Western philosophy, addressed in Immanuel Kant's distinction between the categorical imperative and hypothetical imperatives and in John Stuart Mill's distinction in chapter 5 of *Utilitarianism* between morality and simple expediency. Some philosophers either have not drawn a boundary (and hence not isolated a concept of morality) or have treated the boundary as relatively unimportant, insisting that there are both moral and nonmoral virtues. Arguably, ancient Greek and Chinese philosophers generally belong in this group, as does Hume.

The terminological distinctions outlined play a sporadic role in the exposition of this book, but the view that underlies them is not presupposed by any of the key arguments.

2. This is the beginning of a running argument that ethical philosophy should be restructured around the concept of character. As is often the case in philosophy, much will be directed against views that are close to, although distinct from, the one advanced. The closest rival of character-ethics is virtue-ethics; I wish to suggest the advantages of the former.

Virtue-ethics, however, should not be taken as monolithic. Our ordinary talk about virtues and vices is of excellences and deficiencies in relation to general standards and linked very closely to performances. Virtue-ethics based on this can be faulted as missing the continuous and particularizing role of character in life. However, there is a tradition of virtue-ethics, going back to both Plato and Aristotle, which conceives of virtues as character traits. Clearly virtue-ethics of this sort is much closer to character-ethics. My argument in chapter 5 will be that even this has deficiencies, in that, to the extent that virtue-talk lends itself to treating virtues in isolation from one another, it risks compartmentalization of what is ethically important. The thesis of the unity of the virtues has the effect of bringing virtue-ethics closer still to character-ethics; this, indeed, may be the strongest thing to be said in its favor. Some of the advantages of character-ethics over a crude and straightforward virtue-ethics linked to ordinary speech have already been pointed out. The advantages over subtle forms of virtue-ethics are a more complicated story, to be taken up in chapter 5.

2

Character and Self

To understand the importance of character in human life, we must appreciate who it is that has a character. The question suggests that underlying character there is a person, a definite individual, who in the process of growing up (and beyond) takes on a character. This picture, though, is both oversimple and possibly paradoxical. The possible paradox can be seen if a person asks, "What was I like before I was like anything?"

We might think of character as a second self or, alternatively, as a first self. In either case, we cannot avoid questions about the self. How does one know anything about it? These are exceptionally difficult and abstruse questions. They also are the questions in metaphysics that come closest to the surface of ordinary life. Any adequate account of the meaning of individual life must presuppose some account of, or assumptions about, what it is to be a definite individual; and this requires a view of the self.

A common experience of adolescence is to ask oneself who one is, apart from the highly contingent roles and relationships one has been born or thrust into. The question seems to imply that there is some definite or nearly definite nature within the person which can be discovered. Someone who discovers what it is will be better able to steer a course in life, knowing better what psychic resources are available and what is going to be most suitable or comfortable in relation to his or her nature. A picture that is something like this is involved when someone says, "I just want to be myself." This calls for a two-stage endeavor: introspection in order to find out the nature of one's self, and adaptation so that the circumstances of one's life can better match one's nature.

A view like this appears very common among people who have never studied philosophy. Very different views, however, have been common among philosophers. Many nowadays would regard "I just want to be myself" as literally nonsense: How could one fail to be oneself? If the adolescent expects that there is a definite, enduring nature within herself or himself, many philosophers would consider this a serious mistake. Hume is widely held to have shown, in Book 1 of his *A Treatise of Human Nature*, that there is no such thing. Early Buddhist philosophers in India had launched similar arguments two thousand years earlier in opposing the Hindu tradition that there was something (a self?) which could endure through a variety of reincarnations and which could be liberated from the wheel of life, death, and rebirth.

For the sake of simplicity, we can refer to what the ordinary person believes in as the Enduring Self and abbreviate this as ES. The view often attributed both to Hume and early Buddhist philosophers may be labeled the No Self view and abbreviated as NS. A third view is as follows: What happens when someone introspects for a self in order to organize her or his life is, typically, creation (or the endorsement and perhaps modification of what has been in the process of creation) rather than discovery. There is a self in the sense that each of us constructs one. (The possibility is left open in this view that many people have a bent, or a vocation, for the development of a certain kind of self.) We may call this view the Constructed Self view, and abbreviate it as CS. Something like CS was the view of Jean-Paul Sartre and has been attributed also to Hume by some commentators.

Anyone who has ever thought "I want to be myself" ought to be interested in the resolution of this philosophical debate. Plainly, if there is no self at all that one can be, it would save a lot of trouble and anxiety to know this. If there is a self, it would be helpful to know whether it was an enduring self, waiting to be discovered and understood, or whether what seemed an introspective effort was, in fact, to some degree creative.

The remainder of this chapter will offer a resolution of the metaphysical problem, but it will not be a simple resolution. Part of my thesis is that none of the three classic alternatives—ES, NS, and CS—gives a complete and adequate view as it stands. To sort out the truth about the self will be also to work out how it is that character functions (at least approximately) as the nature of a self and how it is also that one can maintain a sense that there is something like a self that underlies, and takes on, character.[1]

If we look first at the surface phenomena of self, two are especially striking. One is that a core of a sense of a self seems close to the surface of the experience of almost everyone. Virtually everyone, waking up suddenly in a strange environment, will know immediately who she or he is in the rudimentary respect of being able to supply the correct name. It has been suggested by some philosophers that this is not knowledge at all, in that knowledge is a form of success, which presupposes the possibility of failure, but that failure is impossible here because one cannot apply the word *I* to the wrong object. But if there is any merit at all to this suggestion, it is only in relation to cases in which the judgment is of here and now and does not involve either pointing or supplying a name. A person can identify the wrong body as *I* or think that he or she is Napoléon Bonaparte. Normally, however, we have little difficulty in this element of knowing who we are.

Related to this is the ability that almost everyone has to identify himself or herself very readily as the person who did or thought such and such. At first glance, it might appear that this takes place as a part of the memory of what various people did and thought (or said they thought) and that the only thing that is peculiar is that everyone remembers best what she or he did or thought, something that can be explained on the assumption that almost everyone is preoccupied with herself or himself most of the time. But the phenomenon is a little more subtle than this. As Sydney Shoemaker (1975) has pointed out, what one remembers strictly speaking is that someone did or thought *X*, and the judgment that one did or thought *X* requires the additional judgment of one's identity with the person who did or thought *X*, an identification which is not itself a matter of memory. If *S* has a clear awareness that he was the person who broke the front window yesterday rather than someone who was present but just watched, he does not need to appeal to criteria of identity to know that he was the person who broke the window. How does *S* know? It is tempting to say that he just knows. Whether this is an adequate answer or not, the fact remains that this is another instance in which people are in the position to make successfully judgments of the form, "It is (or was) I," in which the grounds of success are not readily analyzable.

A less precise but more suggestive way of indicating the general point is Hume's remark, "Ourself is always intimately present to us" (1739,

p. 320). Everyone has some rough idea of what this means and some inchoate inclination to agree. But if one looks for a precise explanation or for a precisely specifiable experience of a self, the results would seem to be very disappointing.

The second surface phenomenon is a remarkable plasticity in people's sense of what they could be. This is especially striking in the identifications that people are able to make while involved in works of imagination, such as films. People sometimes appear to experience the events of a film almost as if they were the protagonists. This must be qualified: One does not think of oneself as having the protagonist's name or every one of his or her characteristics, and people generally are much more likely to identify with a protagonist of their own sex than with one of the opposite sex. The identification, when it occurs, goes this far: One sees oneself as in the position of the man or woman who is experiencing such and such and who also is doing such and such. Insofar as people's actions are connected with their characters, this is a phenomenon of identifying with people whose characters are different from one's own. There are limits; a film about the life of Adolf Hitler is unlikely to produce many responses of this kind, although perhaps some might take this as a challenge to a skilful filmmaker. In any event, the limits are pretty far out. Someone who is very inhibited can be led to identify with a character who is sexually very uninhibited, and people who would never break even a minor law can be led to identify with a character who, under considerable pressure and in some confusion of mind, commits a murder. Something like this imaginative process occurs also in dreams. People dream of themselves doing extraordinary things. Insofar as actions reflect character, this is to dream of themselves as having drastically different characters. One way of interpreting these phenomena might be to speak of a self which underlies character, remains the same when character changes, and always could have a very different sort of character.

Certainly, we can imagine ourselves, without going to a film or falling asleep, as having very different lives and in the process being different people. Something like this lies behind the saying of the Roman playwright Terence, "Nothing human is alien to me," which was Karl Marx's favorite motto according to his daughter. To understand how circumstances shape human lives is to develop an acute sense of how, given different circumstances, one might have been a different person. Alternatively, one can accept this point as a result of a series of thought experiments without holding any views on the relation between circumstances and character. Geoffrey Madell has said:

> I can describe my present total psychological state, and include . . .
> what my personality traits are. . . . I can now begin to imagine my
> present psychological state . . . to be different in this or that re-
> spect. . . . Now it is very difficult indeed to see how there could be
> any limit to the degree of difference which is allowable."

Madell contends that it would be odd to suggest that psychological states that are different beyond a certain degree could not be one's own (1981, p. 18).

This must be qualified. It is true that we can imagine ourselves in psychological states that little resemble those we have had, but only if there are adequate continuities and causal connections between our present states and those states; normally, many of these continuities and connections are provided by the factor of memory. Any one of us could imagine becoming a bug, in the manner of Franz Kafka's "The Metamorphosis"; but if we imagine a bug that has no memory or trace of human psychology, the inclination to say, "That would no longer be I" is strong. In any event, the changes that we can imagine in what we are suggest the same disturbing question that began the chapter. Who or what is it that acquires a character and can imagine itself as having a different character?

The simplest way of viewing all of this is as follows. Everyone is born with a Self, which remains strictly self-identical throughout that person's life, in that, whatever character the person develops or however he or she changes, the Self remains itself. This might explain how it seems to make sense that one could be very different from what one is: The same Self might have a different character. It also might explain one's ready apprehension of elements of who one is and one's ready ability to know what one had thought or done. We somehow are (normally) in touch with, or have special access to, our Self.

Thus ES is the most natural view for someone who is just beginning to think about the self. Something like ES is suggested by Plato's remarks about the immortality of the soul and is (or may be) implicit in the doctrines of at least two major religions, Hinduism and Christianity. Only a view at least somewhat like ES could make sense of the notion, traditional in India, that a human being could be reincarnated as, say, a frog, and still in some sense remain the same. Given ES, one can readily imagine the Self continuing its self-identical existence in some separate realm after the death of the body. Doctrines of personal immortality do not strictly require ES, but it is easier and simpler to believe in personal immortality if one holds ES than if one does not.

If ES is intuitively plausible and accommodates the phenomena we have mentioned, then, why not accept it? There are two major difficulties. One is that it is very difficult to understand what the relation is supposed to be between the Self and the other elements of the person who has the Self, such as the character that changes and those reflective processes that include thinking about the Self. If you think about your Self, is what is thinking distinct from the Self it thinks about? If the answer is yes, this suggests a bizarre form of alienation in which one's conscious life is led by something other than one's Self. If the answer is no, then there is a problem in explaining how a Self can have coherent self-referential thoughts, linked to the problem of how the reflective Self that thinks about itself can change in various ways (becoming, say, more analytical or more intuitive or senile) while *ex hypothesi* (under ES) remaining the same.

The second major difficulty is epistemological. What we are aware of within ourselves is constantly changing or, at least, subject to change; if there is a constant enduring Self, this does not appear as an object of our ordinary introspective experience. (Something like this is part of the point Hume makes in Book 1 of his *Treatise*.) Unless there is some special way of getting at the enduring Self, we might wonder whether it is there at all. If someone claims that we do constantly have contact with our enduring Self (which is why we are so good at knowing who we are), then it needs to be explicated what this contact consists of and how it enables us to identify ourselves and our activities so readily.

Both of these difficulties are involved in making sense of any search for self. When Hume, in Book 1 of his *Treatise*, looked for and failed to find the enduring self of traditional metaphysics, the question naturally arose: What had been looking for (and failing to find) Hume's self? This might seem a point against the NS view, but there are difficulties at least as great for the ES view. Suppose that someone looks for her or his self, and claims to find it. Is what looks for the self here, in fact, part of the self that is looked for? It would seem very hard to deny this. But any subject–object relation, such as is involved when X thinks about Y or X looks for Y, involves a conceptual separation between what thinks or looks and what it thinks about or looks for; and it is hard to reconcile this separation with the supposition that the two entities are the same. This point would be made by some philosophers in terms of levels of discourse. However it is put, it contributes to what Gilbert Ryle spoke of as the "systematic elusiveness of 'I' " (1949, pp. 186–89).

One attempt to overcome the difficulty of imagining one's self in a subject–object relation with itself is to posit a different kind of relation, one embedded in a special kind of experience. It has sometimes been pointed out that, although reflective experience takes the subject–object form of X's thinking about (or looking for or wondering, doubting, or worrying about Y), we all have unreflective experiences that do not take this form. Our consciousness can take on various contents or qualities without any of this involving a duality between a pole of consciousness that presents itself as experiencing and another pole that presents itself as being experienced or reflected upon. Could we have unselfconscious experience of our Self?

There are two difficulties with this suggestion. One is that, in fact, in our unselfconscious moments we seem to be in touch with all manner of things except our self. On a sunny, pleasant day, when we are feeling entirely relaxed and not at all intellectual, if we are in contact with anything, it is the sun, the clouds, feelings of warmth, and so on. It is difficult to give a rendering of such experiences in which the self appears as an item.

The other difficulty is that even if someone were to have contact with her or his self in an unreflective way that did not involve a subject–object mode of awareness, it would seem by definition that this could not present itself as awareness *of* her or his self. Therefore, if someone is looking for evidence of a self or for information about it, this cannot present itself as an entirely unreflective mode of experience.

This second difficulty might not be insuperable if there were ways of moving back and forth between reflective and unreflective modes of thought, so that what occurred in unreflective experience could then be, as it were, transcribed and examined in a reflective mode. Something like this has been the strategy of some forms of mysticism. It is difficult to generalize about mysticism, which has emerged in different forms and with different presuppositions in a variety of religious and cultural traditions. But this much can be said: Many forms of mysticism have centered on the mystic's attempt to eliminate distractions (i.e., attention to aspects of the world that are thought of as unimportant) as well as all reflective thought in order to concentrate on contact with her or his true being or self. At the center of this kind of mysticism is meditation, which is a temporary state sandwiched in between experiences of more ordinary kinds. It would be a contradiction in terms to have a meditative experience and simultaneously to articulate it. Indeed, in some quarters, it is taken as self-evident that mystical experiences are ineffable. However, mystics do sometimes talk about their experiences—afterward. It would appear that there are mechanisms for recalling unreflective experiences and for articulating them in reflective terms.

Thus, if there is any evidence at all for ES, it might well come from meditative experience. A natural response to this could be to regard the metaphysical issue of the self as really, at bottom, experiential. David Hume should have meditated, it might be said. Contemporary doubters might be similarly advised.

There are two reasons why this response is not entirely satisfactory. One is that difficulties remain in the analysis of meditative experience, not to mention the analysis of the mechanism by which unreflective experience is supposed to be put in reflective terms. We may put this to the side, though, because of the seriousness of the second reason. Even if we concede to mysticism everything about meditative experience that mystics normally claim, it looks as if the view that results from this cannot be as strong as most people would want ES to be. If there is something that endures, it appears on examination to fall short of being what most people would want to think of as the self.

This is best seen in the context of classical Hindu philosophy. In the *Upanishads,* and in texts that are in the tradition formed by the *Upanishads,* meditation is supposed to peel away layers of personality, like the peeling of an onion. This might seem intuitively right as a guide to finding an enduring self: After all, how we think and behave can and does change, and we are looking for something that endures. But the image of the onion might give us pause. After all, what is left when all of the layers of the onion have been removed?

The Hindu spiritual search focuses on coming in contact with one's *atman,* thought of as the inner nature that remains when all of the layers have been peeled away. The central claim of Hinduism is that *atman* is identical to Brahman, the universe viewed pantheistically (somewhat in the manner of Baruch Spinoza) as divine. To say, of course, that your *atman* is identical to Brahman and that my *atman* is identical to Brahman implies that there is no real difference between your true inner nature and my true inner nature—or for that matter between either of our true inner natures and the true inner nature of any passing frog or (on the most obvious interpretation) any piece of furniture. The recurrent analogy in the Hindu literature is with drops of water in a spiritual ocean.

One of the puzzles that this philosophy presents is that of reconciling the rigorous pantheism of the theory with the many gods and goddesses of folk Hinduism as well as reconciling our identity with one another with the obvious individual differences that any spiritual teacher must take into account (not to mention the sharp caste distinctions that were so important in traditional Indian society). The solution to this puzzle is that the philosophy, in effect, claims that reality can be considered on two separate levels, each of which yields a different picture. Both pictures are true, although one is a deeper truth. There is some loose analogy with two-level views in Western philosophy, such as Kant's presentation of the distinction between noumenal and phenomenal reality or (a better analogy) the current tendency to think that an ordinary object such as a table both is entirely solid and at the same time (as modern physics tells us) is a largely empty space through which tiny particles move.

The puzzle about self that classical Hindu philosophy presents is this: If each of us has an *atman* that is identical with Brahman, in what sense does the endurance of this *atman* throughout a life, and beyond to a further life, represent the endurance of an individual self? Even though the natural translation of *atman* is self, we need not assume that the two terms are equivalent or that (given the doctrine of the *Upanishads*) what survives death is (in Western terms) an individual self. Consequently, it would be a mistake to identify the Hindu doctrine of *atman* at all closely with the views of Western philosophers, such as Bishop Butler and Thomas Reid in the eighteenth century who posited the existence of an enduring self. It also would be a mistake to render the early Buddhist doctrine of *anatman,* the denial that there is an *atman,* as simply the denial that there is an enduring self (in the Western philosophical sense), although that does look like part of the doctrine of *anatman.*

All of this suggests that, even if meditative experience does disclose something, this cannot be identified with a permanent individual self. Clearly, much depends on what one expects an enduring self to be. A strong assertion of one is found in the doctrine of the immortality of the soul central to most forms of Christianity. What lasts throughout a person's life, and into an immortal afterlife, is the same soul, even though the moral character and perhaps even the temperament of the person whose soul it is might change. Part of what makes the soul the same will be some underlying continuity in the psychological life of the person, a causal connectedness between earlier and later stages which carries with it resemblance of at least some of the particulars and also some degree of memory. The soul in heaven may well be purified in relation to what it was in the person's early life when sins were committed (which later, let us say, were repented); but that celestial soul will retain some individual characteristics and will retain some memories of its earlier state as well as attitudes toward that earlier state (regret, nostalgia, or whatever).

Examine in contrast the career, as it is seen in traditional Hinduism, of a human who, as a result of sinful behavior, is reincarnated as a frog. (For some discussion of reincarnation as an animal, see Karl Potter in O'Flaherty 1980.) It hardly seems part of the picture that this tadpole will remember its previous human life, let alone have attitudes of regret or nostalgia toward it. Indeed, one might ask, in what respects will the psychology of the young frog resemble that of the human being whose reincarnation it is? Perhaps there might be some broad similarities: eager, anxiety-prone humans who sin might be reincarnated as especially eager, nervous frogs? But this hardly amounts to much continuity.

If the *atman* of the frog, which of course is identical to Brahman, is in some sense the continuation of the *atman* of a now-dead human who has sinned, this must be true because of what underlies personality characteristics and the like; after all, the eagerness and nervousness of the human or of the frog are just outer layers around their *atman*. This suggests the following analogy: To die and to be reincarnated as a frog involves a process somewhat like that by which an audio or video tape on which something has been recorded then has something else recorded on it. The mind on which the character of Bloggs—sinful Bloggs as he was—had been inscribed then has inscribed on it the character of an eager, nervous frog.

Even if reincarnation were to move in a more favorable direction, this is hardly what most people would look forward to as immortality. Two questions should be separated. One is what the Hindu tradition sees as the continuity involved in reincarnation. Is it as abstract and tenuous as the story of Bloggs suggests? The other, which is more important to our investigation, concerns what *we* would count as survival, as continuing to be the same person.

Let me declare uncertainty about the first question. There is no reason to assume either that all Hindu views of the nature of reincarnation agree entirely or to assume that in the Hindu tradition the doctrine is worked out as precisely as doctrines central to a creed tend to be worked out in Christianity. Certainly, some Hindus have believed that in cases in which someone is reincarnated as a human being there can be faint memories. Even these views leave open the question of the sense in which the new person can be regarded as the *same* as the person who died. If X who is ten years old has thoughts that seem like memories of the life of Y, who died ten years ago, could these not be interpreted as being, as it were, thought-broadcasts from the past rather than as memories had by someone who is the same as Y? Early Buddhist texts, such as *The Questions of King Milinda,* raise worries akin to this. Many of the challenges focus on the very unclear criteria for what would count as the same person if there is no visible continuity between Y's life and X's life. Even if there is some causal connection, a telling analogy is this: If a lit candle is used to light another, is the flame on the second candle the same as the flame on the first? Or should it be regarded as a new flame produced by the first? The question is unanswerable in the absence of criteria to determine what is to count as a new flame or as the same flame, and the Buddhist suggestion is that if factors in Y's life have some causal connection with X's life, we are in the same position. Perhaps Hindus would be in a better position to respond if they claimed strong, intricate and readily verifiable connections between one life and the next, but this claim has not generally been made. Furthermore, the analysis of *atman,* as lying between layers of individuality—therefore as separate from these layers—suggests that what is transferred from one life to the next is primarily not a matter of whatever it is that gives an individual life its character or flavor.

The question of what we would count as survival, as continuing to be the same person, is even more difficult to answer in a precise and definite way. If an element in us endures and remains unchanging, we would count this as survival only if this element had a much closer connection with our individuality than the Hindu *atman* has. The quandary is that the elements in our psychic life that do have a close connection with our individuality appear to keep changing.

There is no reason to assume *a priori* that this would not be true of life after death. If we ask what kind of postmortem existence would count as survival, there is a continuum of imaginable cases. At one extreme, the continuity posited (or at least assumed by most believers) in traditional views of immortality, in which people continue with almost all of their memories and psychological characteristics, would be generally taken to count as survival, even though the continuity posited need not include any bodily continuity. At the other extreme, if it were said that someone had been reincarnated as a frog with no memories of human life and no major continuities of character, it would seem implausible to maintain that the same person continued in existence. Intermediate cases might be more difficult to adjudicate. For example, even if the Christian doctrine of heaven is entirely correct, we have no accounts of what celestial life is like in the long run nor have we longitudinal studies of the psychology of heaven dwellers. Might Saint Augustine after a millennium and a half in heaven lack all memory of having stolen pears as a child? Suppose that he lacks all memories of his life on earth (after all, that was a long time ago), and indeed has been completely transformed by the influence of his surroundings of the last millennium and a half. In what sense is he still the same person? A story by Jorge Luis Borges, "The Immortal," deftly creates a comparable case among an immortal group of humans. After a very long time, an immortal might literally not know who he or she is. There might not be enough long-term continuity in such a life for us to be sure that there was a definite answer.

This does not represent a new point; something like this has been suggested by a number of recent writers, most notably Derek Parfit (1984). It suggests difficulties of two sorts for ES. One, the most obvious, is that the continuities of what a person is that we can know about are often a matter of degree (rather than all or nothing), and we can imagine cases in which the degree is such that we would not know what to say. A more fundamental difficulty is this: To examine what we do know about the continuities in people's lives, in relation to various actual or imaginable cases, is to realize that ES (as we have been construing it) claims something that goes beyond the actual or even the imaginable evidence. You are much the same in your thoughts and behavior as you were ten years ago, although there are some differences; but ES claims that you are the same, period. That is, the same in a way that would seem to have to do primarily not with thoughts and behavior but with something else. The difficulty might be put this way: The advocates of ES want something to be true, but it is not clear that they are able to tell us what it is.

We have already suggested that ES is implausible if construed as claiming that there is an enduring, unchangeable psychic element closely linked to our individuality. An alternative interpretation of ES has to do with senses of identity. Bishop Butler's view, echoed in recent years by Roderick Chisholm, was that ordinary material objects, such as pieces of fruit, can be spoken of as remaining the same in a "loose and popular" sense, but that people remain the same in a "strict and philosophical" sense (Butler in Perry 1975; Chisholm 1976). This needs to be examined with more care. In the end, it seems much easier to understand Butler's "loose and popular" sense of identity than the "strict and philosophical" sense.

Ever since Heraclitus pointed out that you cannot step in the same river twice, it has been widely understood that we commonly refer to things as *the same* even if they have undergone changes or variations, so that they are strictly speaking *not the same*. The Connecticut River has different water flowing through it than it did last month or the east bank may have shifted a millimeter in places or the pollution index of the water may be up or down. If we choose to dignify changes of this sort by renaming the river, our language would be infinitely complicated because, after all, the changes are continuous. What Heraclitus, in effect, was saying was that human language and thought would be impossible unless we pretended that things were the same which strictly speaking were not the same.

If, however, the Connecticut River suddenly split into a number of streams, we would hesitate to say that it was the same river; if it moved fifty miles west our hesitation would be extreme. Whether we are talking about a river, a chair, a piece of wax, or a peach, it is clear that, on the one hand, we are willing to tolerate some change and yet call what we are talking about the same; on the other hand, there are limits to how much change we would tolerate. If a chair were entirely burnt, we would not normally point to the heap of ashes and say, "That is the same chair" or even "That is the same as the chair that . . ."; on the other hand, we might speak of the entirely burnt wax as the same piece of wax. A chair that had all of its legs and its back replaced might well not be spoken of as remaining the same chair; there would be no similar hesitation in the case of a human being with an artificial limb or a transplanted heart.

Two points emerge. One is that there are conventions that determine whether something that has changed may yet be spoken of as the same chair, the same piece of wax, the same river, and so on. The other is that these conventions are plural: there is no reason to think that the conventions for what counts as the same river will be exactly the same as, or parallel to, the conventions for what counts as the same chair. If we want to know whether something counts as the same X as something encountered earlier, part of what we must know are the rules of language governing what we call sameness in X's.

Because language is a cultural artifact, we cannot assume that all languages will incorporate the same rules. Any usable language will have to allow us to call something the same river or the same chair, even if there have been changes in it, but there is no reason why the content of these rules could not vary from language to language. The variations might be especially striking if we encountered an intelligent nonhuman group and learned its language.

Thus, if we wish to characterize the "loose and popular" sense of identity, in which rivers or pieces of fruit can remain the same even if they have changed, we would have to give prominent attention to the role of linguistic convention in judgments of identity. We also would have to acknowledge that linguistic conventions themselves can change and that they may vary from one group to another. What would a "strict and philosophical" sense of identity be? Neither Butler nor Chisholm gives an entirely clear account of this, but the likely outlines of an answer emerge if we bear in mind the contrast with "loose and popular" senses of identity. X and Y would be identical in the "strict and philosophical" sense only if we could be in a position to affirm their identity without knowing anything about linguistic conventions and only if a judgment that they are identical would be correct in any language.

This raises a number of thorny and technical issues about the ways in which linguistic conventions play a part in judgments of correctness. The remarks that follow will be crude and untechnical; but they will be, I think, sufficient to dispose of any ideas that ES is at all plausible if ES is construed as a claim about senses of identity.

A widely held view has been that correct statements fall into two groups: (1) Those (such as ordinary scientific and other factual statements) that are true in virtue of both conventions of language and facts about the world and (2) those (such as statements in arithmetic and formal logic as well as everyday tautologies) that are true merely in virtue of conventions of language. In recent decades, this dichotomy has been challenged by philosophers who have pointed out that our conventions of language are adjustable in the light of facts about the world and that our sense of the facts conversely is conditioned by linguistic structures. But none of this subverts the claim that conventions of language always are a factor in the correctness of a statement. Any correct claim has to be made in some language, and the factors that make it correct must include the structure and conventions of that language (as well perhaps as considerations that are not merely linguistic, popularly known as facts).

If this is true of statements in general, then *a fortiori* it must be true of statements of identity. To know whether X and Y are identical we must know the conventions of our language that are relevant to X and Y as well as the facts about X and Y. If this is identity in the "loose and popular" sense, then all identity is identity in this sense. The demand for human identity in a "strict and philosophical" sense, then, is a demand that human identity be exempted from the laws of language and truth. One of the reasons why this demand seems so deep and powerful is that it never could possibly be satisfied.

Let me sum up the case, as developed thus far, against ES. At first, the claim that each of us has an enduring self looks like an empirical matter. If so, the proper tactic would seem to be that of Hume, namely, to look introspectively for a constant element underlying the psyche. It has been objected that ES could not possibly refer to an element of experience because a complete self could not possibly be experienced introspectively by a self that was looking for it and was distinct from what it was experiencing. However, this objection can be disallowed in the light of claims of meditative experience in which there was no distinction between experiencer and what was experienced. The more serious difficulty is that in traditions, such as classical Hinduism, which claim experience of a constant underlying psychic reality, this psychic reality (*atman*) does not correspond to what we would normally consider an individual self. Consequently, even if one accepts reports of meditative experience as evidence, they do not constitute evidence of an enduring self. An alternative is to take ES not as an empirical claim but as a logical point about the sense in which a person is self-identical throughout a lifetime. Here, the problem is not lack of adequate evidence but rather what looks like incoherence. Enduring Self appears to be a demand that statements of personal identity be exempted from the general rule that the criteria for acceptability of statements are conditioned by the linguistic system within which the statements are made. Is there any basis for this exemption beyond a strong wish for we-know-not-what?

If ES represents a natural first opinion on the metaphysical issues, then NS is a natural second opinion. We all assume that we have enduring selves; but when we look for them, either we find nothing at all but psychic flux or what we find is rather far from what we would have termed individual selves. At this point, it may seem both correct, and also liberating from egoism, to say that there is no self . . . there.

The last word of the previous paragraph should be allowed, for the time being, to hang. It is another example of the extreme difficulty of discussing the metaphysical issues of self in such a way as to do justice to common sense, while avoiding language that does not commit us to, or at least point the way toward, some peculiar-seeming points of view. All of us, including Hume, have the sense that looking for the self is not a random search, that there is, as it were, a place—but, of course, not really a place—to look. We will pass this by for the moment, but we shall return to it later.

It is often said that we can understand a term or a statement only if we have a clear sense, in the case of the term, of what counts as not it, and in the case of a statement of what counts as its denial. This is especially true of statements that themselves take the form of a denial. If it is meaningful to say that there is no self, then we must have a clear conception of what it would have been to have had a self. This suggests one respect in which NS looks problematic. Hume had some idea of what he was looking for when he failed to find a self of a certain sort. But this idea was very rough, not readily explainable at any length; in his own terms Hume, in fact, lacked an ''idea'' of what he denied was there, in that there was no impression that provided him with such an idea. All of this suggests that, if advocates of ES turn out to have great difficulties in explaining just what it is that they want to claim, the advocates of NS have similar difficulties.

It would be very tempting to pursue this line of thought a step further and to declare the issue of self a nonissue, comparing the advocates of ES and NS to people who are playing tug-of-war with a nonexistent rope. There is some similiarity here with debates in the philosophy of religion about the existence of God: there is a great difficulty, conceded by the most intelligent representatives of both sides, in specifying fully the nature of what is supposed to be at issue, and claims are made on both sides that are underdetermined by empirical evidence. A verdict of *meaningless issue* is arguably a cheap and too easy way of avoiding problems of this sort. A paradigm case of a meaningless issue would be one in which nothing at all could be said to specify the nature of what is supposed to be in dispute and relative to which there could be no empirical evidence whatsoever. At the other extreme are issues of the sort considered in elementary science courses in which a very full specification of what is at issue can be given and decisive empirical evidence is available. That the issues of self and of God are not at this extreme—one that is comfortable—is no reason to construe them as being at the other extreme.

We, instead, should regard the form and detail of our concepts as well as the claims we make using our concepts as part of what is at stake. We cannot assume that our major alternatives are to answer yes or no to a sharply defined possibility. In the end, it may be most reasonable to answer yes to something very different from what we originally had in mind.

Thus, someone can answer no to one kind of self, and yes to something very different that can be construed as a self. In one very plausible interpretation, this, in fact, was Hume's position (Baier 1979). Indeed, a reflective look at the way we ordinarily think and talk about ourselves suggests that a thoroughgoing NS position would be grossly implausible. People use words such as *I* and *me* confidently and unhesitatingly in a variety of contexts, and people often have no difficulty at all in determining that so-and-so is the same person they encountered years ago. It may not be so easy to explain exactly what all of this means, but it looks more like a problem of philosophical analysis than a phenomenon of lack of clarity: There is little to suggest that ordinary people find the discourse of selfhood unworkably vague or, in most ordinary contexts, indeterminate in the judgments it yields.

Something like this seems to be recognized in the early Buddhist classic on the self, *The Questions of King Milinda*. Careless commentators attribute an NS view to this work; but, as in the case of Hume, what is denied is merely the kind of self postulated by ES. What is left is a self that certainly is not an item within a person; neither is it merely the sum of elements of personality, but it exists on account of them (see *The Questions of King Milinda*, vol. 1, pp. 63–65).

We can take it as given that, despite the falsity of ES, we somehow do manage to have a workable conception of individual persons that tracks people through their lives. Thus, X will have a self at least in the (minimal) sense that X has developed a consistent and meaningful usage of words such as *I* and *me* and also in that we, viewing X from the outside, can identify X as the same person at various points in her or his life. There may be more to the self than these elementary factors; but the immediate point is that, even if ES is false, people somehow manage to have selves.

This suggests that, insofar as the concepts of I and me are not innate, selves are constructed during a life rather than being present at birth.

If we accept this, part of the explanation of the genesis of self is surely that of Kant: The concept of I is a unifying factor that makes coherent experience possible. "It must be possible," Kant says, "for the 'I think' to accompany all my representations" (1781, pp. 142n., 152). In this portrayal, the (phenomenal) self is an element of the framework of personal experience rather than something within the framework; it is ever present but has no character whatsoever. Kant says that the "self-consciousness" which generates the representation "I think" cannot "itself be accompanied by any further representation" (1781, p. 153). The powerful imperative to have an "I" is a crucial factor in any analysis of self, and one weakness of the recent philosophical literature is that so few of the contributors take account of Kant's work.

My suggestion is that Kant's account of the use of "I" gives us part (but only part) of the truth about self. In fact, people do normally have what are termed self-images. The "I think" that accompanies or can accompany consciousness is formal and empty, in that it would or could occur whatever we were like. But, in fact, no one is entirely protean; all of us are like something. Consequently, each of us lives with an "I" that is cautious, takes commitments seriously, and is concerned with propriety; or with an "I" that is rebellious and anxious to be distinctive; or whatever.

This needs to be spelled out; in the process, some crucial distinctions need to be observed. One is between, on the one hand, what has to be true of the "I" that a person uses and, on the other hand, what happens to be true and is treated as important but does not have to be true. A related distinction is between the primary function of a unit of language and the secondary functions that it fulfills either because they follow from the primary function or because it is easy and convenient to associate them with the primary function.

The first point to make is Kantian. Knowledge and experience need to be integrated within a framework. The existence of a framework allows for both theoretical and practical connections among items. Memories can refer back to earlier experiences. Hopes, plans, or predictions can refer forward. Items can have meaning or significance in the light of other items. One might regard the "I think" that can accompany items in a person's consciousness as like a badge that permits items that wear it to recognize one another and cluster together. Because of the need for integration of consciousness, something like this is the primary function of I.

There is more than one way in which integration of knowledge and experience could occur. It might be possible for a species or a colony of organisms to treat all its members as constituting an I. If termites were intelligent, this is what they might do: A single termite might remember what happened to any other member of the group and hope for good experiences for any of them, because every thought or experience would be considered a thought or experience of the I that was the group. Such an integration would be workable if the system of communication among organisms within the group were highly effective and there was a high degree of sensitivity to what was happening to other members. Otherwise there would be too severe and continuous a disengagement among lines of thought and experiences of the I, so that the group-self would manifest severe symptoms of split personality. It is worth emphasizing that the degree of communication and sensitivity that would be required for a workable group-self stops short of perfect communication and entire sensitivity. No self is perfectly integrated in the sense of remembering everything, planning for everything, or relating every item of experience to every other item. Individual human beings get along with a moderate degree of integration: Some things are remembered, and there is an intricate but incomplete network of relations among items of experience. A colony of termites could sustain a group-self with a similar degree of integration.

Even though entire integration is not required in the construction of self, plainly there is some minimum degree. Someone who forgets everything and notices very little of what we think of as happening to himself or herself could not attain a concept of self. Because of such minimum standards, there is no realistic prospect of the formation of a human group-self. We are not sensitive enough to, knowledgeable enough about, or sufficiently coordinated with, one another. The natural arena within which the human construction of self will occur is that which we currently think of as the individual human life. One way to appreciate this process is to think of the starting point in relation to the lives of individual human animals. Humans, unlike termites, swarm rather badly and usually do not have a gift for subordinating the needs of the individual organism to larger social purposes. On the other hand, within the life of a single human there are normally broad continuities. There are memories, and projects that take some time to complete may play a large part. Given these biological facts, we can assume that by and large any individual human organism is likely to construct one and only one self, the outer boundaries of whose experience are coextensive with those of the organism's experience. This assumption will be defeated in the case of an organism that is deficient in some crucial respect (e.g., it never remembers anything) or that severely lacks the ability to integrate projects and items of experience (in which case we might be drawn to speak of multiple selves) or that has a highly chaotic and unpredictable sequence of thoughts and experiences. The assumption will be defeated also if there were a case of a human whose seeming-memories, projects, and experiences were highly integrated with the projects and experiences of organisms now dead. In such a case, we might well be tempted to speak realistically about reincarnation, thus treating the outer boundaries of the self's experience as wider than those of the organism we can see. The assumption also would be defeated if there were a group of human beings that were in crucial respects like termites. Again, we might view the outer boundaries of self as broader than those which outline the individual organism's experiences.

Before we proceed further, two points of view on the construction of self need to be disentangled. One, which is of primary importance, is that of the being (an organism or a group) that is constructing a self. The view suggested is that the construction has a dual relationship to the integration of psychological elements. On the one hand, it is possible only if there is, or will be, a fairly high degree of integration; on the other hand, it facilitates integration. If we understand the psychological life of a person through the metaphor of a bundle, then we might think of the concept of I as playing a crucial role in the bundling. A second point of view is that of qualified language users who decide whom or what to regard as an individual. Normally, a human organism will regard herself or himself as having a single self, with the life of the organism as its outer boundaries, and this will coincide with the view of outside observers. It is conceivable, though, that someone's attempted construction of self can deviate from this norm. In such a case, the considered judgment of qualified language users can be (but need not be) that the deviation is a mistake. At one extreme, we may encounter an organism that claims to be several people. There is always some hesitation in accepting such claims, but there is no clear reason why they have to be rejected out of hand. But if each of the purported separate personalities appears to have a fairly high degree of knowledge of, and complicity in, the projects of the others, we would be strongly justified in insisting that the organism, in fact, had only one self. At the other extreme, if we encounter an organism that insists on using I in reference to a social group or in such a way that people now dead are included, if the degree of psychological integration with plans and experiences of other organisms in the group—or of the deceased "former selves" were not high, we might be justified in regarding the extension of I as a mistake. In other words, a person's judgments of the outer boundaries of who she or he is are corrigible.

If it is clear that the concept of I helps to integrate items of consciousness, it is much less clear what this has to do with individuality. On the one hand, I has associations with egoism and selfishness. We normally assume that someone who constantly views the world in terms of *I, I, me, me* takes his or her individuality too seriously. On the other hand, the symbol I has built into it no individual identity, character, or flavor. Anybody, among beings satisfying a wide variety of descriptions, could be an I. Thus, in its primary function, the word looks impersonal, but this leaves open the possibility of secondary functions that are quite the reverse.

The double-sidedness of I is apparent when a person thinks of who she or he is, with particular attention to what she or he is like as a person. People do by and large have self-images. These can involve distortions, exaggerations, or downright falsehoods: It is well-known that the great majority of us have self-images that are at least slightly more flattering than the corresponding images of us had by onlookers. But there is no reason why a self-image cannot be largely accurate. Someone can think of herself as a highly reliable, resourceful person, and be such a person in fact. However, even the case in which a self-image constitutes what we would normally call self-knowledge presents difficulties. As Sartre pointed out in *Being and Nothingness* (1945), there is some sense in which the highly reliable, resourceful woman does not have to continue to be highly reliable and resourceful; as Sartre keeps saying, she does not have these properties in the way in which an inanimate object has its properties. What this all means, even if it is true, may not be entirely clear (we will explore it in chap. 3). A first step is to notice that the woman's reliability and resourcefulness have to do with choices she continues to make, whereas there is no sense in which the properties of an inanimate object are based on its choices or can be changed by different choices. In general, at least, some of what has been chosen could be chosen differently. Indeed, as I have argued elsewhere, self-knowledge cannot be separated from decision about and prediction of one's future (Kupperman 1984–1985).

Whether or not one is comfortable with Sartre's talk of a nothingness associated with openness of choice and whether or not anyone's character could be different from what it is without contravening the laws of nature, it remains the case (as the earlier quotation from Madell points out [see p. 23]) that one could imagine anyone, including oneself, as having a very different character. No one's use of I, in other words, connotes an essence that that person must have.

If we put these points together, we have the following view of the concept of I. On the one hand, I, like here and now, is a place-marker: It indicates what will be taken as a fixed point, as an origin in the coordinate system of the world. It intrinsically has no more content than this. On the other hand, it can be used to refer to something like a content: to the relatively stable characteristics that a person has. This second use, though, unlike the first, is to something conceivably unstable—one might almost say disposable. The I of my self-image imaginably might not be me a year from now.

Is this the whole story? Our investigation, if all the points made have been accepted, has given us a shadowy self: a being who has taken on characteristics but can be imagined without them. This entails the rejection of NS insofar as everyone does have a self of some sort. But this shadowy self changes its characteristics and always can be imagined as changing them drastically; this entails the rejection of ES. Is the truth then simply that what we call the self is a result of the creative, integrating activity of thought—and also perhaps that, when we strip away what is disposable, it is nothing but that activity?

Both in what it claims and in what it refuses to claim, CS is an attractive view. It arguably has been held, in one form or another, by thinkers as diverse as early Buddhist philosophers (if I am right that they too, did not espouse NS), Hume, Kant, Sartre, and most recently Jonathan Glover. Søren Kierkegaard (1849) puts one form of CS very nicely:

> The self is a relation which relates itself to its own self, or it is that in the relation (which accounts for it) that the relation relates to its own self; the self is not the relation but (consists in the fact) that the relation relates itself to its own self. (p. 146)

One difficulty is brought out by the Hindu philosopher Sankara when criticizing Buddhist philosophers. If the self is a synthesis of elements of empirical consciousness, then, Sankara suggests, it cannot be explained how the synthesis is brought about, "For the parts constituting the (material) aggregates are devoid of intelligence, and the kindling (*abhigvalana*) of intelligence depends on an aggregate of atoms having been brought about previously" (Sankara, vol. 1, p. 403).

Whether this is a telling objection is debatable. The kindling of intelligence may simply happen, under appropriate conditions, without anything like intelligence having been involved in creating these conditions. It should be stressed, in any case, that even if CS is correct, the construction of self will not normally be *conscious* in any sense that suggests that the person constructing a self repeatedly thinks of herself or himself as making choices that contribute to constructing a self. Indeed, the crucial "choices" frequently are not thought of as choices of any sort: Bloggs simply does *X* instead of *Y*, perhaps with no thought whatsoever. Both philosophers and ordinary people may say things like, "Bloggs chose to distrust his friends and family," when strictly speaking what they mean is simply, "Bloggs *did* distrust his friends and family, even though no one compelled him to distrust them and from the point of view of folk psychology alternatives were open." The construction of self does not require any thoughts about the construction of self, and typically occurs without them.

It is worth pausing, though, to ask about the conditions under which the construction of self can occur. Philosophers such as Kant, who treat *I* as a synthesizing term, have tended to insist that the synthesis must be brought about, which is not the same as explaining how it is brought about or what must first be the case. Part of the difficulty is that, as is clear in Kant's account, if items are to be judged as pertaining to the same self, they must first be brought into relationship with one another to be considered for such a judgment. For the self to be synthesized, there must be a single consciousness or something very like it. One may ask what makes *this* possible?

In other words, there must be a story to explain how it is possible to integrate items of consciousness sufficiently well to arrive at a workable I. This story can be told in many different ways, depending on the philosophical assumptions of the person telling it. Someone who believes that the mind is nothing but the brain and the central nervous system might say that the grounding of experiences in a single biological system creates a network of mutual relationships that makes possible the integrating work of I. Someone who holds an opposed (dualist) view of the mind might speak of the tendencies toward collected thought of the human psyche as preconditions of the construction of self. However one tells the story, a person has something, a psychological field, that can be interpreted as neurophysiological or as mental—or in yet other ways— that is prior to the construction of self and whose properties (actual or potential) make possible the construction of self. If CS is taken as saying that in normal human beings a self is constructed without saying anything about preconditions, then to that extent CS is deficient. At the very least, CS leaves out something that is important, something that points at least a little in the direction of ES.

Indeed, why cannot we think of this something that is prior to self as really being, in some fundamental way, self? Could it be that we have come full circle and that the correct view is after all a form of ES?

Let us suppose that you began life as a growing psychological field; you began to develop the concept of I only after a year and a half or so, and perhaps it was much longer before you had developed anything like a definite character. The psychology of a newborn infant is somewhat impoverished, but definite tendencies (e.g., aggressiveness or cheerful- ness, or their opposites) may be manifested. Anyone who believes that heredity plays a significant part in people's characters will believe that the psychic nature of the newborn need not be entirely bland or neutral. Indeed, a person's life may be marked by lingering predispositions, either inherited or acquired in these early years, so that only when acting in accord with these does the person feel energetic, zestful, and truly alive. The discovery of an appropriate mode of life might be spoken of as the person's discovery of her or his true self or authentic self (see Meyers 1987; Glover 1988, pp. 136–37, 178–79; Norton 1976). Strictly speak- ing, of course, what is discovered is not a full-fledged self but merely directional markers.

Thus, it may well be that if you are a psychological field, you have never been entirely characterless. On the other hand, when you think of who *you* are, you are unlikely to think of the psychological field with which your life began. We tend to think of the self as richer and as having more character (even if it is changeable) than can be assigned on most views to a psychological field with which one begins life.

The issue here is complicated by the fact that, on the one hand, the concept of I does not appear and does not exist even as a possibility in the very first phase of human life, but on the other hand, when the concept of I does emerge, it is used retroactively in connection with everything the organism did or experienced in that first phase. One can regard this retroactive appropriation of experience and behavior as acknowledgment that the self precedes the use of I; or, alternatively, it can be regarded as a convenient way of organizing our talk about infants and of acknowledging the psychological connections between an infant who is not yet a person and the person that infant will become.

This leaves us with two possible views of the infant derived from these two possible views of self. One is a qualified form of ES; the other is a qualified form of CS. I will spell out both and also give reasons for thinking that the latter is preferable.

1. We might answer the question of what we are in terms of a psychological field. Some might identify this psychological field with the neurophysiology of a single organism; dualists would have a different analysis and, consequently, a broader range of options as to what the boundaries of the field are. In either case, a newborn infant would be regarded as already having a self. As the child develops and becomes more self-conscious, this self becomes overlaid with formulations (by the child and others) of what it is; there is not only self, but also self-consciousness. There will be a sense in which all of the formulations will be mistaken, in that (even if they seem accurate) what they describe will be adopted ways of being and acting, which will not do justice to the primal self of the newborn infant. The primal self, the true self, is a wide range of possibilities, as we realize in our dreams and fantasies. If character is our way of being and acting in matters of importance, then, in this view, character cannot be self. It is merely a structure that a self erects.

On this view, it is, of course, true that a person's self normally endures throughout her or his life. It does not change: How would something whose nature is indefinite change? It is not surprising also that attempts to find self that are like Hume's in Book 1 of his *Treatise* fail. Hume was looking for an item within the psychological field, but this was a category mistake. The field itself, which was intimately present to him, was what he should have been looking for.

2. It can be argued that the psychological field which is present in a newborn infant and which continues throughout that infant's life would more accurately be termed a protoself. How can someone genuinely have a self if he or she is incapable of the concept of I and a self-image? A normal human being begins life with a protoself, and a self begins to appear in the course of early childhood. It is constructed within the

protoself, typically not by conscious decisions but rather by the formation of habits and attitudes and the emergence of characteristic ways of thinking and behaving. This constructed self, in fact, is very largely what is analyzed in chapter 1 as character. The major difference between what we would call the nature of someone's self and what we would call that person's character is that we might include in what pertains to our self characteristic ways of thinking and acting in matters not normally considered important (e.g., tastes in food or in clothing styles), whereas our ordinary use of *character* emphasizes matters of importance. With this slight qualification, we can think of character as virtually equivalent to the nature of the self that is constructed as we grow up.

One might think of the choice between this view and the form of ES stated before it to be one of language: What do we choose to call the self? But if this is so, there are reasons within language to prefer the form of CS just stated (in which character approximates the nature of self) to ES. The main reason is that there is a strong association of *self* with individuality, not only in the weak sense in which (on any view) our uses of I represent different origins of coordinate systems on which reality is mapped, but also in the strong sense in which to have a self is to be a certain sort of person. The individuality of the self, on the form of CS that has been presented, has to be taken cautiously: There is a sense (linked to what is imaginable) in which one does not have to be what one is and in which one could become different. Our conventions of language allow us to call someone the *same person* who has changed her or his character as long as the changes are not too extreme and there is adequate continuity and causal connectedness. (As the changes become more extreme or abrupt, we become increasingly hesitant.) Despite the ways in which one could be different and yet be oneself, our normal way of talking fits the view that to have a self is to have the possibility of self-knowledge and that self-knowledge will be of something more robust than the collection of characteristics and tendencies that someone may have inherited. Linked to this is what I judge to be our great reluctance to regard very young infants as having a self, although we certainly recognize them as having psychological fields and—in a sense related to rights and to likely future selves—perhaps as persons.

If all of this is correct, it makes sense to view a person's life in terms of CS and to view the normal human being as constructing a self, to the nature of which her or his character is an approximation, within a psychological field.[2] This leaves open questions of how this construction takes place, how free it is, and how much responsibility we have for our characters. These are central issues of chapter 3.

Notes

1. In the end, any full understanding of what character is will have to include the background of a metaphysical account of the self. At the least, the perspective on character had by someone who takes an ES view of the self will be radically different from that of someone whose perspective derives from a CS view: The former might attempt to identify character with the permanent nature of the self or, alternatively, could be expected to treat it as much less important than such a nature. The central argument of this chapter connects the term *character,* the meaning of which I have taken (with minor qualifications outlined in chap. 1) to be fixed by ordinary language, with *self,* which has come to function more as a metaphysical term of art. This can be taken as an attempt to ground the best available metaphysics of self in an approximation to the ordinary language of character.

2. Some readers may object that three, rather than two, possible views of what the self is ought to have been considered. The form of CS defended, they may say, is individualistic. There is much more to us than our characters plus such things as tastes in food and clothing styles. Someone who is asked, ''Who are you?'' typically replies, as was pointed out in chapter 1, in terms that include such matters as occupation, family connections, nationality, ethnicity, and so on. One could argue that the only authentic I is a social and communal I and, thus, that the self goes far beyond character.

There is a good deal to be said for this point of view. Let me begin by offering my opinion that the formation of our characters always is tinctured by our time and place, the structures of our society, and our roles within the society. Thus character is not as starkly individualistic a concept as it might first appear to be. Whether a change, then, in social setting must need be reflected by a change in character is a further question. It could well be that it sometimes is and sometimes it is not to any appreciable extent. To take an extreme hypothetical case: If there were time travel, Mark Twain's Connecticut Yankee in King Arthur's court might remain a Connecticut Yankee for years.

It must, in any case, be conceded that, as most philosophers since Plato and Aristotle have recognized, the individual person entirely apart from social setting is an abstraction. Character always functions in a social medium, even if it means (as in the case of Daniel Defoe's Robinson Crusoe) carrying around the social medium in one's head. My reply is to grant all this, but to point out that *the self* also is an abstraction; it is a metaphysical term of art. Thus virtually all of Western literature of self has been intertwined with the problem of personal identity, of determining the conditions under which X is or is not the same person as Y.

Two senses in which X can be spoken of as the same person we knew some years ago can be distinguished. There is first of all a sense, which according to John Locke (1690, Bk. 2, chap. 27, no. 26, pp. 226) is forensic, in which X is the same person as Y if and only if it is appropriate to bestow upon X credit or blame owing to Y. If X is the same person as Y in this sense, we usually mark it by our willingness to call them by the same name. This first sense of *same person* is the sense of the philosophical literature, and it is the sense that is employed in this chapter.

Second, there is a more colloquial sense in which we might say that Mary is not the same person since she lost her job and was divorced or that George was not the same person after the Germans took over his country and he joined the Nazi party. If someone's social setting changes drastically, she or he may well become a different person in this more colloquial sense. But it is not necessary: Mary may remain the same person after unemployment and divorce and George may well be the same person even under a Nazi regime. The relation between social setting and what it is to remain the same person in this sense, in other words, is contingent. This is true also in relation to the first, less colloquial sense of *same person*. None of this is to deny that the social setting is enormously important and that very often changes in social setting and roles are causally decisive in making someone a different person in the second sense. The point is merely that *self,* if it is viewed as a metaphysical term of art tied to factors that make someone the same or not the same, has a contingent rather than a logical relation to changes in social setting and a logical rather than a contingent relation to changes in character. If someone's character changes very abruptly in extreme ways, we would thereby hesitate to call her or him the same person in the first sense and would also deny that she or he was the same in the second sense. An extreme and abrupt change in social setting which was unaccompanied by any appreciable change in character would not justify such a response.

3

Character and Responsibility

The view developed in chapters 1 and 2 was that character approximates the nature of self. Roughly speaking character is to the major matters of life as the nature of self is to all of life. It was argued that self in human beings is typically developed within a psychological field. It therefore is perhaps not coextensive with that psychological field. If we can use the word *mind* in such a way as not to beg the ongoing controversies between dualists and physicalists, the position as regards character can be put most simply and untechnically. You are born with a mind but not with a character. By the time you are ready to consider reflectively what character you would like to have, however, you already have one. The possibility is left open that not everything in your mind falls within the compass of your character (or the slightly larger compass of what could be termed the nature of your self). If character is style of thought and action in matters of importance, then, we might decide to say that a stray thought or impulse does not reflect your character, even though we could at the same time hold that your response to the stray thought or impulse does.

This suggests a number of questions:

1. How are the boundaries—if there are any—to be drawn between thoughts and impulses that are part of what you are and those that are not?

2. How could we make sense of a division within the mind between what is self and what is not?

3. Is there any sense in which a person is responsible for thoughts and impulses that are not part of what she or he is?

4. If people typically have developed characters *before* they are in a position to make mature, reflective decisions about what they want them to be, are they responsible for their characters?

5. Are people responsible for acts that flow from their characters?

A brief phenomenology of human psychology is in order in approaching the first question. Each of us, while awake, experiences an ever-shifting array of thoughts and feelings. Two facts about these collections of thoughts and feelings are especially relevant. One is: If we may judge by people's reports, the collections usually are somewhat chaotic. Many people who speak in an extremely clear and coherent way report that they often have thoughts which are by no means clear and do not cohere at all with those that they articulate. Let us imagine someone who can read minds, in the sense that she can have experiences very much like those of hearing words that are formed in other people's minds just as if the words had been vocalized. The suggestion is that the mind reader would "hear" thoughts that would conflict with the sincerely made utterances of people around her (and which might well be embarrassing); the suggestion is especially that what she would "hear" would be much more confusing and chaotic than the spoken words of the people around her. The unspoken might well be to the spoken rather as an orchestra tuning up is to one that is playing a composition.

Barring amazing advances in neurophysiology, none of us is in a position to say with great assurance that this is the case. But it certainly seems plausible. We should bear in mind that the chaotic nature of the unspoken is at best a contingent truth. It is imaginable that someone might achieve, over a period of time, an inner discipline of thought, so that reading her or his mind would be like listening to an orchestra play a composition. Devotees of religions such as Buddhism seem to claim that adepts can achieve an inner discipline of this sort after a good deal of training.

The second fact is that apparently most people have thoughts pop into their heads without any immediate control on their part. A distinguished Cambridge philosopher once remarked in a talk that one could easily in the presence, say, of an older person one genuinely respected have a thought such as "You pompous twit" that not only was unwelcome but ran counter to one's basic attitude. My conjecture is that this is not an altogether uncommon experience. Along with entirely unwelcome thoughts, a person might unexpectedly have thoughts (e.g., of the next meal or of long-ago experiences) that were neither especially welcome nor unwelcome, merely irrelevant to the current line of thought. Finally, thoughts might pop into one's head that were welcome but not necessarily willed into existence, like Mozart's musical ideas.

The phenomenology of control is more complicated than it might at first look. Even if one cannot control the initial occurrence of a thought, there might be some control over whether one then dwells on it or conversely chooses not to think of such and such. The control might be very inadequate: A determined effort not to think, say, of elephants might lead to many random images of elephants. But there is no reason to think that it is impossible. Monks and nuns determined not to think of sex sometimes report success. This success, it should be noted, may depend less on efforts of will in self-censorship than on creation of routines and habits that are not conducive to the offending thoughts. Someone who was determined to have a number of creative musical thoughts à la Mozart also could do some things to make their occurrence less unlikely. One step, of course, would be to get musical training. Others might include exposure to interesting music, eliminating certain kinds of distraction, reserving calm periods of time, and so on. All of these taken together would not be guaranteed to work; in this sense, the occurrence of musical ideas (or ideas of any sort) cannot be controlled. But that does not mean that nothing we do can affect their likelihood.

There are various primitive ways in which someone might be said to endorse or accept a thought or a desire. One might say it aloud with an air of "This is what I believe" or "This is how I feel." One could dwell on it or look forward to periods of time in which one might have such thoughts or feel such desire. Alternatively, one might ignore it, rather as if it were an irrelevant interruption of some inner conversation. One could reject it with horror, try not to have such thoughts or desires, and speak only sentences that expressed contrary sentiments.

It is very tempting to believe that the formation of self within a psychological field involves, first, the occurrence of various thoughts and desires, and second, a process of endorsement and rejection in which a person accepts some of these—coming, as we say, to identify with them—and rejects others. One then can say, as Harry Frankfurt does, that when a person decides on a desire, making it fully his own, "To this extent the person, in making a decision by which he identifies with a desire, *constitutes himself"* (1987, p. 38). In Frankfurt's view, "It is these acts of ordering and of rejection—integration and separation—that create a self out of the raw materials of life" (p. 39).

This view is enormously plausible. It corresponds to much in common experience. The boy who is on his way to being a carefree and inconsiderate man not only has a variety of carefree and inconsiderate thoughts and desires but, typically, is happy (or at least not too unhappy) at having them, and is likely to dwell on such thoughts and desires more than on those of a contrary nature. One must acknowledge that, at least for most people, self-definitions—what someone decides to be or, at least, to see herself as being—play a major role in increasing or decreasing the frequency of various patterns of thought and action and, thus, in the formation of mature character.

Is the self a structure of endorsed thoughts and desires? Can we say that those that are random and not endorsed or that are rejected lie outside of the self? One appeal of answering yes to these questions is that it seems neatly to solve the problems of responsibility. A person, on a view like this, is responsible for her or his self (and, *a fortiori,* character) by virtue of having arrived at that self/character as a result of deciding to accept certain first-order desires (and thoughts).

Nevertheless, I cannot agree. To get at the differences between my view and the one just stated we can begin by looking more closely at the formation of character in real life.

First, it is clear that if someone who is growing up endorses or decides to accept a pattern of thought and desire, this endorsement is likely not to take the form of explicit positive judgment. The boy is unlikely to say, "I like carefree and inconsiderate thinking." Something a little like this is possible, but what is more likely is that the boy simply will be content with, or not dissatisfied with, such a pattern of thought without any reflective judgment's taking place. Second, there exists the possibility that reflective judgments will be negative but not have sufficient power or persistence to stem a tendency toward a certain way of life. Extremely lazy people might think, when they reflect on the subject at all, that it is better not to be lazy; they may accept their occasional desire to act energetically and reject contrary desires; all of this could be consistent with the formation of a character trait of laziness. (Something very similar appears to be true, *mutatis mutandis,* of many adult alcoholics, to judge by the account developed in Herbert Fingarette (1988). Thus, it would seem naive to suppose that if someone accepts certain patterns of thoughts and desires and judges others negatively that the former will be part of her or his character and the latter will not be. Endorsements can be effective only if they have an appropriate relation to our habits of thought and feeling—and perhaps also to the situations we allow ourselves to be in. There appear to be many cases in which someone in the process of becoming a person of type X thinks, "It would be better to be a person of type Y rather than type X," but thinks this without any appreciable effect on her or his habits of thought and feeling. There may be, also, a smaller number of cases in which someone thinks, "It would be better to be a person of type Y than X," but at the same time has feelings of self-hatred or self-disgust that motivate a drift toward becoming someone of type X.

Because of these possibilities, if there is a division within a psychological field between self and nonself, there is no reason to think that all of the items on one side will have been endorsed or accepted by the person whose self it is or that none of the items on the other side will have been endorsed. The lazy person can have stray thoughts that point in the direction of exertion, can endorse them when they occur; yet we can truthfully say, "That isn't him." Anton Chekhov beautifully portrays this kind of person, which is why many of his plays are both funny and depressing. But one readily can encounter this kind of person without going to a theater (see Higgins 1987, esp. p. 326).

None of this is to deny that endorsement normally has an important role in character formation. Frankfurt surely is right that acts of integration and separation normally play a major role in creating "a self out of the raw materials of inner life." This has been suggested also by Heinz Kohut among others (1977, p. 177). At the least, any judgments we make of approval or disapproval of tendencies of thought are likely to correspond to strengthening or weakening those tendencies in ourselves. But as Aristotle pointed out long ago, in the last analysis, habit is the crucial factor in character formation. Patterns of thought and desire can be as habitual as actions. When habit runs counter to what we approve of in ourselves, usually habit will win.

Are we entitled to speak of a division at all within psychological fields between self and nonself? Both an answer of yes and one of no have considerable initial plausibility. Yes seems right because it seems intuitively obvious that a stray thought of acute hostility that is not acted or dwelt on does not represent the self of a consistently and genuinely gentle person; thoughts and feelings that occur very occasionally and run counter to the basic pattern of thought and feeling can be viewed as like the static that may accompany a radio or telephone message. The answer of no also looks plausible because many psychologists will tell us that even stray and seemingly uncharacteristic thoughts and feelings can be indicative of an individual's psychology, sometimes in important ways. Furthermore, if someone has strong and persistent thoughts and desires that run counter to the way that person speaks and acts, are not these subversive thoughts and desires an important part of what that person really is like?

The following seems reasonable in the light of how we normally assess what a person is like. In ordinary cases, we will give the heaviest weight to persistent patterns in what a person does and says. Whether we give any significant weight to a thought that at the time is unbidden and unvoiced may depend on how revealing it is. Even if Sigmund Freud is right in suggesting that all thoughts are connected with a person's experience, preoccupations, and psychological mechanisms, some connections may be much more significant than others. We might say, "How revealing that Bloggs (as he now tells us) thought of food at a moment like that!" Other stray thoughts, like the image of a foreign city that a certain smell can evoke, may count for nothing or next to nothing in an assessment of what a person is like. My suggestion is that instead of viewing the psychological field as divided into self and not self, we normally think of a continuum of relevance and importance. Some items, especially behavior in morally problematic situations, are clearly relevant and very important; others may be less relevant and important; and the continuum extends to some stray thoughts whose relevance and importance would normally be taken to be vanishingly small.

To speak more narrowly of character rather than broadly of the nature of a self: My view is that we give heaviest weight to actions and thoughts that are connected with other actions and thoughts in such a way that we would consider them representative. It is tempting to say simply that we give weight to what is characteristic, not to what is uncharacteristic. But this would be misleading, in that if someone only occasionally behaves uncharacteristically in moments of stress, we might well include that in a description of her or his character. (To deny this would be like saying that only one murder would not count.) As we noted in chapter 1, part of someone's character may be that in some unusual circumstances, certain kinds of behavior become not altogether unlikely for that person, although they would be for most people. There is no sharp line to be drawn between thoughts and actions in relation to matters of importance that count toward character and some that absolutely do not; at most we can say that some things count more heavily than others. Even this difference cannot be closely correlated with the factor of a person's endorsement. As we have seen, someone can reflectively endorse a pattern of thought and action that differs sharply from what we would judge to be her or his character.

One reason why it might seem tempting totally to exclude stray thoughts and impulses from our assessment of character is this: Most of us believe that no one can help what her or his stray thoughts and impulses are. Most of us are, on the other hand, prereflectively inclined to link character with moral responsibility. It therefore seems to simplify matters and to allow us to maintain our habits of thought if we totally exclude stray thoughts and impulses from what pertains to character.

A number of assumptions are at work here that might not survive careful examination. We shortly will look at the nature of the link between character and moral responsibility. We already have seen that the answer to the question "Can people help what their stray thoughts and impulses are?" is no and yes. None of us, perhaps, can have immediate willed control over whether a thought or an impulse comes to us; but, to the extent that we have control over the formation of habits and routines, we can affect the likelihood of various thoughts and impulses coming to us at times in the not-too-near future. It is tempting to say that stray thoughts and impulses are extraneous to character because we have not reflectively endorsed them. But we have already seen that much in a person's character may not have been endorsed and that, indeed, a person may have endorsed, ineffectively, what runs counter to her or his character.

It is true that if someone endorses a stray thought or impulse, this is likely to count more heavily in our assessment of that person's character, simply because it is very likely then to be connected with other kindred thoughts and impulses. We also become much more likely to hold the person responsible for the thought or impulse. This is not to say that responsibility requires control: that is a debatable point we have not yet examined. Rather, even if responsibility does not require control, it can yet be true that we hold people much more responsible for what they have endorsed and repeated than for occasional thoughts and impulses that they have not endorsed. Our normal practice of not praising or blaming people for stray thoughts and impulses that they do not endorse can be grounded in factors other than lack of control.

What is most important is that we do praise or blame people very freely on the basis of their characters. This leads us to the most difficult question of this chapter. On one hand, praise and blame are normally taken as expressions of our holding people responsible for whatever they are praised or blamed for, so that it seems plausible to say that we normally hold people responsible for being energetic or lazy, kind or mean-spirited, and so on. On the other hand, it is rarely if ever plausible to say that a person is energetic or lazy, kind or mean-spirited, and so on, as a result of conscious control over her or his character; and it is far from clear that most people *could* have sharply different characters as a result of conscious control on their part. Third, most people (especially if they do not think about the ramifications) might find prephilosophically plausible the generalization that X can be responsible for Y if and only if either Y is the result of X's conscious decision or X could have controlled whether Y was the case. We cannot have it all three ways. In particular, if it is true that whether someone is kind or mean-spirited, and so forth, is not normally the result of that person's conscious decision or to any considerable degree under that person's control, then, either we should fight back our normal tendency to praise kind people and condemn mean-spirited ones or we should abandon (in the case of character) the assumption that responsibility presupposes the actual or possible control.

David Hume favored the last alternative, and I agree with him in this. He contended that moral qualities are largely involuntary, "It being almost impossible for the mind to change its character in any considerable article, or cure itself of a passionate or splenetic temper, when they are natural to it." Hume sees no reason why virtue and vice "may not be involuntary"; for all that, he also sees no reason why we should not esteem virtue and blame vice (1739, p. 608). Hume returns to the subject of control of character in his essay "The Sceptic." Again character emerges as largely involuntary: It is not always "in a man's power, by the utmost art and industry, to correct his temper, and to attain that virtuous character, to which he aspires" (1742, p. 169). Philosophy does not have the power to change character by the direct and immediate effect of rational conviction. But a study of philosophy may gradually modify a character—in the only way in which characters can be controlled and modified—by a constant "bent" of mind and by repeated "habit" (p. 171).

The issue here is typical of some in this book, in that it is a mixture of empirical questions with questions of how concepts should be deployed. It is natural to expect that recent psychological investigation would be helpful. There is no reason why it could not be, but I give reasons in appendix A why the philosopher concerned with character often should not count on psychologists to have assembled useful data. There do exist longitudinal studies of change and continuity of personality (see Brim and Kagan 1980; West and Graziano 1989). But none that I am aware of is a study of change that might directly result from being willed, and there would be difficulties (discussed in app. A) in conducting such a study. We are left, then, with the observations of sophisticated and perceptive lay observers such as David Hume.

This is not to say that Hume's remarks on this subject are entirely impeccable. The first passage quoted (from *A Treatise of Human Nature*) mixes the difficulty of changing one's character with that of changing a passionate or splenetic temper: Many psychologists would place the passionate or splenetic temper under the heading of temperament, regarding temperament as foundational to character and perhaps as peculiarly stable (see Goldsmith et al. 1987). One way of viewing the relations between temperament and character is to see the man who was born with the passionate temper as having various possibilities as to how it will be directed or integrated within his life, many of these possibilities including systematic control of, although perhaps not elimination of, the passionate temper.

Jonathan Glover has recently suggested "probably, for most of us, self-creation is a matter of a fairly disorganized cluster of smaller aims: more like building a medieval town than a planned garden city" and that "it is absurd to suggest that all of our psychological characteristics can be altered substantially and at will, or even that more than a few can be entirely altered" (1988, pp. 135, 136). Self-creation "can be at best partial" (p. 179). Let me suggest that the processes of self-creation are greatly conditioned by where their starting points are and that it would be useful to distinguish three stages: The child's creation of the outlines of a character against the background of temperamental and other constraints, the fine-tuning and filling in of details that takes place in late adolescence and early adulthood, and later fine-tuning along perhaps with attempts at revision. The strongest examples one encounters of what sounds like conscious control concern fine-tuning and filling in of details, especially in late adolescence and early adulthood. An important part of this process is articulation of values and ideals. As Charles Taylor has pointed out, articulations "shape" what they articulate (1976. p 296). Richard Warner has developed the point that motivation by self-concepts plays a crucial role in imposing "a certain order over time on one's mental life" (1987, p. 96).

One should neither ignore nor exaggerate the possibilities of willed change of character during adolescence and early adulthood. Erik Erikson has spoken of the process of identity formation as having "its normative crisis in adolescence," but he also has said that "the community often underestimates to what extent a long intricate childhood history has restricted a youth's further choice of identity change" (1968, pp. 23, 160). Self-concepts, when they are not fantasies or wishful thinking, can bring about change; but such change may be very gradual, and the self-concepts available to an adolescent may also be limited. There are cases of exceptional willed change, but these do not conflict with the basic Humean view that normally people do not (for the most part) have their characters as a result of conscious decision and cannot shape them at will, and that in this sense character is largely involuntary.

The thesis that character is largely involuntary (which I will refer to as Hume's thesis) must be carefully distinguished from theses that might seem closely similar but that are both distinct and clearly false. One is that people's characters do not (at least past a certain point in their lives) drastically change. To maintain this would be absurd. It is not uncommon for a mature person's character to change drastically over a period of time, especially as a result of illness, continuous frustration, the experience of living under a different form of government, committing oneself to a different sort of work, and so on. Anyone's character is likely to be affected, at any point in life, by social norms, a person's social class and family relations, how that person spends most of her or his time, and so on; as these factors change, a change in character will be the natural (although not inevitable) result. What Hume denies (I think correctly) is that one can will a drastic change in one's character over a short period of time; he also denies that it is always in a person's power to control a change of her or his character even gradually over a long period. Changes often occur, but usually they are largely not under the control of the person whose character is changing. Words such as *largely* need to be emphasized because we generally can control our immediate reactions to changes in circumstances and how we act on various particular occasions, and these cumulatively do have a lot to do with changes in character. I can accept or reject the dominant values of my social class. If I lose my job and have to work on a factory assembly line, I have some control over what I think about as I work and how I organize my free time. To say that a person has control over any given one of a number of factors that contribute to change of character is not however to say that a person has control over the entire process. The correct thesis that long-term change of character is, at least for the great majority of people, largely involuntary must be distinguished from the false thesis that we cannot control any of our reactions to changes in circumstances or how we behave on any particular occasion. The truth is located between two attractive overstatements: On the one hand, the view that people always, in effect, chose their lives and, on the other hand (as we may think if we dwell on our limited patterns of response to contingencies), that a life lives a person rather than the other way around.

It has to be said that some aspects of character may be less difficult to control than others. At one extreme would be those that are keyed to a large variety of actions and also to patterns of perception and desire. The degree to which someone is considerate or selfish is at that extreme and seems especially unlikely to be controlled by a single or a small number of acts of will. Herbert Fingarette's work on alcoholism suggests that it also is less easy to control than might be supposed, in that it, too, involves a way of organizing a life rather than a small number of discrete choices (1988, chap. 5). Aspects of character reflected in taking other people's money might lie toward the other extreme, if for some people they are less deeply implicated in the structure of a life and, hence, less difficult to change. My suggestion is that the possibilities of control not only may vary from individual to individual, but also are always matters of degree. The summary judgment that people have little control over their characters is compatible with cases in which an individual has a fair amount of control over some aspects of character. Cases of very little control, however, represent the norm.

Hume's thesis also must be distinguished from the false claim that people seldom make genuine choices that, in effect, determine how their characters will develop and change. We do often have control over circumstances that will gradually mold or reshape our characters: These include what college we attend, what kind of person we marry (if we marry), and what kind of career we aim for. A man who, say, is deciding between a career as an accountant and one as a debt collector for a loan company is deciding something that has considerable relevance to what his character will be in twenty years' time. Choices of these sorts may be the most important decisions related to our future characters that we make. However, the relation to change of character is usually indirect and subtle and is both difficult to generalize about and hard to predict. Indeed, people are often in a very poor position to know what changes in their character a certain kind of marriage or career is likely to bring. There may be cases in which the relation between change of situation and change of character is more predictable. An example is a study showing that American teenagers who spent one-month homestays in Japan "increased in flexibility and independence and became less conventional compared with the control group" (Stitsworth 1989). The decision to go to Japan might have been, for some, a decision to modify their characters. Even here, though, the relation between the decision and the change of character is indirect. Thus, although our ability to make decisions that lead to changes in character is an important qualification on Hume's view (one that he acknowledges in "The Sceptic"), it still allows us to say that the great majority of people have rather little control over their characters, especially if control is taken to mean direct control.

Why does it seem, at least at first, so counterintuitive to hold people responsible for characters over which they have had little control? Why should responsibility seem to presuppose that something be voluntary? Here is one suggestion. The language of responsibility, of praise and blame, can be understood only in relation to the way in which it normally functions. If we look first at actions, we see that there is no point in praising or blaming actions over which (whether because of compulsion, the effects of hypnosis, or for some other reason) the agent had no control. The point of blaming an action is to make it less likely that the agent, or someone else, will perform such actions in the future. But if an action is involuntary, there is no reason to think that blame will diminish the likelihood of such an action's occurring again. Thus, if our primary attention is on actions, it looks as if there is a close functional link between responsibility and the voluntary.

A closer understanding of this requires examination of the concept of the voluntary and also of the way in which morality functions as a regulated system of praise and blame. We may begin by defining *voluntary* as immediately controlled or controllable by an act of the will.

If Bloggs does *Y* but could have prevented himself from doing it if he had tried, then *Y* is voluntary. (In the special case in which Bloggs does *Y* and could not have prevented himself from doing it if he had tried—but only because of an impediment or obstacle which Bloggs did not know about and which did not in any ordinary sense *make* Bloggs do *Y*—then, *Y* also counts as voluntary.) We should bear in mind the word *immediately* in our definition of voluntary. Perhaps, as Hume suggests, Bloggs could modify his character gradually by cultivation of certain habits and bents of mind; but if it is true that Bloggs could not immediately change his character by an act of will, then Bloggs's character is largely involuntary.

If actions simply flowed from character like water from a pipe, then if Bloggs's character is (largely) involuntary, it would seem that all of his actions would be (largely) involuntary also. The relation between character and actions, however, is much more complicated. Selfish people do not always behave selfishly; nasty people do not always do nasty things. Part of the reason is that to have a character trait *X* is to have a propensity to do things of sort *X* and does not require that one constantly, on every occasion, do things of sort *X*. As we have seen, it does not even require that one usually or often do them. A large part of the reason why people do not in every case do what we might think best expresses or reveals their character is that whether an action is performed or not can be determined by features of the situation that is immediately present, including incentives, pressures, or threats. The person who is capable of extraordinary cruelty may never behave cruelly except when under considerable pressure or when offered considerable incentives. Character certainly does have a causal role in behavior: In many cases, part of the explanation of why someone behaved in such and such a manner must be that he or she is such and such a person. But another part of a causal explanation of behavior will be features of the situation, which may include incentives or threats; and, in a great many cases, pointing out these features will be nearly the entire explanation. (Why did Spike not take the money? Everyone was watching, and. . . .) Incentives or threats can lead the nasty person to behave in a perfectly civilized manner, although leaving unchanged the nasty character that would produce (if suitable opportunities arose) nasty behavior.

It is central to the functioning of morality that praise in moral language can be an unusually strong inducement to behave in an appropriate way; also blame in moral language (as when someone's behavior is called vicious, immoral, or wicked) can exert unusually strong pressure.

Clearly praise and blame (or the anticipation of praise or blame) can have the appropriate effect as inducement or threat only if an action is under the control of the agent. If Bloggs cannot, by an act of the will, change the way in which he is about to behave, then the promise of praise or the threat of blame would be utterly pointless. For this reason alone, it makes sense to hold people responsible only for voluntary actions. There is an added reason, though, not to blame people for involuntary actions. Morality works as a system of influence within a general population partly because it is not exceedingly demanding, so that most people can feel that they pretty much meet the demands of morality. If these demands were greater, and major lapses much more unavoidable, the response might well be despair or apathy. Because of this, any kind of behavior that is optimal but requires unusual personal resources (i.e., heroic or saintly behavior) is generally considered supererogatory rather than morally required (see Kupperman 1983, chap. 11). The same reason that leads to creation of the category of the supererogatory also would tell against any tendency to blame people for actions that they could not control. It would be demoralizing as well as ineffective.

It is, on the other hand, neither ineffective nor (to any significant degree) demoralizing to praise or blame people for characters that are largely involuntary. Because of the link between character and action, such praise or blame can be taken to reflect on action. Let us suppose that Bloggs is selfish and that he is unable through any effort of will immediately not to be a selfish person. But he *is* able to prevent himself from performing selfish actions. If we blame him for being a selfish person, this may well be an incentive for him to avoid performing selfish actions (especially when these are likely to be known about). Furthermore, our blame may have the effect that he would prefer not to be a selfish person: although this will have no immediate appreciable effect on how selfish he actually is, it may induce him to try to convince himself (by performing some unselfish actions) that he really is unselfish.

Thus, even if character is largely involuntary in the sense defined, holding people responsible for their characters is not ineffective: It can modify the way they behave. (This is *not* to say that people, including philosophers, normally praise or blame as a device to modify behavior; to equate the function of an utterance with a speaker's intention would be like saying that people in agony normally scream in order to get help.) Holding people responsible for their characters also is likely not to be (to any significant degree) demoralizing because of people's abilities to persuade themselves that they are much nicer than they really are. It is, after all, usually much more difficult to deceive oneself about specific actions one has performed than to deceive oneself about one's character. Sartre, in his well-known discussion of bad faith, glides between cases in which someone deceives himself or herself about whether he or she has performed an action of a certain sort and cases in which self-deception is about the character exhibited by a series of actions (1943, pt. 1, chap. 2). No doubt both kinds of self-deception take place. But to deceive oneself about whether one has performed an action of a certain sort (say, mailing a certain letter or a specific sexual act) is, in the ordinary and readily classifiable case, abnormal; to deceive oneself about the character exhibited by a series of actions must, on the other hand, be considered normal because there is often plenty of interpretative leeway in whether an action or a few actions are regarded as exceptional and unrepresenta-tive or as expressive of character. Thus, we may well not be reliable judges of our own characters. As Hume remarks, "No one can well distinguish *in himself* betwixt the vice and virtue, or be certain, that his esteem of his own merit is well-founded" (1739, pp. 597–98). If we tell Bloggs that he is selfish, he is likely not to be demoralized, especially after he performs a few conspicuous unselfish actions and convinces himself that he is really a very unselfish person.

Arguments of the sort just given are so easily misunderstood that I should say more about the form of the argument. It is, first of all, not an attempt to convince anyone that we should hold people responsible for their characters. The starting point is that we *do* talk as if people are responsible for their characters, and this is engaged in even by people who also say things like, "Of course, he cannot help being such an awful person." The question naturally arises as to whether this way of talking is incoherent or rests on a mistake. My argument is that the answer is no. When we understand the ways in which judgments of responsibility function we can see that our practice in this area is not incoherent and does not rest on any obvious mistake. It should be emphasized that reduction of the meaning of our judgments of responsibility to their functions is no part of the argument and would be absurd: We would know what it means to hold someone responsible for something, even if we had no idea what point if any this kind of thinking has.[1]

A further function of praise or blame of character is related to the formation of character. Hume may be right in suggesting that it is unusual for someone consciously to prefer a character different from the one she or he has and, as a result, gradually to modify his or her character in a controlled way in that direction. (Anyone who doubts Hume on this might ponder something which is slight by comparison with change of character: The difficulty often experienced by someone, anxious to reduce weight, in effecting a long-term change in her or his eating pattern). But praise or blame reaches children as well as adults, both because we sometimes praise the character tendencies of children and because children are exposed to the general ways in which characters are praised or blamed in their society. Thus, the general pattern of praise and blame of character in a society or in the group within which a child grows up can affect the formation of character.

The formation of children's characters is, of course, at the center of moral education, and we will consider this topic at greater length in appendix B. One remark about the facts should be made now. Children do sometimes reflectively and explicitly prefer to become one kind of person rather than another kind. If this is both widespread and also effective, then my scepticism (which agrees with that of Hume) about the extent to which people can control their own characters would need to be restricted to the case of adults. My sense is that it is unusual for a child to exert considerable control over the development of her or his character—albeit less unusual for adolescents to exert control over the fine-tuning of their characters—but this might well be mistaken. Psychological research on the role of children's reflective judgments in the formation of their characters is needed and might be possible without gross invasion of privacy. Even if it were to turn out that children's reflective control over the formation of their characters is both widespread and effective, there are two reasons why this would not create a strong case for saying that people are responsible for their characters *because* they chose them. One is that it seems highly likely that the cases in which we are most anxious to hold someone responsible for her or his character will turn out to be just the cases in which someone drifted into having a certain kind of character without any reflective control (or much apparent capacity for such control). The second reason is that we do not normally hold children responsible for decisions in the way in which we hold adults responsible. We excuse the harmful actions of a small child because we are ready to see the child as responding or reacting to influences and other psychological forces, and we also say that the child did not know enough to make an informed decision. Surely, this attitude also would be appropriate to any reflective decisions about character that the child may make. Because of

all these factors, whatever the facts about children's character development turn out to be, the best case for not considering it absurd to hold
adults responsible for their characters remains the one outlined earlier:
Holding people responsible for their characters, even if these are largely
involuntary, is effective and functional in a way in which holding people
responsible for involuntary actions is not.

Even if someone's character is involuntary, it does not follow that
actions that flow from that character are involuntary. Thus, there is no
impediment to holding people responsible for actions that flow from their
characters. Suppose that Bloggs performs a selfish action; and suppose
that we explain it by saying that Bloggs is a selfish person and that this
was a splendid opportunity for him to behave selfishly, in that Bloggs
stood to gain a great deal of money and thought that he could escape
censure. Let us assume that Bloggs simply grew into a selfish character
without any conscious decision on his part as to what kind of character he
would have, and let us also assume that he could not become an unselfish
person overnight. It still makes sense to hold Bloggs responsible for
selfish actions that flow from his selfish character, for a number of
reasons. First, even if Bloggs cannot become unselfish overnight, he
could, as we say, make an effort to become gradually less selfish.
Blaming him for actions that express his selfishness can help to prompt
him to move in that direction; this can be meaningful and useful, even if
we do not expect a very high degree of success. Second, even if we do not
have much hope for a change in Bloggs's character, the connection
between character and behavior is, as we have already noted, scarcely
mechanical: Even if Bloggs remains a selfish person, he could curb his
selfish behavior, and under pressure he might. Third, holding Bloggs
responsible for selfish actions will function to discourage others from
behaving selfishly and might add to a climate of opinion that encourages
children to develop unselfish characters.

All of this leads to the conclusion that it makes sense to hold people
responsible both for their characters and for actions that flow from their
characters. Insofar as the subject matter of ethics includes what we hold
people responsible for, this places character and expressions of character
squarely within the domain of ethics. Indeed, many readers may wonder,
how could character not be central to ethics? Surely, the goal of any
ethical system is to encourage people and show them the way to be good;
surely, also, to be a good person is to have a good character. The second
half of this book will superimpose a complicated story on these simple

claims. Part of it also will be the way in which character functions not only in ethical decision, but also within the structure of values for which people should aim in their lives.

Note

1. We can distinguish within a framework governing criteria for responsibility between "X is responsible" and "It might be advantageous to hold X responsible." For example, in our familiar framework someone is to be blamed for an action only if the action is both wrong and voluntary. In the famous case in which it was thought advantageous ("as an example to the others") to execute admirals who did their best to win a battle, but lost, we would insist that—wherever the advantages in fact lay—the admirals were not to blame.

Separate from such intraframework judgments is the question of whether a framework governing criteria for responsibility that someone posits or proposes is appropriate. One relevant factor, surely, is whether it is, in fact, the framework of ordinary moral discourse. There is a burden of argument on any proposed revision. The framework of ordinary moral discourse links the voluntary to responsibility for actions, but not to responsibility for character. Some might attempt to shoulder the burden of argument at this point by contending that it would be advantageous not to hold people responsible for their characters. I have argued the opposite of this.

Others might argue instead, that there is a general principle: " 'Ought' implies 'can,' " from which it follows that, by and large, we should not hold people responsible for their characters. My reply is " 'Ought' implies 'can' " has been advanced and widely accepted mainly in relation to actions and that some separate line of argument is needed to extend the principle to characters (against the grain of ordinary moral discourse). In addition, John Kekes recently has argued, " 'Ought' implies 'can' " is itself a normative judgment rather than some kind of analytic truth (1990). This reinforces the judgment that significant advantages need to be shown if we are to be convinced to apply the principle to responsibility for character.

Finally, the line of argument of this chapter would be challenged by anyone who held that (1) there is a fact of the matter as to whether someone is responsible for her or his character, and (2) this fact of the matter is independent both of how we actually talk in such matters and of whether it is advantageous that we continue to talk in such a way. No one to my knowledge has made such a case. Indeed, philosophers who are moral realists (among whom I count myself) generally are either realists about rightness or wrongness, obligation, values, or some combination of these. Realism about responsibility as an independent moral notion would represent a further claim.

II

THE PLACE OF
CHARACTER IN ETHICS

4

Ethical Theory and Choice

We may begin by saying a little about choice. There are clear-cut examples of what we would call choices, as when Bloggs thinks, "shall I do X or Y?" and, then, does X, even though (if he had wanted to) he could have done Y (or, at least, had every reason to think he could have done Y). In these clear-cut cases, choice involves something (an action, thought, or desire) that is voluntary (in the sense defined in chap. 3) and also involves explicit consideration (followed by rejection) of an alternative. The first of these features seems to be essential to what we would call choice. We would not, that is, say that Bloggs has made a choice if, in fact, something outside of his own will made him behave as he did and he could not have behaved otherwise, even if he had wanted to. Were determinism to turn out to be true, we still could speak of Bloggs as making choices in cases in which the causal determination of his behavior (or thought or desire) is routed through what he wants, so that he is causally determined to do (or think or desire) X; if all of this were the case, we still could say that if *per impossibile* he had wanted to do (or think or desire) Y he could have. Thus, there can be clear-cut cases of choice, even if determinism is true; my own view of determinism (that it is science fiction) will not enter into the discussion that follows.

What of the second feature of clear-cut cases of choice, that there is explicit consideration (followed by rejection) of an alternative? Is this also essential to what we would call choice? The answer seems doubtful if we examine cases such as this. Bloggs is driving a car and is looking at the road but thinking of something else. An animal appears in front of the car, and Bloggs immediately, "without thinking," swerves so as to miss it. Only a moment later does what he has done register on him. In this case, not only did Bloggs not explicitly consider an alternative to his action, he did not even explicitly consider his action. Did Bloggs choose to swerve? If Bloggs looks straight at the animal and does not swerve, does this mean that he chose not to swerve? If there is a man in front of the car and Bloggs looks straight at him, has no thoughts that he can report afterwards, and drives straight ahead, does this mean that Bloggs chose to run over the man?

Linguistic intuitions may vary from person to person and from case to case. My suggestion is that most people cannot classify these as cases of choice without some sense of stretching language, but they cannot comfortably classify them as cases not of choice, either. We readily speak of choice when there is explicit awareness of, and response to, possibilities and when response takes the form of voluntary action; we readily refuse to speak of choice when what is done is involuntary. These cases all fall somewhere in the middle.

Someone who is most struck by the fact that, in every one of these cases, Bloggs could have behaved otherwise, might try to emphasize this by regarding them as unqualified cases of choice. Existentialists sometimes have suggested that everything that we do, think, or desire that is not involuntary involves "choice." This view implies that we are constantly making choices, even if we are not reflectively aware of doing so, even if these "choices" are not marked in what we say we are doing (or thinking or desiring) or in any inner monologue.

For the purposes of this book I will use *choice* in this broad sense, regarding any action, thought, or desire as chosen if we could have acted, thought, or desired differently if we had wanted to. (In the special case in which we could not have prevented ourselves from doing something if we had tried—but only because of an impediment or obstacle which we did not know about and which did not make us do whatever it was—what we do, think, or desire also counts as chosen.) *Chosen,* thus, will be used interchangeably with *voluntary* as defined in chapter 3. Nothing in the argument that follows hinges on this linguistic decision, which is merely designed to simplify the presentation of a broad range of cases. The reader should bear in mind that much that is, in this broad sense, chosen is not consciously chosen. There is no intention to obscure the differences among what we will speak of as choices.

These differences can be considerable. Imagine at one extreme Smith, who takes Immanuel Kant more seriously than Kant perhaps meant to be taken. When a man appears in front of her car, Smith forces herself by an effort of alertness to register this explicitly: "There is a man in the way of my car; if I do not swerve, he will be killed." She also utters a maxim, "One should avoid taking (human) life whenever possible," which she knows is validated by the categorical imperative. One hopes that there is still time for Smith to swerve. At the other extreme is Bloggs, who thoughtlessly swerves. Smith makes what is by any standard a moral choice. Bloggs makes what I will call a choice, although he himself might well be hesitant afterwards to speak of himself as having made a moral choice. The important points here are: (1) however we talk about "choice," we would hold both Smith and Bloggs about equally blameworthy if they hit the man in front of their car, and (2) any adequate ethical theory has to make sense (and be useful) in relation to both kinds of case.

One reason for emphasizing the range of what might be called choices is that a good deal of ethical theory has focused exclusively on cases like that of Smith. The subject matter of ethics has been presented, that is, as consisting of cases in which something of importance is at stake and someone explicitly weighs alternatives and then decides to do one thing or another. Ethical theories have been designed with a view toward telling people how to make these decisions.

Such views disregard the mechanisms of selective attention and reflection that everyone has, not to mention the possibilities of pure thoughtlessness. They also disregard continuities in human commitment and action. Many of the choices that loom largest in people's lives involve continuing engagement with the objects of choice: Commitment to a person, to a group of people (such as a family or community), or to a political or social cause typically takes this form. Our difficulties in seeing this clearly run deeper than the level of ethical theory. The very language of choice, which is strained in speaking of unreflective and thoughtless choices, also loses its clarity when we speak of continuing choice over a period of time. If Bloggs works loyally over a period of twenty years to promote the well-being of X (where X can be a person, a cause, a political party, or whatever), do we regard this as one choice that Bloggs has made, or as many? If it is many choices, how many are there? Some might answer in terms of the number of occasions on which Bloggs has stopped to think about whether he should continue to promote the well-being of X, but the thrust of the discussion thusfar is that Bloggs can be regarded as making choices even when he has not stopped to think but, nevertheless, could behave differently. The problem, here, is parallel to that of how we speak of a case in which, over a period of ten minutes, Jane sees Spot running. How many perceptions does this comprise?

One response is, "Say whatever you like"; and I agree that nothing hangs on what we decide is a single choice or a single perception. What does matter is this. Many of the most crucial "choices" in our lives turn out to be clusters of an indeterminate number of choices, most or all of which point in the same direction, which are such that many are not reflective or explicit. Any model of choice in human life must take account of this. Ethical theories which focus on explicit choices in which alternatives are weighed leave this out.

There is a gap here between how we would like to see human life, and what it really is like. We would like to see our lives in terms of discrete choices, usually not occurring all too frequently; the periods in between these can seem a free-play zone in which we are just living and not choosing. Why is this picture so seductive? There are intellectual reasons: The picture is simple, and, if we cling to it, choice can seem easy to describe. The major appeal, though, is that a life of continuous choice can seem and feel much more strenuous than the one which this picture tries to convince us we have. Only a puritan like Jean-Paul Sartre could find an image of continuous choice, with a corollary of continuous responsibility, positively appealing. Nevertheless, commitments often *do* involve continuous choice (in the broad sense of *choice* we have adopted). Many of these choices become quite predictable once an initial choice, which may be explicit, has been made. But, all the same, inexplicit, unreflective choices—many of which flow from commitments—are a continuing feature of human life.

Let us return to the selective attention and reflection I have contended are important features of everyone's life, even in relation to matters of importance. Two truths about this selectivity need to be borne in mind. One is that it is, in fact, essential to human life. We cannot possibly take everything in or treat everything as problematic. If some facts register and some situations are treated as problematic, this is so that most things need not register and so that during most of life we will not have to pause for reflective decision.

This much is incontrovertible. In addition, there are some philosophies, such as the Taoism of China and also Zen Buddhism, that emphasize the value of spontaneity, of the free unreflective exercise of our capacities. If we have to think about what we are doing, such philosophies suggest, that will spoil both our performance and the value of the moment. This does not mean that we should go through life like mindless two-year-olds; a great deal of training and discipline is required for someone's spontaneity to be able to yield excellent performances and beautiful moments. But the ideal life, in such a view, has no room at all for reflection about problematic situations.

A more moderate view is this. Self-conscious reflection has its uses, but any one of us is likely to have more than enough in her or his life. It is arguable then that any decision that a case calls for self-conscious reflection can be viewed as having a built-in cost, the diminution of spontaneity in our lives. The importance of the case and the usefulness of reflection in dealing with it, then, will have to outweigh this cost in order to justify the reflective pause.

The second truth about selective mindfulness is this. If it is granted that spontaneity and unreflective activity must play a part in anyone's life, it has to be conceded also that many choices (in the broad sense of choice) that are of ethical importance are made without reflection or even the agent's explicit awareness that a choice is being made. These choices, nevertheless, can be made very well or badly. Bloggs does very well when, without thinking, he swerves to avoid driving over someone. Schmitt does very badly when, without reflection or any explicit awareness that he is making choices, he does his job as a concentration-camp guard. Many questionable practices, such as slavery, the exploitation of women, mistreatment of strangers and foreigners, and so forth, have been carried on by people who seem in many parts of their life to have been nice, likable sorts; it may not always have occurred to them that anything in what they were doing called for reflection or explicit choice.

Against the background of all of these facts about choice, a great deal of ethical philosophy of the last two hundred years looks both oversimple and overintellectualized. To avoid irrelevant complication, we may restrict the discussion that follows to morality, which governs those choices the simple ones of which are such that, if they are made wrongly, we would speak of immoral or morally wrong behavior. The most serious lapses of recent ethical philosophy are in relation to morality. Many philosophers have treated morality as if each of us is a computer which needs a program for deciding moral questions; the ethical philosophy is built around, and delivers, this program. Ethics, then, in this view is at work only at those discrete moments when an input is registered and the moral decision-procedure is applied.

Even if ethics is restricted to explicit use of a decision-procedure, we have seen that a crucial step before we can implement a decision-procedure is that we notice that a situation is problematic and then reflect on it. Thus, priority must be given to the moral agent's sensitivity, to her or his awareness that a case is morally problematic (see McDowell 1979; Herman 1985; Kupperman 1988). Second priority goes to the agent's conscientiousness, as reflected in the willingness to reflect seriously on what seems morally problematic. Moral error can be (and frequently is) the result of insensitivity, of failure to recognize a course of action as morally problematic, or of a tendency to worry morally about the wrong things. It probably happens less often that a moral agent recognizes a course of action as problematic but through light-heartedness or irresponsibility does not reflect on it. But this, too, is a possibility. Hence, even if an ethical philosophy has a generally reliable decision-procedure on offer and even if application of this is all that is needed, a great deal must happen before this decision-procedure is brought into play.

One way of understanding this process is to take in two basic facts about the way in which moral categories (as embodied in familiar moral rules) function. One is that they affect our perception of the world as well as structuring our praise and condemnation (see Kovesi 1967). In a situation in which a great many objects, of various sizes and shapes, are in motion and many activities are in progress, including (in one way of seeing things) that someone's purse is taken, most observers are likely to structure their perception of the scene so that the taking of the purse is among the facts registered; indeed, if it is noticed at all, it is likely to play a prominent role in the perception of the scene. Traditional morality not only tells us that stealing is wrong, it also gives us a structure of experience in which acts of theft are distinct and are likely to be salient features of any scene in which they play a part.

The second fact is that the nature of morality, as compared with other kinds of normative judgments, is that it is normally taken with especial seriousness. We readily can imagine individuals and groups within a society who are largely indifferent to what they agree is morally wrong. But if this were the dominant attitude toward what purport to be moral judgments, we would doubt that this society had a morality (Kupperman 1983, chap. 1). Consequently, although we cannot assume that any given individual or group of people will be conscientious in reflecting on what he, she, or they recognize to be morally problematic, we can take it as a realistic demand that people do reflect on what they recognize to be morally problematic.

Where does all of this leave ethical theory? Before we can begin to answer this question, we have to look at some actual ethical theories. It would be impossible in a work of this size to provide detailed discussion of all that have been proposed in the last two hundred years, but we certainly can look at some main contenders. We will begin by examining in some detail two important and influential theories: Kant's and the classical utilitarianism espoused by Jeremy Bentham and J. S. Mill. In chapter 5, we can broaden our account to include comments on more recent theories, such as John Rawls's theory of justice (1971), and we can look also at recent virtue-oriented accounts of ethics provided by such philosophers as Philippa Foot and Alasdair MacIntyre.

The major danger in any discussion of ethical theory is excessive simplicity, especially in assuming that a thing can have only one function or can perform its functions only in one way. Ethical theories fulfill a variety of functions beyond that of providing a moral decision-procedure. This is especially important to note about Kant's theory and classical utilitarianism. An unsympathetic view of these theories would be that they are elaborate attempts to prove what we already know, for example, we always knew that it is wrong to kill innocent people or to steal, but Kant and J. S. Mill purport at last to show systematically that this is so. This unsympathetic view is unfair for a number of reasons, one being that Kant's method arguably has some implications that do not (and did not) coincide with common moral opinion and that classical utilitarianism has radical implications at least in the part of morality that is associated with social and political decisions. But the main reason why it is unfair is that these theories are much more than rational structures that support a familiar morality. Kant and the utilitarians, in effect, offer ways of interpreting and making sense of moral thinking. To the extent that we accept what they say, we emerge with a much more highly developed sense of what is meant by moral judgment, what the rules of evidence are, and of how we can understand the moral discourse of others and of ourselves. All of this is important to any ethical theory worthy of the name, and there is no intention of slighting it in what follows. Nevertheless, my focus will be on the ways in which theories such as those of Kant and classical utilitarianism provide moral decision-procedures; like most people, I will regard such decision-procedures as lying at the heart of ethical theories, even if the theories have far more to offer.

My three main claims about the moral decision-procedures at the heart of Kant's theory and classical utilitarianism are:

1. The decision-procedure is parasitic upon and presupposes a classification scheme of features of the world that we are supposed to treat as salient.

2. Even given such a scheme, the decision-procedure also is indeterminate in the results it yields.

3. The decision-procedure is oriented toward single decisions, viewed as disconnected from other decisions, in a way which ignores or slights the moral importance of continuity of commitment.

The first two of these claims need not be taken as criticisms. They will seem so to someone who harbors the image of human beings as moral computers and who believes that an ethical theory ought to deliver a morality program that will provide valid and unambiguous solutions to all problems. Ethical theories, indeed, sometimes have been presented in this way, but one of the points of this chapter is to disabuse Kantians and utilitarians of this hopeful and naive view. Indeed, the first two claims count against any presentation of a theory which ignores the need for sensitivity in applying the theory to concrete cases or which ignores the fallibility even of applications made by sincere well-meaning people. It may well be that no ethical theory will be immune to the first two claims. The third claim, on the other hand, does look like a serious criticism, in that it ought to be possible to develop an ethical theory that does not ignore or slight the moral importance of continuity of commitment.

In order to see how these three claims hold for Kant, we must focus on the pivotal concept of a maxim. Kant's categorical imperative in its various forms is not anything like a superrule: One does not apply it directly to concrete cases. Rather, it is a testing procedure for maxims that are to be applied to concrete cases. One way of grasping its function is to think of the categorical imperative as if it were a computer morality program. (Even if, as I have suggested, the categorical imperative does not lend itself to precise and unambiguous use the way a computer program might, the comparison can be useful in some respects.) In order to relate the morality program to real life, something about real life must be put in language that the computer can recognize and deal with. The maxim accomplishes this. A simple example is the case in which a man is tempted to perform a complicated series of actions which include putting some money in his pocket. He intones the maxim, "I will steal when I really need some money." This maxim then can be tested by the categorical imperative, and it fails the test. He cannot will that his maxim be a universal law (otherwise he would will that he himself be stolen from by someone else in need); he is treating another rational being (the person stolen from) as a means rather than an end; and he is not behaving as if he were in an ideal moral world, the Realm of Ends.

The example above can elicit two responses. One is positive: Kant has insights that cannot be dismissed. Kant's characteristic philosophical method is to examine a distinctive mode of thought and to analyze what one is committed to by engaging in that mode of thought. The results include aesthetic disinterestedness (in the *Critique of Judgment*) and space, time, and the categories as conditions of experience of and thought about the world (in the *Critique of Pure Reason*). To think morally is to enter into a mode of thought that requires universalizability, concern for others, and due regard for ideal standards. Hence, the formulations of the categorical imperative can be taken to represent—or to approximate—*a priori* truths about what it is to think morally.

As contemporary writers such as R. M. Hare (1981, chap. 5) have pointed out, anyone has the alternative of not thinking morally. Someone who does not enter into the world of the *Critique of Pure Reason* is an imbecile, but it is possible for a reasonably intelligent person without flat contradiction not to enter into the moral thought examined in the *Critique of Practical Reason* or the aesthetic thought examined in the *Critique of Judgment*. However, if one does think morally, one cannot legitimately treat oneself, because of special self-regard, as an exception to rules that one would apply to others; one is similarly bound to take account of the wishes and well-being of others, and so forth.

The formulation just given of what Kant got right is deliberately broad in order to leave open the possibility that Kant's own version of what is implicit in moral thought is overstated or excessively neat in its outlines. This leads me to the second response, which focuses on what Kant mainly got wrong: his insistence on generality. In Western culture, morality traditionally has centered on rules and principles. This is mirrored in, for example, a tendency to describe someone who is very moral as a woman (or man) of principle. Kant seems to assume that this feature, too, is essential to morality in something like a logical way, that the maxims which are central to his version of morality must take the form of general rules. This assumption, though, however attractive it may be, is unwarranted.

Examples may help to make the issue of generality more clear. We may begin with familiar broad general rules, such as "One should not steal" and "One should not make false promises." These are general, in that they apply to ranges of cases that are not required to be closely similar to one another; the possibility is left open that one instance of stealing can be different in important respects from another, but both are declared to be wrong. The rules are broad, in that they cover a very wide variety of cases in which a fairly unspecific label (stealing or making false promises) can be applied. Examples of less broad general rules are: "One should not steal unless one is very poor and the theft is from a Fortune 500 company" or "One should not steal unless the theft is to save someone's life and there is no other way to accomplish that end." Here, the variety of what is forbidden is narrower than for "One should not steal," but the rule still is general, in that the possibility is left open that one case covered by the rule can be different in important respects from another, even though the rule imposes the same interdiction or gives the same permission to both. Theft from Fortune 500 companies can take drastically different forms, as can a refusal to steal from something that is not a Fortune 500 company. An example of a maxim that is not a general rule is, "Stealing is wrong in any case that is in relevant respects similar to the one at hand." This maxim leaves open the question of what will count as relevant similarity; but it cannot be applied to cases that are different in important respects from the case at hand; hence it is not general. Philosophers, such as R. M. Hare (1963), have distinguished between generality, which links a case with all those that share some general description, and universalizability, in which the link is with all those that are similar in relevant respects. Hare argues, in effect, that all the logic of moral discourse yields is universality of maxims, not generality; this position seems to me to have survived attack very successfully.

Not only are Kant's maxims general rules, but much of the time he talks as if they will be broad general rules, such as "I will not make false promises" or "I will not steal." Rigorism, the view that there are broad general moral rules which are valid with no exceptions, has become highly unfashionable; and some commentators have been prepared to argue that Kant (despite appearances) was not seriously a rigorist (see

Paton 1953–1954). This reinterpretation illustrates some of the difficulties that attend any criticism of Kant, such as mine: The principle of
charity of interpretation can be held to apply with especial force to the
work of a great philosopher, and some skilled and conscientious Kantian
scholar will be able to argue that Kant did not really intend the emphasis
on generality and breadth of maxims for which I am criticizing him. The
issue, here, is complicated by two factors. One is that it must be conceded
that an emphasis on general and broad maxims is not so pronounced in
Kant's *Metaphysical Principles of Virtue* and that in the *Foundations of
the Metaphysics of Morals* (where it is pronounced) the emphasis must be
gathered from the examples presented rather than from explicit statements. Second, I am prepared to argue that broad general rules are
important to morality, although not for reasons that Kant indicates. Any
morality, even if held by only one or a few people, is implicitly a social
morality by implicitly claiming that it should be held within a society.
Further, any social morality can be viable and effective only if portions
that are of great immediate practical importance can be taught to, and
applied by, children and adults of limited intelligence. (Something like
this is true even of traditions that are less rule oriented than ours, such as
that of classical China.) The sum of these two points is that viable
moralities need to contain broad and simple elements; I would argue that
only rules of a highly general kind can meet this requirement. In addition,
as James D. Wallace has pointed out, familiar moral maxims serve (for
all of us) as reminders used in inculcating and sustaining character traits
(1988, pp. 64–65). Arguably, also, a morality that centers on broad
general rules is less vulnerable to some forms of perversion than one that
does not: It becomes less easy to claim that, even if what one wants to do
goes against prevailing norms, there are special justifying circumstances.
Finally, insofar as moral rules structure perception as well as dictate
conduct, broad general rules provide a readily shared, morally useful way
of seeing and portraying reality. Thus, I do not think that Kant was
entirely misguided in his emphasis on broad general maxims.

 This is not to say, though, that all rules within a viable morality must be
highly general or that sophisticated people who accept the morality could
not arrive at rules of very limited generality (or at ways of arriving at
judgments which, strictly speaking, did not involve rules at all) to which
the broad general rules could be regarded as merely crude approxima-
tions. Broad general rules provide a useful starting point and core of any
morality; but there should be more to a morality than a core, and positions

beyond the starting point may have their advantages. There is no requirement in logic or in the nature of moral thought that maxims take the form of general rules. Nor, if we do rely on rules, can we infer that for any given morally problematic case there is a single general rule that clearly and incontrovertibly is appropriate to that case. Suppose that Bloggs is thinking of embezzling a large sum of money from a Fortune 500 company. Is the appropriate maxim, "I will steal when I am strongly inclined to" or is it "I will steal when I am strongly inclined to if the victim is a Fortune 500 company (and its shareholders)"? Or should the maxim mention that the theft takes the form of embezzlement or that the sum of money is large?

Kantians would argue that these questions are irrelevant and that however one formulates Bloggs's maxim, he cannot without contradiction will it to be a law applicable to everybody and, therefore, what he wants to do is morally wrong. We might agree with the conclusion without conceding all the steps of Kantian argument. Hare's example of the animal lover who joins the fox hunt in order to subvert it suggests that the fact that a practice would not continue to exist if everyone behaved as one did within it need not demonstrate the immorality of a person's behavior (see 1964). (It would be impossible to have Fortune 500 companies to steal from if everyone stole from them; also, it would be impossible to have fox hunts to subvert if everyone subverted them.) In any event, there are cases, such as the notorious one in which a man steals from an extortionate pharmacist the medicine needed to save his dying wife, in which it is clear that how one formulates the maxim is crucial. We arguably could endorse as a law applicable to everyone the maxim of stealing to save a life that could not be saved otherwise; we cannot so endorse the maxim of stealing when one very much wants to.

The crucial point is: Even if one were to accept Kant's categorical imperative in all his formulations as entirely valid, the categorical imperative cannot be related to concrete cases without the interposition of a maxim; and cases do not, as it were, have maxims written on them. Indeed, any fair reading of Kant's ethics discloses his enormous reliance on a moral tradition as a source of a classification scheme for viewing morally problematic cases and as a source of maxims. The morality looks different if the maxims that are tested by the categorical imperative are much more complicated and less broad than the ones Kant uses as examples, and it looks very different if the maxims pick out radically different features of situations than those picked out by our traditional outlook.

In this respect, Kant's decision-procedure is parasitic upon and presupposes a classification scheme of features of the world that we are supposed to treat as salient. We can also see how, even given such a scheme, the decision-procedure often is indeterminate in the results it yields. The case of the man who can get from an extortionate pharmacist the medicine that would save his dying wife only by stealing it illustrates this. The classification scheme embedded in traditional morality treats both property rights and the preservation of life as salient: Thus, there is warrant to see what the man wants to do either as theft or as preservation of life or as both. Whether his maxim passes the test of the categorical imperative depends, though, on how the maxim is formulated; in that respect, the conjunction of Kant's decision-procedure with the classification scheme of traditional morality is indeterminate. The widely discussed cases of moral dilemmas generally have this feature.

Finally, Kant's decision-procedure is designed for single decisions, with the assumption that in any normal life, occasions for moral reflection are only intermittent. The largest part of life, as Kant portrays it, is governed by what he calls hypothetical imperatives, which are not moral at all and with which he is not much concerned. In the larger part of life, we simply do what we think will make us happy; occasionally, we are called on to make a decision which requires a maxim to be tested by the categorical imperative, and only here does morality play a part. This particular division between morality and the rest of life has a number of peculiar features. One is that if moral reflection is about our duties and if ethics (as Kant seems to construe it) is concerned exclusively with moral decision, then relations with other people, including our families, are relevant to ethics only insofar as they generate duties. The caricature of the Victorian who, nursing his or her seriously ill spouse, murmurs "I am only doing my duty" fits this Kantian view of ethics. The most worrisome thing, though, about the Kantian view is the way in which it lends itself to an atomism of moral life. Commitments to other people are just one variety of continuing patterns of choice that give a life its character. Someone who takes the Kantian view seriously cannot maintain a proper sense of the continuities in his or her life, and cannot grasp the ethical importance of those moments at which the thorough Kantian would feel justified in hanging out the Off Duty sign.

Suppose that you have taken on a responsibility to another person or to an organization or cause. Kant does recognize ongoing responsibilities, but these are either responsibilities to improve oneself or general responsibilities to contribute to the well-being of others. This does not leave Kant in a good position to account for your special sense of responsibility to *this* person, organization, or cause. It could be argued that a special responsibility of this sort arises out of having made a promise; indeed, something like this is a highly traditional view of marriage. But even in cases in which a promise, explicit or implicit, can be argued to be a factor, the Kantian view, by presenting the responsibility as a kind of debt, leaves out something of great importance: the ways in which ongoing commitments become part of one's sense of the person one is, so that continuation can be right, in part, because it is integral to what one has been doing. To organize an entire moral life along Kantian lines is like organizing a walk by treating each step as a separate decision. It is also to overlook the inadequacy of any life in which all responsibilities are general ones which anyone (or anyone positioned as one is) would have, and none grow out of special personal commitments.

This is not to say, of course, that all commitments must be forever. People can change their allegiances and their relationships, although it is built into the concept of commitment that (if one was genuinely committed) one does not change lightly and that under normal circumstances a considerable degree of continuity is likely. The behavior of someone who takes lightly commitments that normally would be regarded as serious is usually viewed as unworthy or shabby rather than as perfidious. Think of someone who is only slightly helpful to friends in need. The model would not be that of breaking a promise so much as that of the moment at which someone's human connectedness turned out not to be what one might have presumed. None of this is flatly denied by Kant, but there is no room for it in his scheme.[1]

Classical utilitarianism has been treated by many as thoroughly opposed to Kantian ethics. Indeed, there are major differences; yet I wish to argue, using J. S. Mill's *Utilitarianism* as my major reference point, that my first two claims about Kant's ethics apply also to classical utilitarianism. The third may apply to Mill in a less-strong form than the one in which it applies to Kant. It may seem at first preposterous to suggest that classical utilitarianism is parasitic, as I have argued Kant's ethics is, on a classification scheme of features of the world that we are supposed to treat as salient. One of the differences between Kant's ethics and utilitarianism, after all, is that Kant's method is (through use of a maxim) to focus on a limited number of features of a morally problematic situation, and thus, in effect, to ignore all others. Kant's ethics, thus, requires that some features of the world be treated as salient. Utilitarianism, with its emphasis on consequences, in effect treats all features of the world from this point on as consequences (treating the word *consequences* very broadly) of whatever leads to them. Everything is relevant; so, it might seem, nothing need be salient.

This leads to an especially sharp contrast between Kantian theory and classical utilitarianism if we take the two approaches in the abstract. If utilitarianism is applied to a concrete case, though, the contrast begins to look slightly less sharp. Commentators frequently distinguish between act utilitarianism (widely attributed to Bentham), which dictates that among the actions that we could perform we choose the one that has the best consequences, and rule utilitarianism, which dictates that we follow that moral rule which, among the available alternatives, is such that general respect for it in a society would lead to best consequences. There are yet other forms of utilitarianism, some of which I think are superior to the two just mentioned; but this complication need not concern us here. There has been considerable scholarly debate about whether J. S. Mill could be classified as an act utilitarian or as a rule utilitarian. Because commentators tend to attribute to Mill the form of utilitarianism they think is strongest, it will not surprise the reader to know that I think he was neither. What is most immediately relevant is this: In every form of utilitarianism, moral decisions must owe their ultimate justification to assessment of consequences.

This leads to a telling general objection to utilitarianism, namely, that it is unworkable, in that we never can know the consequences of anything (Donagan 1977, pp. 199ff.). Immediate consequences sometimes are obvious: If someone shoots a small child through the heart, the child will die and the parents will grieve. Utilitarians however do not restrict their purview to immediate consequences. Eventually, the child, had he or she lived, might have turned out to be the ancestor of a dictator more wicked and pernicious than Hitler. We cannot be sure that an act that has terrible immediate consequences will not have, in the long run, preponderantly beneficial consequences, saving perhaps millions of lives.

One reply to this is that even if we cannot have entire certainty that the long-run consequences of killing the child will be bad, we can say that they are very highly likely to be bad. Thus, it will be pointed out, any utilitarian would tell us that killing the child is wrong. This misses part of the force of the objection, though, which is that we can be entirely sure that killing the child is wrong, even though we cannot be entirely sure that (in the long run) it will have bad consequences. Let us put this to the side and look at cases in which the immediate bad consequences are not so very terrible that it would be difficult for them to be outweighed by what happens in the longer run. The ordinary case in which someone lies, breaks a promise, or commits a petty theft can be of this nature. In the general run of such cases, there are two bad consequences: the suffering of the victim or victims and a slight tearing of the fabric of social trust. But, without imagining anything so unusual as a malevolent future dictator, one can imagine many cases in which there are indirect good consequences of a variety of sorts (e.g., the victim has a spiritual awakening, all the people involved come to realize how much they need each other, onlookers are sufficiently shocked as to reform their lives, etc.) that are such as to outweigh the immediate bad consequences. When confronted with petty lapses, we might well deny that we *know* that the consequences will be bad, even though we know that what has been done was wrong.

This is a point about the consequences of actions, but a similar point can be made about the consequences of societal respect for a moral rule or of anything. It is true that we can make reasonable estimates of the future (at least in many cases), but the point remains that these estimates fall well short of certainty: Sometimes we are in a position to say that something (e.g., that people generally keep their promises) will have better consequences than any alternative will without being in a position to say that we can be sure of this. This is especially true in relation to rules or general policies because of the pronounced difficulty in saying just what the major alternatives are. Alternatives to the rule that people generally keep their promises will include rules that people generally keep their promises in certain kinds of situations but not necessarily in others. They also may include rules that center on social conventions yet undreamed of, which in some respects are like promising, in others different. It would be foolhardy to claim near certainty that general respect for the familiar rule has long-run consequences better than those of general respect for any alternative.

The best utilitarian response to this set of objections is to concede the point. The utilitarian position then would be: *If* we had complete knowledge of the future (and had other archangelic qualifications), then we could solve all moral questions by the test of best consequences; the utilitarian could at the same time specify useful ways of approaching moral problems for all of us who lack angelic qualifications (see Hare 1976, 1981). Utilitarianism in this version becomes first and foremost a specification of an ideal morality, and in its pure form is not intended as a specification of *our* morality. Even if this response is adopted, the utilitarian needs to explain just how we, with our limited knowledge of the future and other limitations, are to make moral decisions. In fact, act utilitarians have tended to say that we should perform the actions that seem likely to have better consequences than the alternatives would, and rule utilitarians have tended to say that we should follow the moral rules general respect for which seems likely to have good consequences. The question, then, becomes how we make even the tentative estimates of consequences that this requires.

This cannot be solved by specifying ideal conditions for knowledge of the future. Morality must be designed for human beings whose knowledge is not ideal. If one reads the portions of utilitarian works in which actual moral decisions are discussed, one possible answer becomes clear. Utilitarians generally, like Kant, rely on established moral rules to provide the framework within which moral problems are approached (see Mill 1861, pp. 24–25; Moore 1903, pp. 155–65). We do not have to try to calculate whether stealing or murdering someone might have good consequences; the experience of humankind tells us that such actions generally have bad consequences. What is appealed to is not a rigorous scientific demonstration in which the alternatives of each action or policy are carefully worked out and consequences charted for each alternative. It is rather a commonsense experiential map of the world in which we have a rough sense of what usually has, as far as one can see, good consequences and what usually has, as far as one can see, bad ones. It is not my intention to impugn this approach to consequences: In the vast majority of cases, it is the best we have got. But it is neither rigorous nor scientific. It proceeds by placing individual cases within a class of cases about which there is some rough knowledge of consequences.

Thus, classical utilitarianism as a system of advice on how to behave morally is, like Kant's ethics, parasitic on a classification scheme drawn from traditional morality. This comment has to be qualified in two ways. First, it does not include the social and political agenda implicit in classical utilitarianism, which was very radical for its time. If money and various forms of privilege have diminishing marginal utility, so that a huge increase for an individual of money or privilege does not normally result in a correspondingly huge increase in happiness, then, a good rule of thumb is that (unless there are countervailing factors having to do with people's motivation and incentives) small increases of money and privilege for large numbers of people will make a greater contribution to happiness than will large increases for small numbers of people and very probably will also outweigh large decreases for very small numbers of already very privileged people. In this area, the theory is driven not by traditional morality but by commonsense assumptions about marginal contributions to happiness. Second, it is open to a utilitarian to devise new general rules or policies and to create a prima facie case that general respect for these would contribute (at least in societies like ours) to human happiness: J. S. Mill did this in *On Liberty* (1859). Despite these qualifications, it is true that utilitarians generally have relied, in considering whether actions that satisfied or violated traditional moral norms would have good or bad consequences, on the classifications provided by traditional morality and on commonsense claims about the usual consequences of actions within these classifications.

Indeed, what alternative have they had, given our lack of real scientific knowledge of the consequences into the far future of actions and policies? The philosophical literature on utilitarianism, ironically, is studded with elaborate discussions of particular cases which have been advanced, usually by antiutilitarians, as test cases for the theory. Many of these have the following form: Something which violates traditional moral norms (e.g., framing a man for a crime that he did not commit in order to prevent a riot, killing an innocent person to save the lives of many others) seems to have foreseeable short-run consequences that on balance are good. The antiutilitarian on the basis of this contends that utilitarians (at least, act utilitarians) would have to endorse behavior that, nevertheless, our moral intuitions tell us is wrong. Frequently, the act utilitarian response is that it is likely that hidden indirect consequences in the long run will tilt the balance, so that the action which shocks our moral intuitions will, indeed, in the long run, have on balance poor consequences. It is not my intention to ridicule these responses. Usually, in fact, they are at least somewhat plausible: Common sense tells us that violations of moral norms, no matter how well-meaning, frequently lead to feelings of uneasiness or guilt on the part of those who commit them, frequently lead to less excusable deviations, and may well weaken people's sense of being able to rely on one another in certain ways. I do want to suggest, though, that neither the antiutilitarian nor the utilitarian is on extremely firm ground in discussion of these cases, because no one can be highly confident of what the long-run consequences will be. Once this is seen, utilitarianism begins to look indeterminate in its concrete recommendations. If utilitarians rely on commonsense classifications and claims about what sorts of actions or policies generally have good or bad consequences, then, their assessment of a case will depend on how it is seen and classified. Utilitarians, like Kantians, then, will be able to disagree among themselves as to what ought to be done in a particular case if they disagree among themselves about the appropriate description of the case.

It is fair to say of classical utilitarianism, as it was of Kant, that the decision-procedure is oriented toward single decisions, viewed as disconnected from other decisions. Can a utilitarian do justice to the continuous pattern of choice that is involved in many kinds of commitments? One reason for thinking that John Stuart Mill is less badly positioned than Kant in this regard is the way in which Mill gives ethical importance to habits of mind. This is clearly evident in *On Liberty,* in which the usefulness of habits of recognition of rights is argued; but it also emerges in some remarks in Mill's essay on Bentham (1838, p. 103) and in chapter 3 of *Utilitarianism,* in the discussion of the best education of people who will take seriously the well-being of others. Insofar as commitments typically are sustained by habits of mind, to a greater extent than by reflective renewals of choice, Mill thus is in a better position to recognize their importance than Kant is.

Nevertheless, although Mill could have written a book that did for human commitments what *On Liberty* does for human rights, he did not. The classical utilitarian literature leaves us with no appreciation of the way in which, in our day-to-day involvements with the people and things we are committed to, calculations of the greatest good of the greatest number are out of place. Neither does Mill, any more than Kant, provide a clear account of the ways in which continuities in a person's life can be such that choices fall out from what she or he has done before, not because of abstract principles or calculations, but because of what is essential to the integrity of that life up to that point.

One final comment should be made on a feature, shared by the ethics of Kant and Mill, which tends toward slighting or ignoring the role of character in choice. This is the impersonality of the decision-procedure. In the philosophies of Plato, Aristotle, and Confucius, examination of ethical judgment began with the nature of the person judging and how he or she became that way. Both Kant and Mill eschew the notion that good ethical judgment presupposes some optimal personal development of the person who judges. Instead, they present decision-procedures that purport to be objectively valid and to be usable by any informed person of moderate intelligence; Mill by implication insists on also requiring appropriate experiences of, and continued capacity for, "higher" pleasures. What is required of the moral agent, besides a clear view of the case, is simply a will to implement the decision-procedure.[2]

Furthermore, anyone is capable, at least on occasion, of this good will. Kant gives the example of someone who claims to be governed by uncontrollable lust: We ask him, if a gallows were erected and he was to be hanged immediately after the gratification of his lust, could he not indeed control it? The answer, Kant assures us, will surely be yes. We can also ask the man,

> If his sovereign ordered him, on pain of the same immediate execution, to bear false witness against an honourable man, whom the prince might wish to destroy under a plausible pretext, would he consider it possible in that case to overcome his love of life, however great it may be. He would perhaps not venture to affirm whether he would do so or not, but he must unhesitatingly admit that it is possible to do so. (Kant 1788, pp. 118–19)

This example is interesting in a number of ways. Its great plausibility points to an asymmetry in commonsense views of the limits within which people have *live options* or what they might term *real choices*. It is widely believed that, as Kant suggests, even the worst reprobate is capable, on any specific occasion, of making a very good choice. There is, on the other hand, a sense in which an Aristotelian wise man or a Confucian sage would be incapable of performing certain kinds of dastardly actions and might reasonably speak of having no choice in the matter. To bring the point home: Would the reader be capable of torturing a small child for money? For virtually all of us, there is no choice in the matter. But in the commonsense view of things, even the most extreme reprobate always can do what is virtuous.

Second, it might be the case that the depraved man of Kant's example is capable of making a good choice on any particular occasion without being capable of drastically reshaping his life. (One might recall the analogy with the difference between a dieter's ability on any particular occasion to refuse tempting food and the dieter's ability to persist methodically over a long period of time.) This suggests that a person's ability to make good choices can look unlimited if we focus on particular choices, viewed as disconnected from one another, and might look more limited if we focus on continuous patterns of choice.

Kant and Mill can present their decision-procedures as impersonal and as making minimal demands on the character of the person who uses them because they believe that anyone of moderate intelligence (and in Mill's case the ability to calculate what is relevant) is capable of implementing the procedure on any particular occasion. This, in turn, presupposes what might be called a snapshot view of ethical choice. As I have pointed out, commonsense psychology holds that a pattern of thought and behavior that is continuous over a period of time makes greater demands on character than does a single decision; by focusing on single decisions these philosophers can discount the role of character development in choice.

Even apart from this, Kant and Mill can present their decision-procedures as making minimal demands on the character of the person who uses them because of inadequate analysis of the interpretative work that must precede use of the decision-procedures. The notion is that either the characteristics of actions, situations, or policies (which for the Kantian yield formulations of maxims and for the utilitarians yield classes of actions or policies that generally are known to have good or bad consequences) are obvious and accessible to everyone or that we can gather what they are by means of a special intellectual tool, such as the utilitarian calculus or Kantian casuistry (see Kant 1797). Our sense of what is relevant and important cannot, however, be analyzed in these terms.

In chapter 7, I will pursue this argument, building a case for regarding the character of the person who is judging as central and crucial to moral judgment. This will be part of an outline of the proper place of character in ethics. First, however, we must look at more ethical theories.

Notes

1. My account of Kant's ethics is intended to be moderately sympathetic; of course, it can be criticized as not sympathetic enough. One line of criticism is as follows. Kant does allow for positive duties of beneficence and the like, which are in effect ongoing. Also, there is some recognition that emotions will enter in the

fulfillment of duties. Indeed, granted that these are imperfect duties, and that we could not possibly be beneficent to everyone (even if we heroically wanted to be), emotions and special relationships would have to play a part. The special sense of responsibility to specific causes and individuals would have to be viewed as falling under the casuistry of applying ends of beneficence.

Let me concede first that any ethical philosophy, viewed as a structure for making sense of, and providing reasons in relation to, how we should live, will look stronger and more plausible in relation to some areas of life than in relation to others. Further, theories have a life of their own and can be developed in various ways. I do not deny that Kant says some things that could be used in developing a somewhat Kantian account that has room for ongoing personal commitments. The suggestion, though, is that such an account is not developed to any significant extent in Kant's writings and that any Kantian ethics that included an adequate account would seem to most philosophers to have a shape significantly different from that of Kant's ethics.

Here are two reasons why such an ethics would seem to me to have pulled Kant's own ethics into a different shape. One is that in many decisions tied to ongoing personal commitments, the question "Could I will the maxim of the action I am considering to be a universal law?" is relevant but is not the most important and decisive question one would ask. Indeed, even if Kant is right in claiming that one could not without contradiction will it to be a universal law that no one ever help others, there certainly are cases in which either of two policies with regard to personal relationships could without contradiction be willed to be a universal law. People often (and, it seems to me, appropriately) make their decisions in such cases by an appeal to sense of self—trying, that is, to maintain their sense of who they are (which includes connectedness to others as well as the nature of one's character)—or, alternatively, trying to move their sense of self in a favorable direction. Respect for law is not the crucial factor in many cases in which one decision will be significantly better than another. Kant himself might well have placed such cases within the rubric of hypothetical imperatives, but to analyze them thus in terms of a search for personal happiness is inadequate both because of Kant's jejune view of happiness and because it neglects the part played in these decisions by our sense of the validity of pulls exerted by other people (for the latter, see Sommers 1986).

The second reason has already been suggested. Any ethical philosophy which includes an adequate account of ongoing personal commitments will have to recognize that our judgments of what is wrong are of more than one sort and are made, so to speak, in more than one kind of voice. Take the extreme case (arguably this does violate the categorical imperative) of a parent who comes entirely to neglect his or her children. We criticize such a person differently from the way we criticize a financeer who has cheated investors. The latter has violated her or his duty; what is wrong in the case of the former is both deeper and different and has to do with failure as a human being. To continue Kant's all-purpose reliance on the concept of duty in relation to both kinds of case is to fail to do justice to the differences.

To sum up: A Kantian could say that we have duties to particular people as part of ongoing commitments, but I question whether this can be both faithful to Kant and entirely adequate. An adequate account of good and poor decisions in personal relationships cannot be based entirely on the categorical imperative, nor can we do justice to seriously wrong decisions by regarding them as violations of duty.

2. This summary judgment fits Kant with less qualification than it fits Mill. Kant's view of what constitutes qualified moral judges was less elitist than Mill's. This may seem ironic in view of Mill's political (radical) activism, but it should be remembered that it was Kant who had a bust of Jean-Jacques Rousseau in his study. There are two major factors in the difference. One is that for Mill, but not for Kant, empirical matters are highly relevant to moral judgment and in some cases (e.g., some public policy decisions) considerable education and skill may be required to assess these. Second, if one takes seriously what Mill says about "higher" and "lower" pleasures, it follows that some decisions (e.g., with regard to government support of the arts) are best made by people who know what the "higher" pleasures are and appreciate them fully.

Still, the qualifications for reliable moral judgment that one can read into Mill's account involve general requirements of education and (in some cases) sensitivity plus, of course, the steady willingness to apply utilitarian theory; a broader development of character and personal priorities is not presupposed in the way it is for Plato, Aristotle, and Confucius.

5

Justice and the Virtues

What is justice? This question has sometimes been taken (e.g., in Plato's *Republic*) as calling for a comprehensive account both of what a good life is and what a good society is. Many twentieth-century thinkers, although they may not like aspects of Plato's account, agree that a global account is called for. My analysis will lead to an opposite view: Questions of justice include a limited subset of questions of morality and also a limited subset of questions concerning optimal societal design. As Plato insisted, in order to know what justice is, we must know what the word *justice* means. In my view, the nature of justice cannot be appreciated without a prior understanding of the limited scope of the word and of the concerns that are related to it.

The place of this discussion in a study of character is as follows. On the one hand, to be a just person counts heavily toward having a good character. On the other hand, I wish to resist a simple equation of good character with a conjunction of various virtues or with the possession of what might be termed a master virtue. Justice has often been nominated for this position, so, in our investigation of virtues we may begin with justice. We will be able to see that there is more both to ethics and to good character than falls under the heading of justice; then, we can go on to consider whether character can be replaced by a consortium of virtues.

We speak of justice in at least three somewhat distinct contexts. One has to do with institutions or conventional arrangements (within groups or societies) that are designed to adjudicate rewards, punishments, liabilities, obligations, or endowments. One might think of the system of criminal justice, which in advanced civilizations will employ police, lawyers, magistrates, and judges; alongside this there can be a system of civil justice, which will decide lawsuits, assess damages, and so on. To ask about justice in relation to what is decided within these systems can be ambiguous. The question can be about the established ways in which rewards, punishments, liabilities, obligations, or endowments are assessed within the system of justice: These established ways can include rules that are supposed to determine decisions, procedures that are to be followed in arriving at decisions, and precedents (prior decisions that create a presumption that subsequent ones will accord with them). If someone asks, "Is that justice?" this can be a question about whether the rules or procedures have been followed or precedents duly taken into account. Alternatively, it can ask whether, even if rules and procedures have been followed and so on, the system is as it should be. The two sorts of question are not entirely separate, in that sometimes the rules or procedures of what is called a system of justice are so fundamentally defective (e.g., allowing laws that punish behavior that occurred before the laws were passed or ones that are kept secret, or that single out people by name for punishment) that one might deny that it really counted as a system of justice. A system that was thoroughly perverted in other ways also might not be considered a system of justice. In these cases, questions of "Is it just?" within the system inevitably lead outside of the system, so that there is only one possible answer. Nevertheless, there are many instances in which a genuine system of justice, which for the most part works effectively and, as we would say, fairly, is defective in a few areas, so that it may look as if what the rules and procedures establish as justice might not count as such from the point of view of an ideal system. If a woman loses an inheritance because of a legal technicality, we may have a double view of the justice of the case. We say that the case was decided fairly and, in that sense, the decision was just, but that from some independent perspective it was not just.

A somewhat broader context, in that it may well not involve legal proceedings, is that of laws governing allocations of rewards, liabilities, obligations, and endowments within a society. Here, again, a double perspective is possible. A man whose income is slightly above the maximum of those who qualify for food stamp assistance may agree that in one sense it was fair or just that he was denied food stamps, but at the same time argue that in another sense, because of his need, the decision was unfair and that the maximum should have been higher or that special cases of various sorts should have been recognized. A wealthy man may agree that, under the existing tax code, his tax bill is just, but argue that the entire system is unjust.

Finally, there are contexts in which no clearly established rules, procedures, and precedents govern in which, nevertheless, what look like issues of justice can arise. If one child within a family is persistently asked to do a great deal of work, whereas another child, for no obvious reasons, remains idle, the first child can wonder whether this is just. I will return to this in a little while, as it is highly relevant to the degree to which justice should be viewed as artificial or as natural.

Four points about justice should be made immediately. One is that questions of justice do seem by and large, as my presentation has suggested, to be questions of fairness. There are cases that fit one concept more clearly than they fit the other. If a police officer beats you up, that is clearly unjust; but you may not be inclined to term it unfair unless, say, it had previously been established that you were in some group of prisoners that was not to be beaten up. Conversely, if someone cheats while playing scrabble with you, say by taking extra turns, this is unfair; but it normally would not be considered to be important enough to qualify as unjust. By and large, though, what is unjust would be termed unfair, and what is unfair and a serious matter would be termed unjust.

A second point is that although (as the case of the child who is discriminated against shows) it is possible for questions of justice to arise totally outside of a system of rules, procedures, and precedents, this does not mean that every question of justice can be settled reasonably without any reference to rules, procedures, and precedents. If two people who were hired at the same time, with comparable experience and qualifications, who do the same or comparable work are paid different salaries, we may feel that this is unjust. But is it unjust for American universities to pay professors of engineering higher salaries than those paid to professors in the humanities? Is it unjust that both groups usually earn significantly more than teachers in secondary schools? There is no clear frame of reference within which such questions can be answered. Whatever intuitive ideas of fair pay we may have, they are not so detailed or so clear as to extend to these cases. It is almost like asking what time it is on the sun. We should not conclude from the fact that sometimes we can view justice from outside any system of rules and procedures that we always can do so.

A simple example of the point is the justice of tipping. If we ask what is a fair tip for a good waiter or waitress, the answer will depend on what country we are in and what the conventions of that country are. To tip someone less than he or she deserves is a minor injustice, but cannot be appreciated except in relation to conventions. It is true that the conventions of a place can be defective if a net result is that waiters and waitresses do not get enough to enable them to keep up a minimal standard of living (we would then say that they clearly have a right to more than they are getting) or if the whole system of restaurant service breaks down as a result of the ways in which tips are arranged (in which case our focus might shift from individual rights to the efficiency of a set of social interactions). But there is a broad range of conventions regarding tipping any one of which is acceptable within its context, and there is no abstract universal way of deciding what is appropriate.

The third point is this. Not all moral questions are questions of justice. Being tortured is not unjust unless it is the result of a judicial or quasi-judicial proceeding or is ordered or executed by someone occupying a role in the justice system (e.g., a magistrate or a police officer). If the torture is the work of the neighborhood sadist rather than an official, it is not unjust, merely very wrong. There is no reason, apart from a craving for neat and simple formulations, to subsume all questions of the morality of torture under questions of justice.

There is one exception to the foregoing, that is, cases in which no one connected with the justice system is involved, yet in which torture violated an agreement. To be tortured if one has won first prize in a competition in which the torture was second prize would be unfair and unjust. Apart from fanciful cases of this sort, the great majority of nasty things that ordinary people (who are not magistrates or police operating in their official capacities) do to one another are not matters of justice. If someone steals from me instead of from Bloggs (who, let us say, can much more readily afford it), this is not unjust—unless, of course, there was some prearranged order of victims in which it was Bloggs's turn. The central point remains that something can be morally wrong in ways other than that of being unjust.

The fourth point about justice may seem at first to run in the opposite direction from the emphasis in this book on character. This is that any institutionalized system of justice should be impersonal. Such a system must not only be foolproof, but also must be proof against villainy, sentimentality, partiality, and a host of other human weaknesses. We cannot in constructing the system assign a favored position to some judgments because they are made by people of good character: good character after all can be claimed fraudulently or mistakenly. Neither should the character of the person whose case is judged matter, except in such secondary and discretionary matters as length of sentence for someone who has been found guilty. If character is allowed to matter in fundamental ways in the operation of a legal system, any possible gains in appropriateness of decisions will more than be balanced by abuses. One of the chief requirements of a good system of justice, in fact, is that its operations are predictable to a degree to which people can feel that they know where they stand. Impersonality becomes an important prerequisite for this. This is especially true in relation to those fundamental entitlements known as rights. There are no rights that Smith has merely because she is a fine person or because all right-thinking people think highly of her.

Immorality can be divided, according to this analysis, into three species. One involves allocation of goods or evils that is unfair or is an abuse of the justice system, giving Peter more than he deserved or treating Paul more severely than he deserved. In order to behave unjustly one either has to be an officer of the law discharging her or his duties improperly or one has to be violating an agreement, implicit understanding, or normal way of transferring goods or evils in one's treatment of someone else. A second species of immorality includes ordinary cases of murder, rape, theft, and torture. It would be farfetched to regard these as cases of unfair allocation of goods or evils. They are not cases of injustice, but they are subject to the justice system; and what is done to the murderer, rapist, thief, or torturer then becomes a matter of justice or injustice. Finally, some immorality neither is unjust nor is subject to the justice system. Deliberate humiliation of members of one's family or friends or betrayal of trust in ways that are highly damaging but do not violate the law, falls into this category.

It is impossible to look closely at issues of justice without developing a strong sense that justice is, at least to a considerable degree, an artificial virtue, as David Hume said it was (1739, pp. 484ff.). Kindness and the absence of cruelty are natural virtues, in that even in a savage society one can be kind and avoid cruelty without understanding or participating in any social conventions that could be held to give one's kind or cruel actions their meaning. Justice, on the other hand, generally speaking, presupposes social conventions governing the allocations of various things. What is involved in paying one's debts and in not cheating people of their share of various goods cannot be appreciated apart from an understanding of the social conventions governing debts and how things are to be shared.

The thesis that justice is (largely) an artificial virtue must be qualified. There are cases like that of the child who is discriminated against, and I think cases of racial or gender discrimination, in which justice could be displayed and appreciated without any background of social conventions required to provide meaning. Other examples are ones in which someone returns or, conversely, fails to return kindness for kindness. These bring out the ways in which we have intuitive and rudimentary ideas that precede, or can stand apart from, systems of justice or results yielded by a system of justice: In the case of the woman who lost her inheritance, for example, they might enable us to view a decision that was fairly arrived at as in some sense unjust. Many of our intuitive ideas, obviously, are themselves shaped by local traditions of justice, but not every one is totally explainable in terms of the influence of various conventions. It would be absurd to minimize the artificial and creative nature of legal systems, but absurd also to discount entirely the role of very basic ideas of fairness like that illustrated by the case of the child who is discriminated against.

To be a just person is to make (and act upon) appropriate decisions in some of the areas in which one deals with other people; for example, it involves paying or tipping people appropriately, treating equally people who are in comparable positions, overcoming personal reactions so as to be fair to people one does not like, and so on. As already pointed out, many of these decisions cannot be made without consulting social conventions, which legitimately vary from place to place. This does not mean, though, that the conventions themselves are entirely arbitrary. They can be faulted as counterproductive, as cruel to those affected by them, or as violating fundamental intuitive standards of fairness. This is merely a sketch of what an examination would be of standards for a just social order. There must be recognition, on the one hand, of the artificial and creative nature of any social order and of the plurality of social orders that can meet reasonable standards. But there must be, on the other hand, recognition that there are, indeed, standards by which a social order reasonably can be judged from the outside and that a system of social justice can be fundamentally unfair or can be inadequate in some other way.

The question of just what the standards are by which a social order can be judged is enormously complex, and I will not pursue it here in any comprehensive way. I do wish to argue that intellectual and aesthetic achievements and the development of character need to be considered in any assessment of the well-being or success of a society. This can be seen best in relation to a theory that points in an opposite direction, John Rawls's (1971) account of how the resources of a society ought to be distributed. Because Rawls's account has been highly influential and is often classified as ethical theory, an examination of what he insists on leaving out of his theory can be highly instructive.

The first point to note is that issues of how resources should be divided are not entirely separable from how various goods within a society can be promoted or augmented. For one thing, some policies of distribution can have the effect of increasing or decreasing the resources to be divided; and this can be relevant to our evaluation of them. Also, if a policy has damaging side effects in relation to goods other than those being divided, this also can affect our evaluation. If, for example, a highly unequal division of money leads to rampant disease and child mortality, this strengthens the case against this division. Thus, although the issues that Rawls raises center on policies of distribution, they cannot be entirely separated from issues of what the important goods of a society are and how they should be promoted.

How do we determine what the important goods of a society are? If a philosopher does not wish to appear to be imposing her or his values on others, it may seem attractive to try to arrive at what amounts to a value-free ethics or, at least, a value-free account of societal values. A first step is to ask what people can be presumed to want, rather than, say, asking what reasonable people would want or what people should want. Answers to this question can vary. In most places, people, in general, can be presumed to want money. In a monastery, the range of priorities can be very different and may not include money. It can be argued, though, that desire for money (at least for moderate quantities of it) is almost universal and that even the inhabitants of the monastery might like to be able to give it away. Various liberties also could be argued to be almost universally desired. To center an account of goods on what people almost universally can be presumed to want is, however, on the face of it, an extraordinary step toward a lowest-common-denominator view of values. Could there be important goods which some people want and others, because of ignorance or other factors, do not want? Could there, indeed, be important societal goods of this sort? Might there, in fact, be factors almost as important in assessing the well-being of a society as its wealth, its liberties, and the equality of distribution of goods within it?

Imagine a society like that depicted in Aldous Huxley's *Brave New World* except for two major differences. One is that we are to imagine a degree of socioeconomic and political equality that fully meets the standards of Rawls's theory. The other is that this society, which we will call Tepid New World, is democratic; indeed, people are entirely free to denounce the character of their society and its prevailing tastes and mores, although it is not likely that many will listen to them. We will suppose the Tepid New World to be like the Brave New World, in that enormous skill and technology have been devoted to instant gratification of people's desire for pleasure and that almost all of the inhabitants live simply for a round of pleasures and (perhaps with the aid of drugs) are satisfied with their world. We may suppose them to have, to the limits of their reflectiveness, the political virtues of civility, tolerance, and fairness but to be sharply lacking in sensitivity and in ability to attend to, and reflect on, problems. As in the Brave New World, the arts (and, one assumes, the impractical sciences) are at an exceedingly low point. There is very little encouragement of artistic or intellectual creativity, and both standards and accomplishments in these domains are virtually nonexistent. Any taste for complex and challenging activities that people might have is satisfied by such things as video games and surfboard riding.

However much Rawls (as a private person) might dislike Tepid New World, he would have to rate it a more desirable social outcome than a society in which there were considerable scientific and aesthetic achievements but in which the worst-off people were materially less well-endowed (say in being able to afford only one television set) than the worst-off inhabitants of Tepid New World. The standards for what counts as a desirable social outcome are determined, in Rawls's theory, by what people would decide in the "original position," a situation in which they determine a society's distribution of resources without knowing what their station in that society would be (1971, pp. 118ff.). The central argument of *A Theory of Justice* is that people in this position would play safe and opt for that distribution in which the worst-off members of society would be better off than would be the case in any other distribution.

Better off in terms of what, one might wonder? Here, the value-free ethics comes into play. Money assumes great importance in Rawls's discussion: The people in the original position are all assumed to want money. It is stipulated, on the other hand, that they "do not know their conception of the good" (1971, pp. 137, 142). Having no standards for cultural or intellectual health, they will have no basis for criticism of the Tepid New World.

Why should we stipulate that parties in the original position do not have any standards relevant to judging the worth of a society other than those Rawls allows? They presumably know what money is; they know the importance of getting enough to eat; why, then, can they not know their conception of the good? Is it that Rawls assumes that no conception of the good can have validity in anything like the way in which scientific, mathematical, or historical judgments have? If so, one would like to see supporting arguments. Rather, is it that, because conceptions of the good notoriously differ from person to person, Rawls worries that if the parties to the original position know their conceptions of the good, there cannot be unanimous agreement on the standards for the just society? If so, one would like to see an explanation of why unanimity is required?

It may be that the explanation for the veil of ignorance that Rawls places over conceptions of the good is instead the following. He may well believe that one never has a right to impose one's conception of the good on others in one's society. Ignorance of one's conception of the good eliminates this possibility.

I agree that it is wrong to impose a conception of the good on a society. There are two strong reasons for this. One is that a workable society needs the willing allegiance of the great majority of its members, allegiance which is more likely to be withheld if people feel that someone else's conception of the good is being imposed on them. Also—as J. S. Mill argued in *On Liberty*—to allow someone to dictate the contours of others' personal and civic lives is to diminish the possibilities of individuality and of happiness.

However, it is not imposition of a conception of the good if public libraries that stock both classics and popular best-sellers stock a somewhat higher percentage of the former than circulation figures would warrant. Nor is it imposition if government agencies spend relatively modest amounts of money to help to support the arts and scientific research. Neither is it imposition if secondary school teachers try to convey the idea that Shakespeare and Mozart are remarkably good, not expelling or otherwise penalizing students who continue to disagree. The word *imposition,* in cases in which a social policy enters the life of an individual, suggests a drastic intervention which does not leave adequate room in which to maneuver. In each of the cases cited, the intervention is not drastic, and there is ample room to maneuver for someone who resists the conception of the good purveyed. Someone can continue to take out only popular best-sellers from the local library, avoid all artistic performances, ignore scientific advances, and so on. Thus, policies that are designed to strengthen intellectual and cultural activities can be implemented in a society without imposing a conception of the good; thus worries about imposing such a conception are not a good reason for depriving the parties to Rawls's original position of their conceptions of the good.

None of this is to argue against Rawls's main recommendations about the distribution of resources. Indeed, one can have some degree of sympathy with a philosopher's conclusions (or at least reserve judgment about them) and also admire the sophistication and elegance of the supporting argument, while believing that the argument has serious flaws. What is most relevant to the line of argument of this book is: Even if Rawls's account of how resources ought to be distributed is entirely acceptable, the view of a good society that goes along with his development of it is seriously deficient. If, indeed, the Tepid New World is unacceptable, it is because the ingredients of a good society include not only the factors on which Rawls concentrates, but also aesthetic and intellectual achievements and the character development of the society's members. One of the appalling things about the Brave New World and the Tepid New World is the characters of the people who live in them. Even if the inhabitants of the Tepid New World have elementary political virtues, there is too much that is not political that their characters will lack.

It may be argued that the preceding line of criticism is unfair to Rawls. It is true that *A Theory of Justice* (1971) has been widely taken to present an ethical theory; but Rawls recently (1988) has taken great pains to insist that it does not present a comprehensive moral doctrine, and that it must be regarded as a political conception. Any superiority of the Tepid New World over culturally vigorous societies in which the worst-off are slightly less well-endowed, it will be said, is political. We are free to admire rival societies on other grounds.

This is to assume that cultural deficiencies are entirely unrelated to the ways in which resources are distributed within a society. But is there any reason to assume this? Surely, subsidies to the arts and sciences can be presumed to be relevant to cultural vitality, as is the attention given in schools to future artists and scientists. That questions of cultural vitality also are, to a degree, political, is evinced clearly in *A Theory of Justice:* first by a comprehensive and blunt-edged attack on a broad range of views that Rawls classifies as perfectionism (pp. 25, 325–32); second by specific policy recommendations that follow from the general position of the book. Thus Rawls remarks, for example, that "the social resources necessary to support associations dedicated to advancing the arts and sciences and culture generally are to be won as a fair return for services rendered, or from such voluntary contributions as citizens wish to make" (p. 329). If I am right, this both results from a blinkered view of what matters to a society's well-being and also would promote an unfortunate result. One might have more mixed feelings about the suggestion that "greater resources might be spent on the less rather than the more intelligent, at least over a certain time of life, say the earlier years of school" (p. 101). One can see the advantages of the recommendation, although anyone who has seen the boredom and misery that can afflict highly intelligent young children in indifferent schools will be disturbed by Rawls's suggestion. In any case, the likely effect on a society's scientific and cultural achievements, again, points a little bit in the direction of the Tepid New World.

The most basic point is one that Rawls might well agree with. Even if he is held to have given an entirely adequate account of distributive justice, distributive justice is only one facet of justice, and justice does not occupy the whole of ethics. There are other virtues besides justice and other matters of importance within ethics. An ethics of justice, therefore, however well it is worked out, must be one-sided.

This point very much applies to any ethics that centers on rights, too. There is a large recent philosophical literature on rights, some of it very good. Because there is no work on rights that is preeminent in the way in which Rawls's work on distributive justice has been and because, in any case, the points I have to make about rights are highly general, I will not focus on any particular account of rights in what follows.

Nothing that I say should be taken to deny that rights are important or that they deserve a major place in ethics. The most interesting questions concern what the general justification of a system of rights, if there is one, might be, and also what the methods are of adjudicating in particular cases whether so-and-so has a right of some specific kind. There is room to doubt whether any writer yet has gone very far toward answering the latter question satisfactorily.

The recognition of rights is keyed, at least in part, to acknowledgment that, as Loren Lomasky puts it, "individuals genuinely are owed some measure of sovereignty over their own lives" (1987, p. 16). But a society of sovereign but extremely shallow individuals cannot be regarded as an unqualified success, even if the important rights to adequate food, housing, and medical care also are respected; indeed, the value of sovereignty is diminished (although not eliminated) if the people who exercise it lack the education and the experience needed for intelligent choice. Rights are important; but, as some theoreticians of rights (including Lomasky) have recognized, so is the promotion of character and of various virtues—intellectual, aesthetic, and moral.

Why have some philosophers concentrated almost exclusively on rights in their approaches to ethics? A fascination with legal-like and political reasoning may play a part. But one suspects also that often, as in the case of Rawls's construction of the original position, a determination is at work not to take into account ideas of the good. It is as if the values and ideals of the sovereign individual form a kind of ethical black box, and scrutiny within is inappropriate. This is to elevate to a methodological principle the tolerance that is so important in a democratic society. It scarcely need be said, though, that it is possible to believe that someone's values and ideals are seriously deficient and yet treat that person in a tolerant fashion. To eschew judgments of values and ideals is to be prepared to endorse a society like that of the Tepid New World. It also is to slight or deny the importance of character development to a society or for an individual.

Could the word *character* in that brief sketch of what an ethics centered on justice or on rights sometimes leaves out be replaced entirely by talk of various virtues? Might this be true of ethics as a whole? In recent years, a larger number of ethical philosophers have paid attention to virtues and vices. This represents a trend away from what I attacked in chapter 4. Might proper attention to virtues and vices supply everything that ethical theory has been lacking so that talk (beyond this) of character would be unnecessary? The title *Virtues and Vices* has been used for books more than once in recent years, but perhaps it should have been the title of this book?

The relation between virtues and vices, on the one hand, and character, on the other, is complex. It might be tempting to think of character as simply the sum of virtues and vices. But then is a strong character merely a collection of strong virtues or strong vices? Philosophers tend to speak of virtues as dormant or out of play during the period when they are not exercised in appropriate performances. It is not so clear, though, that character is dormant or out of play during these same periods. We tend to think of character as suffusing much of a person's life, even periods when the person is not doing anything that would count as activity appropriate to a virtue or a vice.

A virtue can be defined tentatively as a disposition to perform reliably well in some area of life; as Edmund L. Pincoffs says, "[it is] a desirable disposition of a certain sort" (1986, p. 9). We will show shortly that some major groups of virtues carry with them additional requirements and that others require less (rather than more) than reliable performance. The tentative definition, despite its need for modification, establishes a link between virtue and performance. To be honest requires that one perform reliably well whenever matters arise that involve money or other personal advantages, or truth, and there might be some temptation to take advantage of others or to misrepresent the truth. To be compassionate requires that one behave sympathetically to those who are needy or unfortunate. Courage requires courageous performances when suitable opportunities arise. And so on.

All these are moral virtues, in that in many cases they are reflected in good moral choices (such as the decision to make sacrifices for the sake of someone unfortunate or to take grave but justified personal risks in a morally urgent cause). Moral virtues can also be reflected in choices that we might hesitate to classify as moral, for example, when someone tells the truth in a matter in which so little is at stake that a lie would not be considered morally wrong, when someone generously gives up a free afternoon in order to read a colleague's manuscript, or when someone takes significant but reasonable risks in order to win a major prize in a competition. Some people would restrict the term *virtue* to moral virtues; indeed, when someone is spoken of as having many virtues, we normally think of moral virtues. However, there is a rival tradition of considering any excellence as a virtue, and my tentative definition of a virtue as a disposition to perform reliably well in some area of life reflects this. The disposition to prove mathematical theorems economically and elegantly might be spoken of as an intellectual virtue. The disposition to appreciate what the best angle is from which to photograph a scene and the disposition to understand quickly what the problem with an automobile is also would count broadly as virtues. In what follows, however, most of the discussion will be focused on moral virtues and on outlying virtues, such as considerateness, which resemble moral virtues in important respects, even though their exercise is not normally in doing what is morally right or expressive of what we would call a high moral standard.

To describe someone as a good mathematician or a good automobile mechanic is simply to speak of abilities. To describe someone as generous, courageous, and considerate is a more complicated matter. Certainly abilities are part of the picture, but there are other necessary elements; thus, it is easy to give an oversimple picture of these virtues. If we were to construe moral virtues as like intellectual virtues, except that they involve different areas of one's life, we might say, "Smith not only is good at mathematics; she is also good at helping people (and, thus, is generous)." At the opposite extreme we might say, "Smith's generosity is that she often wishes well for other people," and point out that being a good mathematician or a good automobile mechanic (unlike being a generous person) has very little to do with wishing. Both views of virtues such as generosity are one-sided and incomplete.

Someone can be a good automobile mechanic and yet wish that most of the cars that he or she worked on would fall apart or be damaged. Suppose that Bloggs works effectively on cars—for the money or because he does not want to be held responsible for mistakes—but delights in inner fantasies of wheels falling off and brakes failing. Bloggs can count as a good automobile mechanic (although, it is true, we might worry about the reliability of his work in the future). If Bloggs also gives money to the poor because he wants to be thought of as a good person (or even out of a sense of duty), but privately wishes them harm, we would not count him as a generous person. Wishes do matter to moral virtues. At the very least, possession of some moral virtues requires that one's dominant wishes not be of a contrary sort; normally, we do expect that the generous person will wish well to the needy, the honest person will wish that the truth generally be told and understood, and so for other moral virtues. Courage may be an exception to this generalization: We normally term people courageous who advance into danger, despite an overwhelming wish to get away. Still, if the soldier does not particularly wish his side to win and merely advances into danger to avoid worse forms of trouble or to make a good impression, we would not term him courageous (see Foot 1978, pp. 4–5).

It is possible, despite this, that Smith is a very generous person, even though she spends little time in having wishes for the well-being of the needy. She simply and matter-of-factly gives her money and time when it would be tempting to withhold them. She may well appear, and be, a cool, tough person rather than someone who is sweet and warm. Visibly wishing well to others is, in fact, in some respects like trying to look attentive at a lecture: It not only mimics the genuine thing, but also takes energy away from it. At the extreme, someone may wish very hard that the needy be helped and not be at all a generous person if he or she does nothing about it.

Intentions, in the sense of how one formulates what one is about to do, are more closely related to moral virtues than are wishes. Smith can be an honest person only if she formulates some of her choices in terms of returning money that is due, telling the truth, and so on. Her generosity requires that she think of some of her actions in terms of helping, or doing things for, other people. As Lester Hunt (1987) has pointed out, generous actions are spontaneous, in that they are done not because circumstances require them but because one seeks to promote the well-being of others in ways that go beyond what is required. It is possible regularly to help others without being a generous person, if what one thinks one is doing is quite different.

Now it is impossible to prove a theorem in mathematics or to exercise the virtue of being a good automobile mechanic without, in some sense, knowing what one is doing. Perhaps the mathematician or the mechanic will not be able to explain every step of her or his procedure, but there must be (along with the basic ability to do the job well) some ability to recognize how various parts of the procedure fit together if success is the result of genuine skill rather than luck or the mechanical exercise of habit or training. Thus, these abilities are like virtues such as generosity and considerateness, in that their exercise requires appropriate intentions.

The difference comes out when we ask whether the ability or virtue is compatible with frequent occurrence of contrary intentions. Someone can be a good mathematician, although deliberately miscalculating or spoiling proofs, and something comparable is true of being a good automobile mechanic. We might criticize such a person in various ways; but, as long as it remained clear that she or he was capable of very good work in mathematics or on cars, we would not deny possession of that virtue. Someone who is, as we say, capable of great generosity but who repeatedly deliberately harms those who should be helped is not a generous person (see Foot 1978, pp. 7–8). Smith may be very good at helping people, when she wants to; but an appropriate will also is required if she is to count as a generous person.

To sum up the results thusfar: One basic difference between moral virtues and virtues like considerateness, on the one hand, and mere abilities, on the other hand, is that the former at the least preclude wishes outside of a certain range and also require that one will and act appropriately on certain occasions. Abilities, however, also are required for these virtues. There is a level of maladroitness that precludes possession of virtues.

James Wallace has made a useful distinction between virtues that are forms of conscientiousness (such as honesty and fairness) ''that focus in a certain way upon the observance of forms of behavior'' and virtues (such as kindness and generosity) that involve a concern for other people (1978, p. 90). The points just made apply to both sorts of moral virtues. For Smith to be a generous person, it has to be true not only that Smith often (when it is appropriate) wills to help others, but also, when this is the case, that she often succeeds (Foot 1978, p. 4). Someone who never notices when others need help or who is deeply ineffectual when he or she wants to help someone cannot count as a generous person. The abilities required for generosity cover a broad range of skills of perception and skills in bringing about results: Something like this is true also for courage. In the case of virtues of conscientiousness, such as honesty, the abilities requisite for the virtue are usually fairly rudimentary: still, Smith cannot count as honest if she lacks the ability to know what honesty requires, any more than she can count as honest (whatever her actual behavior) if her feelings about deception and fraud are gleeful. The immediate point is that, although moral virtues go beyond abilities, they do require them.

Very broadly then, for X to have a moral virtue is for X to meet three requirements: X must have certain abilities, X's wishes must not fall outside a certain range, and X must will and act appropriately in the situations in which that virtue is tested. It is easy to see how puzzle cases can appear in relation to these requirements. Malatesta has all of the abilities of forcefulness and reasonable risk taking that we associate with courage. In any struggle, he wishes his side to win. In any military conflict, he wills and does what normally would be considered appropriate for someone in his position, so that ordinarily there is no hesitation in calling him a courageous man. He also is a forceful, determined, intelligent risk taker in acts of villainy. Do we speak of him as being, on these occasions, courageous? He meets the first requirement for courage, and it could be argued that he meets the second, in that he wishes for success. Furthermore, these might seem the most dramatic and difficult requirements, in that anyone can decide correctly in the matter of murder, but few of us could manage the nerve, daring, and force of will of Malatesta. The requirement that on those occasions Malatesta fails to meet is the easiest and also the most generic: The requirement of appropriate willing and acting applies in the same way to all of the moral virtues (and to virtues such as considerateness), whereas the requirements Malatesta meets are the ones specific to courage. I am inclined to agree with Philippa Foot that the normally courageous man who uses in villainy the qualities we normally associate with courage is not, on these occasions, displaying the virtue of courage (see Foot 1978, pp. 14–17). But it is understandable that anyone would hestitate in saying this. The way in which we might feel torn is indicative of tensions within our concepts of the virtues and of respects in which they are not entirely adequate to deal with large moral concerns.

To approach ethics primarily through the virtues is akin to what in literature is called genre criticism. This approach consists of placing, say, a poem or a play into one of a small number of classifications (e.g., tragedy, comedy, lyric, epic) and then applying to it critical standards developed for that classification. In much this way, the ethicist of virtues first must ask whether we are looking for courage, honesty, generosity, or whatever, and then apply the standards appropriate to that virtue. Both genre criticism and virtue-ethics can give rise to some perceptive and useful things and can sharpen our awareness of the varieties of excellence. The difficulty in both cases comes when something spills out of its category or when two or more categories arguably are involved in what we are attempting to judge. We want to give Malatesta high marks for daring and at the same time give him very low marks in other respects; to say that he has just now exhibited the virtue of courage sounds like praise, and it becomes difficult to know what to say.

This is one of the problems of virtue-ethics. Although grand ethical theories such as those of Kant and J. S. Mill can be faulted in various ways, at least they got people away from a compartmentalized view of the problems of life. If my analysis of virtue is correct, every moral virtue (however specific it may seem) requires a pattern of appropriate action; and the standards for appropriate action turn out not to be in every case internal to that virtue. In a just war, in which there is no risk of such things as civilian casualties, we can assess what is courageous without going beyond the traditional image of courage. Once there is a question of whether the war is just, though, or whether some daring acts might be for other reasons inexcusable, the traditional image is not enough. We then need, as in the case of Malatesta, to raise general questions of right and wrong. The point here needs to be underlined: virtue-ethics breaks down in cases in which a number of factors of different sorts are relevant.

Another example to the same point arises in relation to Edmund L. Pincoffs's remark that there cannot be too much justice (1986, pp. 92–93). One wants to agree. But imagine a parent who reliably takes care that each day's duties be divided fairly down to the smallest task and that a considered adjudication determine the allocation of any amount of money, however small. A member of such a family might welcome an occasional spontaneous minor injustice. The point, again, is that sometimes, in cases that might seem to center on a single virtue, other values must be kept in mind.

Against this weakness, we might place a somewhat muted strength of virtue-ethics, that is, its implicit reference to what agents are like. If Smith behaves generously, qualifying as generous, this is (as we often say) because of the kind of person she is. This is to bring out what usually remains implicit in virtue-talk, the way in which moral virtues (and some nonmoral virtues, such as considerateness) are linked to who we are in ways which considerably undermine any analogy with abilities and knacks. If Smith develops a knack for quick repair of automobile engines, this need not affect the kind of person she is; when she acquires the virtue of generosity, this has to affect the kind of person she is (see Kierkegaard 1846, pp. 176–77). This is made explicit when we speak of generosity as part of Smith's character. It is true that we speak of people both as "having" virtues and "having" a character, but it looks a much shorter step (as the argument of chap. 2 shows) to thinking of people as *being* their characters. When we link generosity with Smith's character, also, we become much better able to appreciate how she notices other people who need help, how a sense of this plays a part in her image of the

world, and how the attitudes and impulses that contribute to her generosity can suffuse moments when she is not actually doing anything
generous.

What I am suggesting is that an ethics centered on character has most of
the advantages and none of the disadvantages of one that centers on the
virtues. It allows us a sense of the ways in which who the agent is plays a
part in ethical performance. It also allows us, as does virtue-centered
ethics, to isolate areas of excellence or of flawed dispositions in a
person's life, so that we can comment on Bloggs's character where aid for
others would be appropriate, and so on. Character-centered ethics,
however, also readily allows us to focus on what people are like when
decisions are called for that involve factors of more than one kind; and it
lends itself to awareness of the ways in which qualities that are displayed
in good and bad actions also permeate the interstices of life.[1]

One might, in addition, claim advantages in psychological insight for a
view of individuals that focuses on character rather than on distinct
virtues. Such a claim follows from François de La Rochefoucauld's
thesis of the economy of the virtues; that is, what appear as virtues
typically can be understood only in relation to a balanced and mutually
adapted system of springs of action. (For a recent discussion of psychological research that seems related to this, see Cantor 1990.) "What we
take for virtues," La Rochefoucauld suggests, "are often merely a
collection of different acts and personal interests pieced together by
chance or our own ingenuity and it is not always because of valor or
chastity that men are valiant or women chaste" (1665, Maxim 1, p. 35).
Moderation is a prime example: "The moderation of happy people comes
from the tranquillity that good fortune gives to their disposition." In
another view, the moderation of man at the height of success "is a dread
of incurring that envy and contempt which people drunk with their own
success deservedly bring upon themselves; it is a pointless display of our
own greatness of soul" (Maxims 17–18, p. 37). Curiosity, also, may be
integrated in different forms in different characters: "There are various
forms of curiosity: one, based on self-interest, makes us learn what may
be useful, another, based on pride, comes from a desire to know what
others don't" (Maxim 173, p. 56). This and other maxims suggest a
general point: It is difficult to find any virtue that can be sharply separated
from a desire either for superiority or to avoid inferiority.

Confucius also suggests that virtues and faults must be understood as
forming an interrelated system in a way that marks him as clearly a

character-ethicist rather than a virtue-ethicist. A man's faults belong to a set with his virtues, he suggests, meaning I think that the kind of virtues a man is likely to have go along with the kind of faults he has. One, then, might infer certain virtues from the nature of the faults (Confucius IV.7, p. 103). If one accepts this, and also accepts the assumption that no one is perfect, it would follow that we also could infer the likelihood of certain faults from the virtues that someone possesses. It may be that we can understand other people in a more balanced way if we do not isolate for analysis what we see as their virtues and defects.

One question remains for this chapter before we leave the literature of virtue-ethics. Do the virtues (and does character) require practices and a social setting? Alasdair MacIntyre (1978) has argued powerfully for an answer of yes. My own view is more qualified. We can see why if we divide the question.

One way of dividing the question is that of Hume. He is a great proponent of MacIntyre's view, but only with regard to what he called artificial virtues, such as justice. Kindness and the absence of cruelty are natural virtues, which Hume thinks do not presuppose a background of practices. I argued earlier that certain very rudimentary kinds of justice also can be seen in that light. Hume's division still seems to me to be useful. But let us concede that sophisticated forms of kindness and of other virtues do require the background of practices and a social setting and, in fact, typically can be appreciated fully only in relation to a moral tradition. Thus, even if MacIntyre has overstated this part of his case, we can agree that moral virtues are mostly artificial and that the sophisticated and highly developed virtues that we most admire generally are.

Another way of dividing the question is this. We can ask whether the development of virtues requires appropriate practices and a social setting; distinct from this, we can also ask whether their continued exercise requires this. It is possible that the answer to the first question is more clearly yes than the answer to the second. In the analogous case of language, arguably a social setting is required for the language to exist and to be learned, but the last person on earth can speak English to herself and keep a diary. Certain virtues, such as those associated with promise keeping, require a social setting to be practiced: It does not unqualifiedly make sense to speak of, for example, keeping promises made to animals or to humans who do not know what a promise is. But someone surrounded by animals only can still be kind, compassionate, and courageous.

Let us look more closely at the origin and development of moral virtues. It is easy to say that, insofar as they require practices and a social setting, they require a community. This is a logical thesis, but it may gain in appeal from the resonance of the word *community*.

It is arguable that, however broadly or narrowly *community* is taken, it betokens something that the Western nations of the modern industrial world have too little of. I myself believe this; yet the case of another modern industrial nation, Japan, which is not deficient in this respect, suggests ways in which the praise of community might be qualified. Japanese intellectuals sometimes complain that there is too little room in their society for individual initiative and in general for what we might think of as the virtues of individualism (see Nakone 1970). If we look beyond Japan to traditional tribal societies, we see that tightly knit communities often have little room for people whose tastes, outlooks, or ambitions are perceived as jarring or as disruptive.

This is not intended to discourage praise of community. The yearning can have a function even for someone who, to take an extreme case, would be a misfit in any tightly knit community. The sculptor Henry Moore was quoted once as saying that the best strategy for a great artist is to study his or her opposite, as Rembrandt studied Andrea Mantegna; similarly, it is wholesome for highly individualistic people living in an individualistic society to be especially attracted to the virtues of community. This may help to lead to a better balance. But it is desirable to retain some sense of realism in the process.[2]

An entire community can share practices and a moral tradition within which, and in terms of which, virtues can have meaning as they develop. But there is no clear reason, either logical or empirical, why this is necessary. An example will help. We might look at the virtues displayed by, and preached by, Jesus in the New Testament. Most people, of a variety of religious persuasions, will (I think) agree that these virtues are remarkable and that at least some of them were very largely new. What were their roots in a community? The simplest point is: If one is looking for a community of people who valued and, in large part, practiced these virtues, the virtues preceded the community rather than the other way around.

The story, of course, is more complicated than this. Virtues cannot be developed unless they have enough relation to the moral tradition of the surrounding community so that the practice of the new virtues can be intelligible. The words *can be* intelligible should be accentuated because there is no guarantee that the new virtues will be intelligible, especially at first, to most people. Someone who is setting new standards, say, of fairness or kindness to people of other races, will seem puzzling. "What's she on about?" people will ask; "What's the sense of that?" People like Jesus or Buddha or those who first campaigned to abolish slavery will be seen as disruptive rather than as expressive of community values. Nevertheless, at the least, the way must have been prepared for such people, in that what they proclaim must be able to be seen as a variation on, an outgrowth from, or a reinterpretation of what had been accepted before (see Foot 1978, pp. 108–9).

These points about the virtues apply also, *mutatis mutandis,* to character. To the extent that a person can be viewed as creating a character, this self-creation does not take place in a void: It occurs against the background of types of people in a community and in relation to social roles and options that are available. It is impossible not to be, in some sense, a person of one's time, however many prevailing opinions and attitudes one rejects, just as (arguably) it is impossible to write music or poetry that a very shrewd connoisseur of three hundred years hence could not date as being of one's time. These may be perceived as limitations on the freedom of self-creation, but considerable individual variation and creativity are possible within these limitations. Nevertheless, a person's character, like her or his virtues, must be able to be seen as a variation on, an outgrowth from, or a reinterpretation of what has been found before. Tradition and a network of more or less common understandings thus underlie the development of individual character.

None of this counts against the pluralism which, according to Alasdair MacIntyre, "threatens to submerge us all" (1978, p. 210). MacIntyre has softened his hostility to pluralism in recent work, pointing out that "a tradition becomes mature just insofar as its adherents confront and find a rational way through or around these encounters with radically different and incompatible positions" (1988, p. 327). This does not retreat, however, from the basic claim that values come out of a community. Let me suggest that new virtues and more creative forms of character are more likely to develop in a pluralistic society than in a tight-knit community. The disadvantages of a pluralistic society include widespread loneliness and isolation experienced by people whose links to others are very slight; they include also a widespread (but not universal) sense that in a world with many competing standards there is none worth taking seriously. It may be, also, that more work and thought have to go into being a virtuous person in a pluralistic society than in one that is not. But, even if more effort is required, virtues still can be understood, can be practiced, and can be created.

To approach ethics in terms of virtue is, I have argued, a step in the direction of approaching ethics in terms of character. The first step, virtue-ethics, has advantages but also has the disadvantages of a compartmentalized approach to moral judgment. It works well in simple and straightforward cases but not in ones in which considerations of different kinds conflict. In chapter 7, I will argue further for the advantages of character-ethics, but I also will point out some risks and costs.

Notes

1. It might be argued that the preceding account of the superiority of character-ethics to virtue-ethics holds only if the virtue-ethics under consideration is of a fairly crude and simple kind, especially if it treats virtues as essentially separate from one another. Classical virtue-ethics, though, was not crude and simple. It treated virtues as character traits, while respecting the link between virtue and performance. Furthermore, the thesis of the unity of the virtues—that to have one virtue requires that one have all virtues—means that virtues cannot be treated as essentially separate from one another.

I have already conceded this much to the thesis of the unity of the virtues, that we would not speak of a virtue in a case in which qualities normally connected with a virtue were displayed in an act that was morally wrong. This is a linguistic point. There are a number of issues related to the unity of the virtues which are empirical and psychological rather than linguistic. Are courageous people guaranteed to be honest and generous? Are they, indeed, more likely to be honest or generous than is someone who is not especially courageous? Can we infer that someone has (or very probably has) a virtue on the basis of conduct that does not directly involve that virtue?

A classic psychological investigation of these matters is the three-volume Columbia University *Studies in the Nature of Character* by Hugh Hartshorne and others, published between 1928 and 1930. The researchers claimed that virtues are "specific," that correlations among virtuous behavior in various kinds of situations are not high. Rushton has recently argued that when the data are analyzed properly, the correlations in fact are high (1982, pp. 431–32). Even if this is accepted, it remains significant that there is not entire correlation among virtuous behavior in various kinds of situations. The Columbia University researchers did not distinguish between, on the one hand, what counts as virtuous behavior, in that it is in accordance with a virtue and, on the other hand, behavior which is virtuous in the strong sense that it grows out of genuine possession of a virtue. Correlations of behavior in various situations that is virtuous in the strong sense may well be high. Indeed, I do not know of any psychological research which shows that someone who genuinely possesses a virtue of a certain sort cannot be counted on to behave, in other areas of life, in ways which grow out of genuine possession of other virtues. But the data we have, along with common sense, suggest that it is plausible to deny that the virtues are unified in this sense. We think we know that people who are genuinely honest are not always generous, that people who are genuinely generous are not always courageous, and so on for other pairs of virtues.

This is not to deny that virtues can have important and visible links with other areas of a person's character. As A. D. M. Walker points out, "We infer someone's possession, or lack, of a virtue on the basis of his responses in a situation remote from that in which the virtue itself may be displayed" (1989, p. 355). This commonsense assumption of the interrelatedness of character traits is one of the reasons why the thesis of the unity of the virtues is so appealing. Another reason may be our unwillingness to confront the spotty imperfection of even the best human beings. Yet another is that it is arguable that any genuine virtue requires a degree both of intelligence (to know what is appropriate when) and self-control (to keep oneself on the appropriate path), so that it looks plausible to say that there are common links among all the virtues, especially if we overlook the fact that people may be more intelligent and self-controlled in some parts of their lives than in others. Finally, the thesis of the unity of the virtues has the philosophical advantage that, if it were true, virtue-ethics would be immune from the criticisms just leveled in the text and would have no more disadvantages than does character-ethics. Indeed, the two would become indistinguishable.

The thesis of the unity of the virtues appears to be false in more than one way. It is plausible to say that there are people who, by the highest standards, genuinely possess some virtues but lack others. There also is a strong prima facie case to be made for the thesis that it is humanly impossible to have all of the virtues to a high degree. A. D. M. Walker has developed this case, arguing that beyond a certain point the development of one virtue is incompatible with the development of certain others (Walker 1989; see also Sherman 1989, pp. 105–6).

None of this means that virtue-ethics is in any sense "wrong" or deeply inadequate. My running argument is that, as a way of approaching ethics and problems of life, it is less adequate than character-ethics because (if the thesis of the unity of virtues is denied) it lends itself to compartmentalization. Any particular theorist, though, can compensate for inadequacies of her or his tools: The argument certainly does not support the view that any particular work based on character-ethics will be superior to any work based on virtue-ethics. Indeed, it has been noticeable in recent years that the best virtue-ethicists drift from time to time into talk of character, and insofar as a character-ethicist will speak of good character traits as virtues, it is arguable that the best virtue-ethics and character-ethics approach one another.

2. That *community* has become a cant word in America illustrates the Taoist claim that things come to be extolled as virtues at precisely the point at which they are no longer natural, and to extol a virtue is to encourage counterfeits.

6

Value

The previous two chapters suggest an indictment of recent ethical philosophy—from Kant and the classical utilitarians on—for a serious blind spot. Recent ethical philosophy for the most part has not paid adequate attention to, or focused clearly enough on, the role of character in moral judgment. The subject of this chapter is a blind spot that is at least as serious. Values also have been portrayed as if the character of the person pursuing or enjoying them was an insignificant factor. The argument here will be that it is central and that both strength and goodness of character matter to the values available to a person.

Disregard of the importance of character has been part of a larger shoddiness in treatments of value. This has grown out of a concentration on morality. We commonly distinguish between judgments of what ought to be done, the more weighty of which would commonly be termed moral judgments, and judgments of what is worth having, seeking, or avoiding; the latter are judgments of value. In a free and liberal society, we normally do not consider other people's behavior and values to be our business, unless the behavior harms others, risks harm to others, or (if we are not so very liberal) seems drastically offensive in relation to community standards. (Anyone who wants to think of something that would count as drastically offensive can start with mistreatment of the dead.) A philosophical ethics that concentrates on those features of the lives of other people that we consider our business will concentrate on morality. Most of us would agree that the parts of other people's lives that are not subject to moral judgment, along with their values, are not our business. It may seem natural to move from this to the judgment that in these areas of other people's lives the only appropriate standard is what the person wants or would want if properly informed. This leads to a contrast between morality, with regard to which a person can be condemned by standards to which he or she might not subscribe, and the rest of life, in which it will be said that there is no standard higher than the person's own happiness. I will argue that this line of thought is shoddy.

It is not, however, totally wrong. A lot depends, of course, on what in the end a person's own happiness is held to consist in. Muddle increases the more "happiness" is tied to desires or to informed desires. The major problem, though, is an illegitimate leap in this line of thought at the very beginning. Let us agree that another person's values are not our business. This suggests that we should not criticize this person's values in the high-pressure way that is characteristic of moral discourse; for example, we should not term them wicked, immoral, and so on. Such terms will be reserved for harmful—and perhaps for deeply offensive—behavior. Even the sadist's values will be exempt from moral reproach as long as he does not act on them and harm others. If all of this is accepted, it is still a long way to the conclusion that we should not judge another person's values, except perhaps by standards internal to that person's system of desires. For one thing, there are forms of judgment that lack the pressure of moral judgment. Someone can be found inconsiderate, unappealing, and a slob without being in violation of moral norms and without being worthy of the sort of social damage that we may try to inflict on those who are immoral. As J. S. Mill remarks in *On Liberty,* "There is a degree of folly, and a degree of what may be called (though the phrase is not unobjectionable) lowness or depravation of taste, which, though it cannot justify doing harm to the person who manifests it, renders him necessarily and properly a subject of distaste, or, in extreme cases, even of contempt" (1859, p.75).

Even if we were to forgo public comment (even of nonmoral sorts) on other people's values, this would carry with it no requirement that we eschew private judgment, and certainly no requirement that we cannot arrive at unvoiced judgments of the quality of another person's life that do not arise out of standards internal to that life. Thus, a liberal resolution that other people's values are not our business does not imply, although students often seem to think it does, that we are barred from judging other people's values by standards external to their lives.

This is not merely an academic point. If people feel constrained by their misunderstanding of the implications of liberalism to eschew judgments, even unvoiced judgments, of other people's values, they lose an important source of thinking about their own values. This is especially true for students who are in the process of adjusting their characters. What is crucial for them is a sense of what their life should be; inevitably, this involves surveying varieties of life and forming judgments on other people's lives that have applicability to the future shape of their own life. If these judgments are not formed, it is easy to think of one's own life that no external standards (other than those of morality) apply, that apart from moral decisions the life should simply, as it were, shape itself. Thus, extreme reluctance to judge, from outside, the lives of others (apart from those small areas that are subject to moral judgment) lends itself to a sense of one's own life as having no relation to standards of excellence. From this it is a short step to a sense of one's own life as essentially meaningless.

This is an extreme outcome, although I believe that nowadays it is far from unusual. A more moderate position is the one that can be gathered from the quotation from *On Liberty*. Mill clearly is prepared to judge, from outside, the nonmoral areas of other people's lives. On the other hand, these judgments take the form of a quasi-aesthetic appreciation of people's social style along with a practical assessment of their abilities at managing their own lives. As the famous discussion of "higher" and "lower" pleasures in *Utilitarianism* makes clear, Mill also is willing to say that some people lack important values, even if they are satisfied with their lives and do not miss these values. The argument for this claim, however, implies that the satisfied philistine would, if he or she became capable of higher pleasures and experienced them, come to prefer them to equal quantities of lower pleasure; thus, the standpoint from which Mill is willing to judge values is, in the last analysis, from within the value systems of the people whose lives are judged—as the value systems would be if relevant capacities and experiences were present. Style and practicality can be criticized entirely from the outside, but values cannot be.

Mill's moderate position, though, is held together by his wonderful optimism about what people would value if they had the relevant capacities and experiences. What if it would turn out to be the case (as most people seem to think) that many philistines, even after being properly educated, would prefer the "lower" pleasures? What if the empirical basis of Mill's higher rating for the "higher" pleasures turned out to be worthless? It is interesting to speculate about whether Mill would have looked very hard for another argument or whether he would have conceded (as most readers nowadays seem to think that he should have) that equal quantities (however such things are to be measured) of higher and lower pleasures have equal value. Speculation aside, there is no reason to be confident that Mill would have abandoned the assumption that whatever is or would be valuable in a person's life depends on the desires that person has or would have (if given appropriate experiences and capacities).

There is a strain in Kant's thought that comes surprisingly close to Mill's view of value. It is true that Kant extols the importance of the good will, which is the only thing that is good without qualification. But Kant's (1785) account of the goals of life centers on one: happiness. Particular goals vary from one person to another, but, more fundamentally, everyone aims for happiness. Kant sees nothing wrong in this, and also rather dourly believes that, in this life at least, there is no reason to assume a correlation between virtue and happiness. In any event, Kant sees the search for happiness as lying outside the purview of his ethical philosophy, except on those occasions on which an action that is conducive to happiness happens to violate the categorical imperative. The search for happiness is, taken in itself, a matter for prudence; and Kant's ethical philosophy is concerned with morality, not with prudence.

The respects in which the views of value of Kant and Mill are surprisingly close can be appreciated by contrast to classical Greek and Chinese treatments of concepts like that of happiness. Aristotle's account of *eudaemonia* (sometimes translated as "happiness" and sometimes glossed as "well-being") is a good example. In Aristotle's view, a person's degree of *eudaemonia* depended heavily on that person's possession and exercise of excellences, including intellectual abilities and what we would regard as moral virtues. Aristotle clearly would not assign any considerable degree of *eudaemonia* to a man just on the basis that he generally got what he wanted and was pleased as a result; even if the man liked his own life, Aristotle would regard his portion of *eudaemonia* as very small if he lacked (or did not exercise) various excellences.

In contrast, both Mill and Kant are willing to entertain the possibility that someone who is both very immoral and very stupid could have a life of considerable happiness. Mill ties happiness to satisfaction of desire, and (following Bentham) equates it with pleasure toward which, he contends, all desires ultimately point. Kant discusses happiness as the common focus of goal-directed behavior. There is no suggestion in either philosopher, though, that the achievement of happiness presupposes that one's goals be of high quality or desires exercise higher order capacities or even that they point toward morally acceptable behavior. This suggests that the sadist is the best judge of whether he is happy (or, at least, would normally be a good judge). His goals and desires are such that we will condemn and try to prevent the actions they lead to, but if he succeeds in doing what he wants and enjoys it, we will not deny that he has a happy life.

Is happiness pleasure? The most elementary observation is that the two states cannot be simply equated, as Mill sometimes does. The differences are many and complicated, but three especially stand out. One is that we tend to speak of happiness, by and large, in relation to larger units of time than those for which we speak of pleasure. Although we occasionally speak of moments of happiness and of continuing pleasures, by far most of our ascriptions of pleasure are for brief periods, whereas we often judge the happiness of periods of years or of entire lifetimes. The second is that pleasure is normally reactive: One is pleased at, or by, something—usually an experience, a thought, or something that affects one. It is true that one can be happy about various things; but when someone speaks of experiencing happiness, it normally is not reactive in the sense of being keyed to a definite stimulus or experience. There is no English word which is to *happiness* as *pleasant* is to *pleasure*. The third is that self-acceptance appears much more crucial to what we call happiness than to pleasure. Someone who basically dislikes herself or himself can accumulate very many pleasures but can never be happy. Indeed, as Csikszentmihalyi recently has pointed out, pleasure by itself does not bring happiness (see Csikszentmihalyi 1990, pp. 45 ff.; see also Nishida 1911, pp. 115 ff.).

To equate happiness with pleasure is not only to simplify the picture of the goals of life, but also to leave out what we characterized in chapter 1 as the individual's sense of self. This should be construed as a robust and context-laden representation that includes both character and roles in relation to other people. If one's sense of self is unsatisfactory, happiness is out of the question.

There are certain things—good food, comfortable surroundings, and the like—that are so widely pleasing that it is possible to talk about pleasure as the end of life and to create the impression that it really does not matter who or what you are as long as you, so to speak, get lucky in such matters as the material conditions of life, your health, your friendships, and so on. Despite his discussion of the higher pleasures, this is the net impression that Mill's account of value leaves. Kant's remarks about happiness do not create a very different impression. Indeed, to link happiness to goals, although it matches the general human expectation that one will be happy if only one gets what one wants, is to ignore the reality of what people's lives are like when they do attain their goals. Both Kant and Mill do not pay adequate attention to factors other than preference—satisfaction.

Just as one appreciates better the peculiarity of one's own country after travel abroad, so also we can appreciate better the peculiarity of a great deal of recent Western thought on value (including that of Kant and Mill) after survey of a very different point of view. Buddhist thought about states roughly comparable to what we call pleasure and happiness, toward which most people try to move, offers an excellent point of comparison. Two claims which seem basic to Buddhist views are that what is pleasant or unpleasant is comparative, marking what is above or below the normal level of immediate satisfaction, and that pleasure typically involves attachment, in that one comes to crave more of (or a repetition of) what is pleasant and, accordingly, will suffer if deprived of it. Thus, the pleasant entails the unpleasant in the way in which rises (in the level of immediate satisfaction) entail dips; but also, beyond this, the pleasant leads to the unpleasant for two reasons. One is that it is in the nature of human life that not all cravings are satisfied and people do not always get or keep what they are attached to, something that may be accentuated in the latter part of life: there are, after all, the facts of sickness, the vicissitudes of old age, and death. A second reason is that a life oriented toward pleasure will, in effect, alternate fever (when the search for pleasure, with its hopes and perhaps also its frustrations, is in full tilt) with boredom (when one has digested one's pleasure and the habit of craving has not yet led one to fasten on something else to crave). Pleasure always is keenest when preceded by frustration so that even a simple glass of water could be intensely pleasant to someone who has not had anything to drink for days; and the opposite thought experiment of a realm of constantly guaranteed instant gratification points toward entire boredom and draining away of pleasure. Thus, in this view, there is a strong and reliable causal link between pleasure, on the one hand, and frustration and boredom on the other.

Because of all this, Buddhists see the life of someone who seeks pleasures as pathetic and foolish. Such a person is in a position like that of the racing dog who pursues an ever-elusive wooden rabbit; so, we pursue the dream of pleasure that will not be paid for beforehand in frustration and afterwards in boredom. The analogy between us and those naive dogs is strengthened by the typical human attitude toward our futures. Desire propels us forward in time, toward the hoped-for satisfaction. A great many people seem, as a result, perpetually to view their present as lacking in order and resolution, which will be obtainable only in the future. "Right now things are in a bit of a mess," someone thinks. "But next month (or next year, or when I finish that project, or get that new job, or am married, or am graduated . . .) things will be as they should be." But next month (or next year or . . .) comes and it turns out that things are still in a bit of a mess—but then one thinks that next month (or next year, or when such and such happens) things will be as they should be. That magical moment never comes, just as the dog never catches the wooden rabbit.

From the Buddhist point of view, attempts to equate value with numbers of fulfilled desires or of satisfied preferences are not only preposterous, but also question begging. What if the best outcome for a person is that he or she not have any of the desires or stronger preferences? Perhaps a mild preference, which does not involve any attachment and is too mild to be considered a desire, for enlightenment should be at the center of one's life.

So much in any event for the Buddhist view of the search for pleasure. Some people might wish to argue, along the lines already indicated, that life in general is, at best, a zero-sum game for any individual. This, however, is not the Buddhist view. Both the nature and the grounds of the hope Buddhists offer are difficult to understand, partly because they appeal to characteristics of experiences that most of us have rarely, if ever, had and partly because they recognize a variety of positively valenced states of mind that makes Mill's classifications look impoverished in comparison.

Ordinary English is not impoverished in this regard. Pleasure, happiness, joy, delight, ecstasy, bliss, and rapture are all distinct from one another; and there is no reason to suppose that the distinctions are all just quantitative distinctions of degree along a single scale. There is also no reason to assume *a priori* that the points Buddhists make about pleasure, if they are correct, are applicable also, *mutatis mutandis,* to happiness, joy, delight, ecstacy, bliss, or rapture. Many Buddhist texts claim that it is possible for an individual, typically as the result of a long period of intense self-discipline, to attain a quasi-permanent state of joy. The joy comes from a psychological equilibrium in which there is no room for pleasure, anxiety, or suffering; whereas the cause is always inner, some of the Northern schools suggest that aesthetic contemplation of nature can be the occasion of this joy. These claims are worth mentioning, but I am in no position to evaluate them; nor will this book have anything further about joy, delight, ecstacy, bliss, or rapture—important as these may very well be.[1] Instead, we will return to the subject of pleasure and happiness.

Whether or not one entirely agrees with the Buddhist critique of pleasure, the degree to which it is plausible suggests that one need not look for value along an axis that connects goal-directed behavior with satisfaction or one that connects desire with pleasure. Indeed, there is much to suggest that there are many things in life at least as important as the accumulation of pleasures. Some people who have more good fortune than character are said sometimes to report many pleasures, few pains, and yet also a general dissatisfaction with their lives. They may say that their lives ought to have some meaning above and apart from all of the pleasures. Talk of this sort suggests that there is something of important value other than pleasure. There also are cases like that of the philosopher Ludwig Wittgenstein, whose life did not appear marked by a great deal of pleasure and who, for that matter, did not appear to be a happy man. But at the end, nevertheless, he is reported to have said that his life had been "wonderful" (Malcolm 1958, p. 100). Perhaps there is something beyond either pleasure or happiness that is of importance?

Many discussions of value have taken the form of searches for formulae for a good life. The equation of value with pleasure is always one of the first options to be considered, partly because virtually everyone values pleasure, so that it would seem most implausible that formulae for a good life would not include pleasure; and this suggests that if the formula is so very simple as to consist of only one word, that word would be *pleasure.*

This view, hedonism, is implausible not only for the reasons already suggested, but also because of a thought experiment that Plato constructs in his *Philebus.* The hedonist can be asked if he would prefer the life he now has, which is presumably not one of sheer, continuous pleasure, or the extremely simple life of an oyster who (we will suppose) is in a state of great and continuous pleasure. Someone who takes seriously what has been said about the comparative aspect of pleasure may wonder whether such an oyster life can be coherently imagined, but let us suppose that the oyster experiences a crescendo of gratifying sensation (that grain of sand is in just the right place), so that every moment appears pleasant in relation to the last. Plato suggests that the result of his thought experiment will be that virtually any hedonist will be forced to reconsider his or her view: Few will prefer the life of the highly pleased oyster.

This seems to me an effective argument against hedonism: Pleasure may well be (as Plato goes on to say that it is) a part of the good life, but it cannot be the single determining factor of how good a life is. We should pause, however, to ask where this argument gets its strength. In due course, I will answer this, but first we should consider a less positive view of the argument than mine. This is that what Plato presents is simply one of those appeals to intuition, to what we antecedently believe or want to say, with which the literature of ethical philosophy abounds. The ethical philosopher who appeals to our intuitions may claim to be appealing to common sense; a less-sympathetic view always might be that he or she is appealing to prejudice—to what tradition, the bias of our particular group, or sheer thoughtlessness has led us to believe without any supporting reason. Such challenges suggest worries about what form supporting reasons in ethics could take and whether there are any. Is there anything in ethics that genuinely could be considered evidence?

This is not a question to be answered all at once, especially because supporting reasons may well take different forms in different parts of ethics. If we concentrate on value, though, the following seems plausible. Someone is in a better position to make judgments of the value of something if she or he has experienced it and, thus, knows what it is like. This is a cautious claim about the epistemology of value, some features of which need to be explicated. First, although I will concentrate in what follows on cases in which someone forms a judgment of the value of experiences or states of mind on the basis of having had them, what we experience (and can judge the value of on the basis of experience) is not limited to what occurs within minds. We can experience and on the basis of experience form judgments about states of society, styles of family life, and so on. Second, even if we restrict our purview to experiences and states of mind, it is well known that people who have all had a certain kind of experience or state of mind do not always agree about how worth having it was; indeed, as Aristotle and others have pointed out, we tend to regard some people as better judges in such matters than others. Thus, to have had an experience or state of mind cannot guarantee the correctness of one's judgment of its value nor should it enable one to be sure of one's judgment. However, a more cautious claim appears warranted, namely, that it places one in a better position, all things considered, to make a judgment. If someone says, "How do you know that working on an assembly line for forty hours a week is a terrible experience?" the reply "I have done it" is normally considered quite strong. (As an additional note of caution: whatever validity the experience confers is to a value judgment merely of highly similar experiences, such as those likely to be had by people whose degree of restlessness and tendency to want variety of activity are comparable to one's own. It is easy to overestimate the similarity of other people's experiences to one's own and, consequently, to overestimate similarities in value.)

To have had an experience or a state of mind might be loosely compared to being a witness (of its value) if one bears in mind that not all witnesses agree and not all are reliable. If we have no idea whether an unfamiliar set of experiences or an entire way of life is of high or low value, the testimony of someone who has had these experiences or pursued that way of life and who is judicious, balanced, and has had a variety of experiences can be taken as strong evidence in support of a conclusion about value.

The implications of this claim go beyond the subject of value. Some philosophers opposed to "moral realism" have contended that there is nothing which is such that we can say that ethical statements are correct in relation to it and which, at the same time, causes beliefs in the correctness of these statements (see Harman 1975; Williams 1985, chap. 8). At issue is whether there is some interface between ethical judgments and something that is the case. Let me briefly suggest that there can be more than one interface: There, arguably, are instances in which people, despite their upbringing and training, find themselves unable to approve of cruel or vicious actions, and it is arguable also that the very factors that make these actions wrong also cause some people to think them wrong. Virginia Held's example is a good one: a soldier in war decides, as a result of on-the-spot experience, that it would be wrong to destroy a village (1984, pp. 46–47). Thus moral realism does not require that ethics rest on a foundation or is a structure of inferences from a homogeneous collection of data. The immediate implication of my present argument, though, is simply that there is at least one interface. No doubt, people's judgments of value are heavily influenced by the way they have been brought up, which plays a part not only in the statements about value that they are predisposed to accept, but also in what they notice and are sensitive to. My claim is merely that *sometimes* a person will make a statement about value that cannot be given a causal explanation entirely in terms of upbringing and similar factors. Sometimes, that is, the main reason why Bloggs says "*X* is of low value" is that Bloggs has tried *X* and found it *is* of low value.[2] This does not mean that Bloggs's value judgments, even when they deviate from his conditioning, are infallible; it does mean that there are cases in which the high (or low) value of an experience or a way of life plays a causal role in some people's judging it to be of high (or low) value.

Undoubtedly, the best evidence about value comes from direct experience. However, a species of evidence that cannot be entirely dismissed comes from imaginative portrayals or thought experiments. All evidence about value has its risks: Someone who claims to know the value of something on the basis of experience may have been prejudiced or insensitive or may simply have not had the experience that she or he thought. The risks of relying on imaginative portrayals, which easily can be biased, one-sided, or unrealistic in some other way, are especially great; and there are comparable risks in thought experiments related to value. Someone who experienced the life of entirely reliable instant gratification that was discussed earlier might find that it was not boring at all, perhaps because of features that one might not be able to anticipate. Someone who tried a month as Plato's highly pleased oyster might find it a better life than expected. In both cases, if this happened, the rest of us might speculate on whether the original thought experiment had been flawed or misleading or whether, instead, the person's judgment had been seriously impaired by his or her new way of life. The latter would always be a strong possibility. If all witnessing is interpretative, in that it takes place from a point of view within a framework of experience and against a background of prior assumptions, it still is true that the interpretative element in witnessing about value is especially pronounced and especially likely to lead to contradictory testimony. We cannot try new ways of life without changing to some degree who we are and accordingly the interpretative framework within which we experience value. The great disadvantage of imaginative portrayals and thought experiments is the way in which they are vulnerable to questions of realism. Their advantage, though, as compared to direct personal experience, is that our interpretative framework can be held fairly steady and there is much less possibility that we will be befuddled or corrupted by what we are trying to assess the value of.

Everyone has strong direct evidence that pleasure has some value. Everyone knows, let us say, that having a nice meal is better than being kicked in the head. Comparable grounds exist for saying that virtually everyone knows that there are facets of human life, which would be absent in the life of the gratified oyster, that also make a contribution to value that is great enough that a life without them would be seriously flawed. This is what gives Plato's thought experiment much of its strength as an argument.

If there is a one-word solution to the problem of value, then it cannot be pleasure. Might it be happiness? Might we be able to construe happiness as including, or requiring, some pleasures so that the value that legitimately can be assigned to pleasures could be recognized within an equation of value with happiness?

Before rejecting this line of thought, I should say why the equation of value with happiness does seem to me much superior to hedonism. One ground of superiority is this. It already has been suggested that there are people who have many pleasures and few pains but who yet, for reasons that we will need to explore, are not happy. There is no clear reason to rule out the opposite possibility: that there may be people (leading, let us suppose, rather simple and unexciting lives) who have few pleasures but yet are very happy. It seems much more plausible to say that there is something drastically lacking in the lives of the first group of people than to say this of the second group. A second ground of superiority, richer in suggestion of the argument that is to follow, is this. One of the problems with hedonism, because of the largely momentary character of pleasure, is that it lends itself to an additive view of what a good life is. Every pleasure is logically independent of every other and can be treated as separate; we add up the pleasures and subtract something else (pains, displeasure, or suffering as the case may be). This seems to rule out of hand the possibility that periods within a life, or an entire life, can have a value that is more than or less than the sum of the values of the parts. It is this interesting possibility that talk of the meaning of life points toward. There is plenty of room for this possibility within a value system based on happiness, even if there is not within hedonism. This is because happiness is not additive: My happiness during the last calendar year cannot be rendered simply as my happiness during January plus my happiness during February, and so on. That much used (and abused) word *holistic* seems to apply to happiness. in ways in which it does not apply to pleasure.

All of this suggests that the view that the value of a life is simply its degree of happiness has considerable plausibility. The view also has qualities that would make it appealing to any liberal society, in that it does not (at least in the great majority of cases) insist on evaluating lives from a standpoint of values external to them. Whatever Bloggs's goals, interests, and values are, if he is happy that is all that matters: His life, then, has value. It is true that Bloggs might mistakenly think that he is happy, perhaps because he does not know what happiness is or as a result of some elaborate refusal to face up to his own suffering and anxiety; but if, along these lines, we deny that Bloggs's estimate of his own happiness is reliable, it is not that we are rejecting Bloggs's values in favor of some other value system. Admittedly, a somewhat different story has to be told of the case of someone who resolutely rejects happiness in favor of what she or he claims to be higher values and who claims success in realizing these higher values although remaining indisputably unhappy. Here, anyone who equates value with happiness will be in the position of evaluating this life from a standpoint of values external to it. Cases of this sort are rare, though, although they suggest worries for anyone inclined to solve the problems of value with the single word *happiness*.

What makes the issues surrounding such cases especially complicated is that someone who, as I do, rejects the equation of value and happiness might yet hesitate to judge a clearly unhappy life to be a good one. Even if the goodness of a life is not simply equal to its degree of happiness, it may be that happiness is a major element (and perhaps a moderate degree is a necessary element) of a good life. We can see this better if we ask how someone could realize what she or he thinks of as major values and yet not be happy with her or his life. Part of the answer may be that there is a lot in life besides the major values, and, if the other things go wrong, success with the major values may not be enough to tip the balance. This suggests that unhappiness can be taken to imply serious inadequacies within a life. This is just a crude first attempt to deal with the question, though, and we need to look more closely at what happiness is and what counts toward happiness.

We sometimes speak of being happy at or happy about this or that; but, as has already been noted, happiness (unlike pleasure) is normally not reactive in the sense of being keyed to a definite stimulus or experience. Is there, nevertheless, some sense in which a person who is happy is happy about something that goes beyond any definite stimulus or experience? Let me suggest that to be happy is to be happy about one's life, that happiness is a positive emotional response during a period of time to the general character of life, which, of course, includes as a major element one's own character. This view has affinities to that of Richard Warner, which emphasizes the role in happiness of realization of self-concepts (1987, pp. 152ff.). The positive response that constitutes happiness has links, on the one hand, to affects such as cheerfulness and perhaps occasional enthusiasm and, on the other hand, to the absence (largely) of negative affects such as glumness, depression, and ennui. It also is linked to a disposition to make positive assessments of various key aspects of one's life. Happiness is closely linked to satisfaction, in that, whereas someone might be spoken of as happy who is dissatisfied with some aspects of her or his life, we would be highly reluctant to use the word *happy* if the aspects were central or the dissatisfaction were persistent and gnawing. This view comes close to the assumptions of some psychological research. Michael Argyle, for example, speaks of happiness ''as part of a broader syndrome, which includes choice of rewarding situations, looking at the bright side, and high self-esteem'' (1987, p. 124). Entire satisfaction is not required, but perhaps a high level is. Thus, people with complicated lives who are striving for challenging goals are much less likely to rate themselves as straightforwardly happy than are people with relatively simple and static lives, for whom something close to entire satisfaction can be a real possibility. This does not mean, of course, that people with complex and challenging lives will be unhappy. Like the vast majority of humankind they may find themselves somewhere between the happy and the unhappy.

It is not easy to analyze the relation between the emotional aspect of happiness and the way in which happiness functions as a positive assessment of a life or a portion of a life. Clearly, there is a causal connection: People generally feel good if they think their lives are going well; conversely, they are more likely to think their lives are going well if they feel good. Are these, nevertheless, two separable components of what we call happiness, each necessary but neither by itself sufficient? My inclination is to answer yes. We can imagine someone who is genuinely disposed to think that his or her life is going well, sincerely saying so again and again and brightening up slightly when that topic is introduced, but who is much more often glum and unenthusiastic than the reverse. Such a person is not enjoying her or his life and is not happy. The case of someone who is cheerful and enthusiastic much of the time, but who becomes less cheerful when asked how his or her life is going and provides a negative assessment, is more difficult. Plainly, such a person does enjoy much of his or her life, but my sense is that we would hesitate to speak of happiness if there are genuine negative self-assessments of the life. We might say, "Bloggs seems happy most of the time, but when he talks about how his life is going, one wonders whether he is really happy." These are puzzle cases though: Normally, people who are positive about their lives have generally positive emotional states, and vice versa.

If we look closely at the value of happiness, we must take both aspects seriously. As regards the emotional aspect, anyone who has ever been to some degree happy knows that it is very nice; conversely, many know from experience that unhappiness of any significant degree is a great evil. These value judgments, based on experience, are related to judgments we can make of the value of cheerfulness and some moderate degree of enthusiasm and of the low value of perennial glumness and lack of enthusiasm. David Hume, it should be noted, ranks cheerfulness as a virtue; the plausibility of this increases when one realizes the ways in which cheerfulness, besides enhancing the life of the cheerful person, is contagious (1739, p. 611).

What value, if any, can we assign to a person's positive assessment of her or his own life? A tempting answer is, "It depends." Even if there is generally something to be said for a person's coming to terms with her or his own life, we might feel much more positively about a case in which someone comes to terms with a life of what we would judge to be high quality than about one of coming to terms with a life filled with inconsiderate or immoral behavior. It is hard to attach value to the smug self-acceptance of a petty villain.

To the extent that good character is easier to come to terms with than bad character and to the extent that a life marked by good character is easier to come to terms with, good character is conducive to happiness. But it would be wrong to say that it is required. Wicked people can be very satisfied with their lives, which can be marked by all manner of positive emotional states. It would be doctrinaire to deny that such people are happy.

Is a happy life necessarily a good one? It is important to see, first, that the fate of morality does not ride on this answer and, second, that the answer can well be a complicated one. A Kantian arguably could agree with utilitarians that anyone who manages to achieve happiness is thereby better off in her or his life than the average. The Kantian could still insist, on the familiar Kantian grounds, that it is wrong to violate the categorical imperative, even if it happens to lead to such a good life for the immoral person. The utilitarian also can argue that we ought to do what is best for everyone, not just for ourselves, even if it is true occasionally that an immoral person can have a good life (in the sense of enjoying a life with more than the average amount of value within it). This does not mean that immorality generally increases one's chances for a good life; in any case, it certainly does not excuse immorality. Thus, morality can be defended, even if the answer to our question is yes. Even if the answer is not yes, there is the complication that (as we have already acknowledged) the positive emotional states that are part of happiness would seem to have some intrinsic value. Thus, there is a strong case for saying that a happy life is necessarily of some value, even if one does not regard this value always to be great enough that the life can be termed a good one.

Nevertheless, my answer is no. My claim, in other words, is that while a happy life will have to contain some value within itself, in virtue of what happiness involves, this value need not be above the average of lives, so that the happy life need not count as a good one.

We might begin by looking not at a wicked life but rather at one of extreme simplemindedness. Imagine an especially dim-witted and insensitive man whose life consists of a small number of simple routines; suppose that these routines go satisfactorily and that the man is very easily satisfied, so that he is (as the expressive New England phrase has it) happy as a clam. All things equal, to be happy as a clam is better than being miserable: This already has been conceded. The question, then, is: Is being happy as a clam tantamount to having a good life? The answer surely is no. Many of us know from experience that it is wonderful to feel very positive about one's life, but we also know from experience that there are a variety of challenging and exciting experiences which have been stipulated to be missing from the simpleminded man's life but which typically have great value: When these are considered, the simpleminded man's life does not look so very good. Most of us would not trade places with him, and it would be implausible to say that this is just because of inertia or prejudice on our part.

My position here may seem dissonant in relation to normal patterns of thought. We are used, after all, to regarding happiness as the paramount end in human life, the one end for which it is absurd to provide justification in terms of further ends. Beyond this, all of us like to have simple and unified answers to the ultimate questions of life; accordingly, we would like to think that everything that matters in a good life is comprised within, and required for, happiness. Thus, philosophers can be found who argue that someone who is thoroughly stupid or who is immoral cannot genuinely be happy. Other philosophers will argue that, if the thoroughly stupid or immoral person can be happy then intelligence and moral virtue cannot have the values that they are supposed to have. There is, however, no reason to assume in advance that ultimate questions of value do admit of a simple and unified answer. Nor is it at all clear that Aristotle, who is invoked by some of the philosophers I have just referred to, supported such an answer. If *eudaemonia* cannot properly be translated as happiness, we might compare it to a vast holding company whose assets turn out to be very diverse, in that in Aristotle's view a wide range of things turn out to count toward *eudaemonia*.

To go further: Happiness sometimes is a means as well as an end. Imagine a woman who, like Wittgenstein, values intellectual activity and achievement more highly than the usual run of satisfactions. We need not make her out to be an extremist: She values happiness for its own sake, but she values certain other things more so that she would rather be an unhappy great thinker than a happy very simple peasant. Such a person might say, both intelligibly and reasonably, that she prefers to be happy, partly for its own sake, but also because her work goes so much better when she is happy.

We have not yet looked at the putative case of the happy wicked person. There are interesting empirical issues about whether this indeed is a possible case. Kierkegaard, in *The Sickness unto Death,* argues that despair is an inevitable concomitant of sin, which he interprets broadly as a lack of that spiritual wholeness which is equivalent to faith. Kierkegaard concedes that the despair can be, in effect, unconscious and latent; but its presence is displayed when something goes seriously wrong in someone's life. The person who has faith, according to Kierkegaard, will remain happy and serene whatever goes wrong. Someone who is in a state of sin, on the other hand, will lapse into conscious despair, which Kierkegaard interprets as the manifestation of despair that had been beneath the psychological surface all along. Kierkegaard's argument is more complicated and subtle than this brief summary can indicate, and it is not my intention here to engage it fully. Rather, we need to consider one of the more debatable consequences of Kierkegaard's view, which is that there is a sense in which it is psychologically impossible for someone whose life is immoral to be genuinely happy, whatever the appearances might be. Some people also feel attracted to this view after reading Fyodor Dostoevsky's *Crime and Punishment* or Plato's *Republic*. Probably most of us *want* this to be true; and undoubtedly, there are cases in which apparently successful villains turn out to have nagging feelings of guilt and despair, bad dreams at night, and so on. But can we assume that something like this will turn out to be true for all successful villains? Undoubtedly, they will feel despair if something goes seriously wrong in their lives; but so will (as Kierkegaard, in effect, says) virtually everyone, including people who are both virtuous and (by most normal standards) religious who are not totally governed by the idea that everything that happens is determined by a good god and should be welcomed. The vulnerability to despair does not serve, even on Kierkegaard's view, to divide the wicked from the virtuous. One might question also the assumption that conscious despair must be interpreted as the manifestation of despair that had been present all along beneath the surface.

Ultimately, the happiness of the successful wicked is an empirical question. There may be general psychological grounds to suspect that some wicked people who seem happy are not so, but these do not amount to grounds for saying that no wicked person can be happy. If, indeed, there are some successful wicked people who genuinely like their lives, sleep well at night, are remarkably cheerful even when things go wrong, what then? Many people may be tempted, once again, to say that this unpalatable outcome is not true happiness, but the grounds for this denial are far from clear. On the other hand, if a successful villain is happy, is there any reason to conclude that he or she has a life of high value? There is a lot to be said for cheerfulness and sleeping well at night, but there are many other important values in life which the happy villain can be argued to lack, and there seems no clear reason why we have to accept such a person's self-assessment of his or her life.

Many people will want to dig in their heels at this point and say something like this. ''Surely a person's self-assessment does count for something. What after all is the justification, apart from snobbery or preconceptions about value, in rejecting someone's claim that his or her life is very satisfactory? If such a person is satisfied, then this provides as strong a reason as one could wish for concluding that the life is satisfactory.''

There are a number of reasons for not entirely discounting this criticism. For one thing, satisfaction generally is better than frustration, all things equal; and the fact that someone is satisfied with her or his life, whether or not we think it warranted, ought to count for something. Second, lives and experiences are enormously variable: We try to capture them by means of general descriptive labels, but there can be significant differences between two lives or sets of experiences to which the same labels apply. It is easy to jump to conclusions about someone else's life because we have missed nuances that are important to its value. We also may assume that a life or a set of experiences is more closely similar to what we are familiar with or can imagine than it is. Thus, there is a respect in which everyone is in a far better position than anyone else to evaluate her or his own life, in that one is in the best position to appreciate the specificity of one's life. Finally, none of us can claim to approach other people's lives with a mind that is totally free of any tendencies to prejudge, and there may be many cases in which someone is fairer to herself or himself than we will be.

Having said this, I want to say that there are cases in which someone— let us say a jolly, relaxed Nazi or a lotus eater or the very simple man who is happy as a clam—seems very satisfied with his or her life, and we can get a strong enough sense of what that life is like to be confident that the person living it overestimates it. Unless the life centers on harming others, this is a judgment that we can and probably should keep to ourselves; but in any event, it is one that we sometimes are in a position to make. No one has ever advanced a coherent and convincing set of reasons for saying that judgments of this sort are nonsense or have to be false. Conversely, we do ordinarily believe that Smith is in a better position to be confident of her judgment of Bloggs's life if Smith has a strong sense of what that life is like than if she does not; Smith also is in a better position if she approached Bloggs with a fairly open mind and was quick to notice both positive and negative features of his life; and, of course, we are more likely to trust Smith's judgment if she is a judicious person of wide experience. In a variety of ways, there are standards that we apply to someone's judgment of the quality of someone else's life which are akin to standards of evidence. There is no reason *a priori* why Smith cannot arrive at a judgment of Bloggs's life that ranks high by these standards and that yields a lower estimate of value than Bloggs's own judgment.

Usually, most of us have better things to do than to look closely at, and evaluate, other people's lives. If we are someone's biographer or counselor that is one thing, but for most of us it is better not to be intrusive; even biographers and counselors may function better if they are not judgmental. My argument thusfar, in short, has not been designed to promote activities that culminate in judgment of other people's lives, activities which in some cases are harmful. The argument has been simply that such judgments can be made meaningfully and can be correct. From time to time, anyone will find herself or himself making such judgments, and they can have a useful function if they are linked to decisions of who one's friends are, how one spends one's time, or especially the fundamental decision of what one's own life is to be like.

What values should we aim for in our lives? This is, on the one hand, an extraordinarily complicated subject if I have been right in rejecting simple views. On the other hand, I do not have a great deal to add to such a sophisticated recent treatment as that of James Griffin (1986). One merit of Griffin's book is that, unlike philosophers such as Aristotle, he recognizes a plurality of acceptable models of what a very good life can be like. Even if one accepts Aristotle's favorable evaluation of the highly intellectual contemplative life, surely it is also true that lives that center on aesthetic creation, aesthetic experience, effective political and social activities, or on styles of personal relations can be very good; indeed, it would seem doctrinaire to claim to be able to limit in advance the number of major types of very good lives. To see the plurality of types of good life is to put people's choices of life in a new light. Even if we are not born with characters or selves, we are born with tendencies of various sorts; and by the time we begin to think seriously about the kind of life we want for ourselves, some tendencies may have become so pronounced that they point toward a style of life in which one can be most at home and most successful. As writers such as Diana Meyers and Jonathan Glover have pointed out, someone's attempt to get in touch with these tendencies can take the form of a search for a "true self" or an "authentic self" (see Meyers 1987; Glover 1988, pp. 136–37, 178–79). My interpretation is that what such a person is looking for is not a fully developed inner reality, but rather direction markers pointing toward a form of life in which she or he can feel most fully alive. In any case, it may make sense, at least for some people, to regard what David L. Norton has spoken of as innate inclinations as the proper guides to a good life (1976, 190ff.) Any account of what is most valuable should include the insistence that such direction markers legitimately can be different for different people.

This is not to say that there cannot be features that are shared by all, or almost all, varieties of very good life. Many people would want to insist on a moral minimum requirement, that a life cannot be very good if it centers on harm done to other people. In some suitably broad sense of the word *accomplishment,* it may well be that there is no very good life that is not one of considerable accomplishment. I would like to insist on the importance of character in a way that includes the moral requirement just mentioned but goes beyond it. My claim is that a very good life requires a strong (and moderately good) character.

The importance of a strong character can be seen if we reflect on what it is for a life to have, or to lack, a meaning. Earlier I remarked that a cruicial factor is the existence of structural elements that connect the various parts of a life. Linked to this is a persistent tendency that many people have to think that events in their lives are important if, and only if, they can be made into a story (see Arendt 1958, pp. 181–88). It does not matter much if the story is told or is only rehearsed in one's mind for an imaginary audience. Stories are not random collections of sentences; typically there will be a beginning, a middle, and an end as well as some connections among various parts of the story. To have a meaningful life, I suggest, is to have a life that lends itself to being made into a story: A life not only in which there are interesting things, but also in which there are connections so that parts of the life assume significance in relation to other parts. Jonathan A. Jacobs has put the point well, "The unity of a personal life history is constructed and self-imposed. It is achieved through an interpretative and explanatory account of oneself that the individual supplies to himself" (1989, p. 3; see also MacIntyre 1978, pp. 202ff.).

There are two main ways in which parts of a life can be connected. One is that projects which take time to fulfill or to pursue can span different parts of a life, so that one part can be seen as preparation for, or continuation of, another. A life of drift or vacillation is unlikely to be seen as meaningful. A person's concerns and commitments will give unity to her or his life. The other main ground of connection is that provided by character. Even if character changes, in the process growing or deterio-rating, the continuity of character can provide a unifying thread among different episodes. Not only will there be connections provided by continuity in the sort of person who is doing or responding to various things, but other unifying themes may well emerge as a result of the ways in which characters shape events: As Friedrich Nietzsche remarks, to be a person of character is to have one's characteristic experience (1886, p. 80). The life of a person of weak character will lack much of a unifying thread of this sort, in that how she or he behaves or responds will vary so considerably with circumstances and the expectations of others that there will be little unity of style (apart from the negative constant feature of absence of style).

The structure of the argument here should be spelled out. It is in terms of necessary conditions. One step is to claim that a life's being meaningful is a necessary condition for its being very good. This is not highly contentious, in that it would be difficult to praise highly a life that lacks meaning or that we would be reluctant to describe as meaningful. The more contentious step is the claim that a necessary condition for a life's being meaningful is that the person living it have a strong character. The argument for this claim requires analysis of what it is to have a meaningful life. Structural connections within the life turn out to be crucial, and these can be provided either by projects that span different parts of the life or directly by a running theme of the character of the person whose life it is. The argument can be completed only if we show that if a life is made meaningful by long-term projects, this, in turn, requires strong character.

What about a person of weak character who pursues long-term projects? People who would readily yield to temptation or who are extremely conformist in their outlooks may continue devotedly in family or love relationships or work for political and social causes over long periods of time. Perhaps they would yield to temptation or defer to the opinion of the community; but the temptation never comes, and the community never disapproves of what they have been doing. It would be foolish to deny that there are large numbers of such cases and that the continuities contribute to these people's lives. Meaningfulness and value are matters of degree. To have a weak character and also no major continuities in one's life is surely to be at the bottom of the scale in meaningfulness of life and, probably, to have a life not at all high in value; major continuities can be sources of meaning and value for anybody, even people of weak character. We speak of meaningful lives at the high end of the scale and of meaningless lives at the low end; but there is plenty of room in the middle. The question is how meaningful major continuities can make the life of someone of weak character. My contention is that the degree will never be high enough that we would speak as a result of a meaningful life.

This is because to have a weak character is always to have a qualified loyalty to anything, to a relationship or a cause or whatever. We would not speak of someone as having genuine commitments if that person was ready to abandon his or her projects if suitably tempted or if the community disapproved of them. In short, the structural elements required for meaning in life cannot be as strong for someone of weak character as they are able to be for someone of strong character. Loyalty to projects that falls short of genuine commitment is better than nothing, but it is not enough to enable someone to have a life that we would term meaningful.

This completes the case for saying that strong character is a necessary condition for a very good life. Is it a sufficient condition? Anyone who believes that wickedness spoils not only the moral quality of a life, but also its lived quality will want to answer no to this: A genuinely wicked person must have a strong character, but this does not mean that he or she will have a good life. We have already suggested that there can be grounds for assessing lives of happy villains as not very good. There is also an independent reason for answering no. Even a virtuous person of strong character may not have a very good life.

The point is rather like the one Aristotle made about King Priam of Troy. Some kinds of disaster so seriously mar a life that, whatever the quality of a person's inner resources and the satisfactions they provide, no one, imaginatively assessing the life, could consider it very good. The general point is that some of the commitments that give unity and meaning to a life can result in failure or can go sour. Failure need not detract significantly from the value of a life; to have worked well for a good cause counts for a great deal whether or not the cause is victorious. Indeed, people sometimes speak of the nobility of failure. But when the failure assumes the proportions of a disaster, as in the case of King Priam, or when the commitments turn sour because of changes in that to which one is committed, then there can be a significant draining away of value. Thus, for this reason, also, it seems most implausible to claim that strong character guarantees a very good life.

Even if the judgments of value advanced thusfar are correct, and we need some degree of virtue (along with strong character and luck that is other than terrible) in order to have a very good life, this does not mean that very great virtue is required. We can legitimately condemn qualities and forms of behavior without at the same time believing that they spoil the life of the person who exhibits them. Cruelty may give a life a flavor such that we think that no sensitive, discriminating person should want such a life. Irresponsibility along with perhaps a bit of lying and cheating may have a different quality: We can think it probably better both for the world and for an individual that he or she not have these character traits, but at the same time believe it possible that someone with these qualities could be fortunate, against the odds, and have a good life (see Waley 1950). It is far more plausible to ascribe a failure in value judgment to someone who envies the successful villain than to someone who envies the successful rogue.

These judments of value are tentative, and, of course, a great many readers might disagree. What seems strongest is the argument that a very good life presupposes a strong character. There are other ways in which character, through the sense of self that is important to happiness, can be related to the value of a life. In chapter 7, we will gather the threads of these as well as the arguments of chapters 4 and 5.

Notes

1. A really full account of value could begin by marking fine distinctions among positively valenced states as well as among negatively valenced states. I expect in further work to pursue the ways in which suffering, distress, frustration, grief, anguish, despair, agony, and unhappiness are not synonymous. This is of more than lexicographical interest: It will provide a map of some of the ways in which things can go wrong in life. It will also, I expect, provide the starting points for an argument against any assumption of a symmetry between positive and negative values: The things that can go wrong in life are not mirror images of those that can go right, and our obligations to prevent suffering may be different from our obligations to promote the happiness of others.

2. To this it may be replied that there will surely be an explanation of Bloggs's value judgment that rests solely on physical, chemical, and biological facts about the world at that time, along with Bloggs's neurophysiology. Thus, the alleged fact that "X is of low value" does not play an *irreplaceable* role in the causal explanation of Bloggs's arriving at his value judgment. My rejoinder to this is twofold. First, one may wonder how the critic knows that a causal explanation of Bloggs's value judgment that rests solely on physical, chemical, biological facts, and so on, is, at least in principle, available. A programmatic optimism about the future of the sciences or, at least, about the ways in which the world accommo-

dates itself to the sciences, appears to be involved. Second, if one concedes ground to the critic's programmatic optimism, one still could argue that there is ample precedent for regarding some things to be objectively the case, even if they do not play irreplaceable roles in the causal explanations of people's realizing that they are the case. This point is pursued by John McDowell in a carefully limited analogy between ethical qualities and secondary qualities (see McDowell 1985).

7

The Place of Character in Ethics

A character that is both strong and good is not an unmixed blessing. One's character narrows options in life, increasing the number of things one simply could not do. This is morally and personally advantageous if it rules out behavior that is unreasonable, tacky, or simply wrong. But it also can make someone predictable, and there always are risks of becoming too rigid and predictable or of contracting excessively the zone of spontaneity in a life. Furthermore, a developed character can play a part in the complex of routines, habits, and automatic choices that makes time go quickly for people as they get older, except when they travel. Someone, of course, can have rigid patterns of behavior (in familiar situations) and display in an unusual situation that he or she, in fact, has a weak character; conversely, a strong character is compatible with a highly varied texture of life. But if familiar situations repeat themselves, the choices of the person of strong character will also repeat themselves. Someone for whom time speeds away might wish for the less-firm orientation and the less-developed character of youth. All of this should be borne in mind during the remainder of this chapter, which will be devoted to the importance and advantages of good character. One should remember also the disadvantages. Perhaps, indeed, the motto ''Nothing in excess'' applies even to the development of character.

Having said this, I do wish to suggest that a character that is too strong or even one that is too fixed in its patterns of behavior appears to be a less-serious problem in our society than that presented by character which is not strong or good enough. Whatever the case may be, a person's character appears to have a crucial role in the quality of her or his life.

Because of our ability to put ourselves in one another's places while taking most elements of our own characters as givens, there is a strong tendency not to think of character's relevance to the value in a life and to concentrate on how externals fall out. The mean man looks for luck, Confucian texts suggest, whereas the superior man looks within himself (*Doctrine of the Mean,* p. 129; Confucius VII.36, p. 131; IX.28, p. 144; XII.4, p. 163). But perhaps the truth is that all of us, most of the time, think of good lives and unenviable lives around us largely in terms of luck. The account of value given in the last chapter suggests that luck does matter, but it also argues that (as Confucius wished to emphasize) a person's character matters a great deal to the value within her or his life. Whether character itself could be termed a matter of luck is difficult to say. The account in chapter 3 suggests grounds for saying it is, to the degree to which character formation is not under a person's control; on the other hand, the account in chapter 2 suggests that we cannot unproblematically speak of a you who would have developed a sharply different character. To say that you are lucky to have the character you do is a little like saying that you are lucky to be yourself rather than someone else.

If ethics is taken to be the reflective examination of what is good, bad, right, or wrong (as well perhaps as analysis of the meanings and logic of such examinations), then much of ethics should be devoted to questions of value. Someone approaching the subject should be able to find a variety of suggestions of how to construct a life that is very much worth living. These suggestions normally will be theoretical, systematic, or polemical, with very little hortatory flavor; but there is no reason why they cannot, all the same, have a practical use for someone (say, a student) for whom major choices in mode of life are open. Earlier it was suggested that people of student age typically have more control over details and fine-tuning of character than at other times of life. Also, decisions concerning career, marriage, or other forms of close personal relationships can be made with an eye to the likely long-term effects on character. One often cannot through an effort of will transform oneself into a certain sort of person, but one can voluntarily take on a career or relationship whose likely natural effect will be to make one more that kind of person. One also can shun a career or relationship whose likely natural effects are unwanted. Thus, even if it is true both that character is crucial to value and that our characters are largely not within our immediate and direct control, this does not mean that reflective examination of value will lack major practical benefits. It can help people to steer their lives.

Most of the great examinations of value that yield suggestions about life are ancient, for example, those of Plato, Aristotle, and Confucius. But an interesting Edwardian exploration of this territory is to be found in the final chapter of G. E. Moore's *Principia Ethica*. Nietzsche is probably the most important recent philosopher who has approached value in this way. Nietzsche's irony and fondness for fragments of ideas make it difficult to be confident of any interpretation of his views. But it is arguable that his relativism about morality did not extend to the values of different forms of life: It seems unlikely that he would have said that his low rating of the life of the herd and his high rating of the life of the *Übermensch* were correct only from one perspective.

It is not my purpose here to examine Nietzsche's claims about value. His working assumptions as a philosopher of value however deserve comment. Running through all of his work is a strong insistence that he does not want followers and that to be a follower of a view like his would be a contradiction in terms.

There are special reasons why Nietzsche might take this position: He, after all, emphasizes independence and creativity. But any philosopher of value ought to take a position at least a little like this. First of all, even if Nietzsche exaggerates the importance of independence and creativity, it surely is true that any properly reflective person ought to come of herself or of himself to a view of value rather than merely endorsing what someone else says. A philosopher can help this process by making distinctions, producing arguments, suggesting appropriate matters for reflection, and in a general guiding of readers along a path. But to take readers to the end of the path by producing a value system that is like a creed, not only would be presumptuous, but also would subvert their integrity. Second, even if this strong risk is put to the side, it is impossible to produce a systematic account of values that is of such precision that followers or imitators could be confident that they are attaining a degree of value comparable to that of their model. As Albert Camus points out, nuances can matter greatly to a way of life, so that a recommendation of models does not include assurance that imitations of the models are to be esteemed (1942, pp. 50–51; Camus also remarks, "A certain vocation is required"). Two lives that would be described in much the same terms could contain very different values. This is a point that Nietzsche also makes (1883–1891, pp. 186ff., "On the Three Evils"). Third, it very often happens that intelligent people are influenced by, or get ideas from, more than one approach to value; there is no clear reason to think this confused or wrong. Views of value usually are presented with reference to ideals. Someone cannot subscribe simultaneously to two or more conflicting moralities but can acknowledge the appeals, in different ways or in different parts of life, of two or more conflicting ideals (see Strawson 1961).

For all of these reasons, thought about values that is based on exposure to a single system of values alone has grave risks. Any philosopher who writes about values should count on the antiphony of other views. It might be helpful, indeed, to the student of values to have reminders of alternatives or elements of irony or self-doubt presented in what she or he reads.

One of the theses of this book is that the examination of values should center on character. We should not think of ourselves as passive consumers of values trying to accumulate the things or the satisfactions that add up to a good life. Instead, we need to place weight on inwardness, on the factor of who a person is. Sense of self is crucial to happiness, the degree of which, in turn, makes a major contribution to a good life. Beyond this, a sense of life as meaningful requires ongoing commitments or other forms of connection among the stages of a life, which to be maintained in difficult situations call for strong character. Thus, a major element in an emphasis on character is an emphasis on the ways in which the person one is establishes and maintains connections among what might seem like entirely separate moments or episodes in a life. Character is a major agent in integrating a life, making possible both personal integrity and a situation-resistant interconnectedness of lived experience.

Like virtually everything else that I have been recommending, this could be carried too far. It should not rule out moments of careless rapture or minor episodes of acting out of character. No one should lie, cheat, or steal as a form of relaxation. This is not to defend what have been called moral holidays. But there is something to be said for inclusion in a life of occasional lapses into milder forms of irresponsibility or self-indulgence, forms mild enough, that is, so that we would not consider them to be morally wrong or morally faulty. The extreme case of the person who never is late for an appointment, always promptly answers every letter, never eats or drinks too much, and always is courteous can fill many virtuous people with a vague sense of unease. Similarly, someone who is so preoccupied with the importance of an integrated life that he or she always thinks of the future, never acts out of character, and always is pursuing plans should provoke unease. There is something especially disturbing, too, about anyone whose sense of personal integrity demands that projects under no circumstances be modified in response to the needs of others. This goes well beyond what any reasonable ethics would recommend.

Nevertheless, the major loci of value in the life of someone whose character is both strong and moderately good will not be found in isolated moments or in stretches of uncharacteristic thought and behavior. Sometimes the sweetness of moments when, perhaps because of sheer good fortune, everything goes well can stand out; and uncharacteristic thought and behavior can add to the complexity and interest of a life. But these will make their contributions much like beautiful ornaments on a basically sound and attractive structure. Their appeal lies either in the enhancement of what is already good or in their contrast to the dominant tone of the life. If the dominant tone is not good, then the life cannot be, even if it includes some contrasting elements. To emphasize character in relation to value is to do three things. It is to insist on a long perspective, so that one looks at entire lives or sizable portions of a life rather than at isolated moments or brief episodes. Second, it is to insist that a life can be viewed rather as novels, epic poems, and musical compositions that last for more than a few minutes: One can look for major themes and continuities, and the quality of these will have more to do with the excellence of the whole than will a nice moment now and then, although, of course, nice moments do matter. Third, it is to emphasize the inwardness of most, although not all, of what matters, so that a good life is seen as more closely linked to being a good person than it is to some set of items on an ideal shopping list.

To turn from values to morality is to move to a subject which not only is concerned with more stringent demands, but which itself also makes more stringent demands. I already have suggested that we should not attempt to formulate a single ideal set of values and that it really is better if systems of value judgments are not treated as akin to creeds. Character is crucial to the value of a life, but character is a personal matter in a number of senses. First, there are limits to how freely we should judge and criticize other people's characters (or their opinions about value). Second, variations in character can be connected with significant variations in the value of a life, so that unique features of character can be important to value. Sensitivity to nuance is, thus, crucial to all judgments of character. Finally, character also is personal in that there are many sharply different ways in which to have a very good character or a very good life: That someone's character is very different from ours does not imply that there is something wrong either with her or his life—or with ours. Morality is not personal in the first or third of these senses, and there are limits on how personal it can be in the second. All of this gives morality at least the appearance of greater precision than judgments of value can enjoy. It also suggests less latitude in the range of other people's moral judgments that we can respect.

This is especially true in relation to that portion of morality (which for many people is all, or nearly all) that is concerned with prevention of harm to others. If someone propounds an ideal of life which centers on what seem to us to be bizarre tastes and enjoyments, we can smile politely and think that there may be something of value there, whose appeal we cannot grasp. If someone propounds a way of life which requires exploitation of a group of people (say women or some ethnic group), even if we think that there may be hidden charms to the way of life celebrated, we also reasonably can make negative moral judgments; and it would be normal to make them openly and forcefully. In a liberal society, all sorts of people can be accorded a right to their own styles of life, and it need not concern us very much whether or not there are hidden attractions in ways of life very different from our own. How someone chooses to be and to live is personal. But it is not at all the same if someone who exploits or harms others claims to have a personal morality. This is because to make moral judgments at all is to claim that conflicting judgments are mistaken. A personal morality is, thus, more akin to a personal mathematics than it is to a personal approach to leisure enjoyment.

A case can be made for saying that nuances always are morally relevant. There are subtle differences in the intentions with which different people perform actions that would fall within the same broad category: People who steal accomplish their thefts with different purposes and different senses of what they are doing. There also can be significant differences in the style with which broadly similar actions can be performed and differences in the foreseeable consequences. This could be reflected in a quasi-Kantian ethics that does not insist that maxims take the form of broad general rules as well as in act utilitarianism, or in a rule utilitarianism that also does not insist that rules be broad or be limited in number.

If we turn from pure theorizing to the real world, though, we can see that a workable societal morality cannot in its core (except perhaps in limited classes of special cases) take notice of nuances. We should bear in mind that how well it would work for an entire society is normally taken as an important test of whether a morality really is acceptable. Any society requires that there be some rules of behavior which its members can expect that most people will respect most of the time: Only if this is true can life not be too unpredictable and dangerous. These rules constitute the core of a morality, and in an advanced society they typically will concern the kinds of harm to others that in some imaginary social contract people would have promised not to commit. Such moral rules also make possible a shared vision of what is happening in complex social interactions. Any set of rules that fulfills these functions will have to be, at least for the most part, broad and simple, so that it can be taught to children and so that we can assume that people of varying degrees of sophistication share a sense of what is morally salient and what is prohibited. There may be complications, as it were around the edges; but these cannot affect the way the most commonplace cases are approached.

This is to say that societal moralities generally will be devised so that most moral choices (or at least the most prominent ones) are in easy cases, easy in the sense that what should be done will be apparent to someone of average intelligence and sensitivity, even if bringing herself or himself actually to do it may turn out to be difficult. An example is the case in which you can walk away with a great deal of someone else's money or push a thoroughly obnoxious person off a cliff and no one would be the wiser. Virtually everyone however at some point encounters hard cases: situations in which there are unusual nuances or other special factors that might make the obvious choice, the one that at first glance seems to fit a familiar moral rule, not, in fact, the one that should be made.

There are two main types of hard case. In one, factors are present that reasonably would pull one in two or more directions. The problem is first to be adequately aware of conflicting considerations, then to have an appropriate sense of their relative weights. The second kind may have these features, but it has one other: The received morality of one's society points clearly in one direction, and the considerations that point in other directions not only seem to have greater weight, but also suggest that the received morality is flawed. Jonathan Bennett (1974) has written a nice essay about such cases, especially the one in which Mark Twain's Huckleberry Finn has to decide whether to return an escaped slave (whom he has been taught to think of as property) to his owner. Moral progress takes place when people struggle with hard cases in which, finally, elements of received morality come to seem badly flawed or worthless.

Part of the argument of chapter 4 was that perception is a crucial factor in moral choice. Whatever decision-procedure someone is using, he or she first has to formulate cases in terms appropriate to the decision-procedure; this, in turn, requires some degree of perceptiveness and a prior sense of what to look for as salient. This is true even in easy cases: To choose among alternatives is to have a sense of what they are, and the nature of the situation cannot be totally irrelevant to this. In addition, there is no sophisticated morality which regards human suffering as entirely unimportant or as totally irrelevant to moral choice. Suffering however is not always dramatic and highly visible. In some cases, one may have to look closely at people's lives and at nuances in their behavior in order to gain a sense of strong and painful needs. To the extent that these are subtle and that a sense of their importance matters, we might speak of sensitivity as what is required. The word *sensitivity* is closely linked to perceptiveness, yet it has connotations of feeling the weight of various factors (including fine gradations) as well as being perceptive enough to note their presence.

There is another sense in which sensitivity can be important, even in easy cases. We should bear in mind that easy cases are those that are easy to judge correctly, and this does not mean that it will be easy for everyone to act on a correct judgment. In fact, a great deal of conventional immorality appears to be facilitated by an ability many people have not to think about others' feelings or about the texture of their lives. The murderer or the thief may not enter into what it is like to be the victim or have much sense of how it feels to be a parent, child, lover, or friend of someone who has been murdered. It would be nice to be able to claim that anyone who is reasonably sensitive to the sufferings of others would not murder or steal, but this is patently not the case. What does appear true is that many people find it more difficult to bring themselves to victimize others the more they become aware of what it is like to be the victim.

In difficult cases sensitivity can matter considerably. We cannot cease moral reflection on the recognition that the case fits a received formula; we have to assess factors that might pull us in a different direction, and to do this we need an adequate sense of what the factors are. Sensitivity is required to have adequate data on which to base a judgment.

There is another respect in which difficult cases, especially those in which one should come to reject an element of moral tradition, require sensitivity. Most of us do not require much sensitivity in order to avoid committing murders, stealing from our friends and employers, and so on. A clear sense of traditional morality and some degree of firm loyalty to it are all that is required; thus, it is possible to be extremely insensitive and also extremely virtuous in some easy cases. Difficult cases are different, in that by definition there will be strong arguments against the best course of action; naturally, anyone inclined in that direction will feel uneasy, will be likely to doubt her or his judgment, and may be tempted simply to do what most people would do. This is especially likely if the validity of an element of a moral tradition is at issue. To be one of the first to think that slavery is wrong or that debtors should not be imprisoned or that women should be treated equally is to be in a position to doubt one's normality, to be accused of the sin of pride (in one's own possibly wayward powers of judgment), and to be perceived as disruptive of community unity. Very few people will resist these pressures merely because of the appeal of a theory or some other intellectual construction. A vivid sense of what is at stake, of the sufferings or the abasement of those who are victimized by culturally endorsed practices, is likely to be a much stronger impetus. Thus, sensitivity can have a crucial role, not only in providing an adequate set of data, but also in pushing us along paths that are difficult to follow.

We have already noted a number of respects in which reasonable moral judgment can require more than merely the possession of an adequate decision-procedure along with awareness of all relevant factors. More sensitivity is required in some kinds of cases than in others, and sensitivity can contribute to someone's moral life in a variety of ways. More fundamentally and generally we can say, though, that no one can behave reliably as a virtuous person unless she or he has steady preferences for such things as the amelioration of suffering, due respect for human dignity and autonomy, and so on. To know a good answer to a moral problem counts for very little unless one cares, at least to some degree, about what is involved in implementing (or failing to implement) the answer. This is especially true in cases (frequently commonplace and easy cases) in which there are strong temptations. Moral decision-procedures do not encapsulate their own motivation, and, as a large number of philosophers have pointed out, an agent must have either a general motivation to do what is dictated by the decision-procedure (the Kantian good will) or motivations of some particular sort that are aligned with what the decision-procedure dictates (e.g., sympathy for sufferings which ought to be relieved).

It is true, of course, that someone can behave virtuously out of habit or because of lack of any imaginative grasp of just how he or she would go about behaving otherwise. But temptations or other forms of drastically changed circumstances can get people to reconsider their habits and to see their way clear to doing what is wrong. Reliable virtuous conduct requires more than habits or solid persistence in a morally acceptable routine. We might speak generically of what is required as concern, bearing in mind that this can take the form of generalized concern for morality or concern to relieve and prevent misery or concern for the particular individuals who would be victimized if one behaved immorally.

Concern can motivate greater sensitivity and also more thoughtful exploration of alternatives in hard cases. This need not be true of generalized concern for morality: Someone with Kantian good will can remain satisfied with a traditional and easy answer to what some would regard as a hard moral question and can direct her or his concern simply toward the implementation of this traditional and easy answer. On the other hand, if answers that are not traditional and easy suggest themselves, such a person can emerge as an exceptionally determined radical.

Virtuous conduct that is reliable (at least to a high degree) requires that concern take the form of commitment: either a generalized commitment to what reasonably can be said to accord with a good ethical theory or commitment to take seriously factors (e.g., human misery) that are taken seriously by the theory. In either case, commitment often is needed to bridge the gap between past conduct and what someone will do next. Mastery of a philosophical system of ethics will not be enough without some appropriate commitment. There are other respects in which commitment is crucial to virtue. I already have, in chapter 4, attacked what I have called a snapshot view of ethical choice, the tendency to frame decision-procedures as if all choices are discrete. Part of the attack focused on the fact that many moral choices are not completed instantly or in a brief period of time. In cases in which we decide that we ought to help or protect someone or something, the helping or protection is unlikely to be completed in an instant. Typically, a sustained effort over a period of time is required. This might be analyzed as a series of discrete choices, but there are problems with such analysis. One is that it is often far from clear how we are to individuate and number the members of such a series. It may be easy to do if what is required is a monthly payment, but well-nigh impossible if it is general help and protection for a child. A second problem is that a commitment that is viewed in such terms is a qualified one—and it may be important that some commitments not be qualified. "I will take care of this, unless later I decide that it would be better not to" is, after all, not much assurance. In some circumstances, of course, it is perfectly appropriate to say, "I will help and protect you, subject to monthly review." But the deepest political, social, and personal commitments do not lend themselves to this kind of formulation. Of course, any commitment can be reviewed, and it may be that for any commitment (with the exception of fundamental moral commitments) there are imaginable circumstances in which this would be very appropriate. But, in relation to some kinds of commitment, a positive readiness to review implies lack of seriousness, so that a commitment that is thought of as a series of discrete choices looks shallow. This is connected with a third problem for the snapshot view in relation to commitments: For cases of the kind we have been discussing, the analysis (taken merely as an analysis of what is going on) looks artificial and procrustean; the analogy was with analyzing a walk as a series of discrete decisions to move one's feet. Only someone in the grip of a theory would want to impose such a view.

This should not be taken as saying that there is something wrong with ethical theories per se. I have argued elsewhere that, even if what I have been saying about ethical theories is true, they play a valuable and indispensable role in ethical life (Kupperman 1988). But it suggests that a theory is more reasonable if it is not formulated entirely in terms of judgment of discrete choices; a theory many of whose primary evaluations are of character traits, patterns of behavior, and kinds of commitment will better be able to accommodate recognition of the holistic nature of much ethical choice. It is true that it might not be readily possible for Bloggs to change a character trait or a pattern of behavior that does not rate highly, but this is not to say that change to some degree is entirely impossible, especially if Bloggs is willing to work for a gradual change and is willing to modify some of the circumstances of his life that lend themselves to less than desirable behavior on his part. The snapshot view does have the advantage that what it is concerned with, discrete choices, is more readily controllable, in that arguably on any specific occasion any one of us (who is not insane, drugged, etc.) can do (at least approximately) what is right. But it has the disadvantage of falsifying the nature of our moral life. A theory that does not view every commitment or pattern of behavior as a series of discrete choices is in that respect more strenuous, demanding, and perhaps discouraging. But it works with a more accurate model of people's moral lives.

Let me gather together the threads of this and the three preceding chapters. What many people look for in a philosophical ethics is a moral decision-procedure, a way of telling what is right or wrong. During the last two hundred years, leading philosophers have given people what they want, on the whole framing the decision-procedures in terms of discrete choices. These ethical theories also have tended to be framed so that the character, habits, and past decisions (unless they generated specific obligations) of the moral agent dropped out of the picture. The effect is rather like that of the cardboard cutouts in which tourists can insert their faces and be photographed as the cowboy and the saloon lady. Moral choice is presented as totally impersonal, apart from specific obligations that may have been incurred.

Philosophical ethics of this kind usually either ignores values or settles for the bland philistinism of preference-satisfaction. If the philosopher turns his or her hand to societal design, the societal values emphasized will also be impersonal in a way suited to the realm of cardboard cutouts. Money and various liberties will be most prominent. This is certainly not to deny the importance of liberty or of money. (For that matter, there are moments in anyone's moral life when a snapshot view works extremely well, with no residual difficulties.) But anyone who wants to build an extremely good life merely with the ingredients of liberty, money, and various preference satisfactions that might be associated with the possession of liberties and money, may well become aware that there are elements of a different sort that are essential to a very good life. These are less impersonal: They include a person's sense of self and a sense of structural connections that give unity and meaning to a life. The argument of chapter 6 was that a very good life requires a character that is both strong and at least moderately good.

Reliably good moral choice also requires good character. In the two appendixes I will take up, among other things, psychological data that suggest that there is more to being a genuinely virtuous person than can be inferred from the ability to check the virtuous alternatives on questionnaires administered by psychologists. As was noted in chapter 5, moral virtue is more than a set of skills or abilities; it requires, among other things, the willingness to act in certain ways. Even possession of this virtue and that virtue cannot add up to being a genuinely virtuous person unless there is both the ability to weigh and balance relevant factors of various sorts (which in some cases may include factors normally relevant to more than one virtue) and the willingness to modify one's normal (and normally virtuous) conduct in response to a reasonable judgment. As was pointed out, in some cases the habits and attitudes that support different virtues can conflict, and the limitations of approaching such cases in terms of individual virtues are like the limitations of genre criticism of the arts. We need something which is more than the sum of virtues—and that is good character.

Aspects of good character include appropriate concerns and commitments. These are distinct from any set of abilities and also distinct from any combination of habits and cognitive skills related to morality. Someone who scores high on moral-development questionnaires and who has always manifested habits of behavior in accordance with honesty, generosity, and so on, may surprise us when a really appealing temptation appears or when others expect him or her to conform to new standards. This typically will be a case of inadequate concerns and shallow commitments, adding up to a weak character. Kant would speak of it as a failure of good will, but that diagnosis seems to me not to scratch the surface. This is linked with my running quarrel with Kant in this book, which is that he (like many ethical theorists of different stripes) persists in abstracting individual moral choices both from the character of the agent (apart from the umbrella requirement of good will) and from one another.

This quarrel does not amount to entire opposition. An impersonal, highly abstract moral theory, which is basically what Kant, utilitarians, rights theorists, and so on, have offered us, has the great advantage of a common tool which a variety of people (who may be conscientious in ways subtly different from one another) all can use and adapt to their lives. Such a theory, indeed, makes a contribution to character, in that the way we see (and talk to ourselves about) moral problems is an important part of character. It would be wrong, therefore, for anyone to think that there is an opposition between theory-based and character-based approaches to morality. Ideally, there should be complementarity, and my quarrel is with theorists who do not express full recognition of this.[1]

Full recognition includes acknowledgement of the ways in which a person's sense of self is a factor in moral choice and in which sense of self heavily depends on unifying elements in one's life. This carries us back to the importance of commitments. Philosophers like Kant have tended to slight commitments unless they took very clear-cut forms (e.g., a promise) that generated specific obligations. But most commitments are not so clear-cut: They represent, rather, ways of connecting oneself with other people, institutions, and causes that amount to patterns of life. Typically, if someone's behavior changes and a connection is dissolved, no one can say, "But you promised . . ." or point to a specific obligation that was violated. If someone's behavior changes lightly or frequently, our criticism will take different forms. Allied to this is the point that our most important responsibilities (say, to a child or to a political movement) may be ones that we take on. These responsibilities are experienced in very different ways than as the implications of impersonal general rules of conduct. How these responsibilities are taken on and maintained is crucial to a person's character.

There are four major facets of taking character seriously in relation to moral choice. First, the setting of a moral choice must be understood to include the person the agent is as well as the kinds of commitments she or he has made or is in the process of making. In some cases, as when someone has an opportunity out of the blue to steal a great deal of money, these elements of the setting may be far less important than the impersonal elements constituted by the nature of the temptation and the societal conventions with regard to property rights. At the other extreme, the setting of a case like Sartre's of the young man who must choose between joining the Free French and staying with his aged, dependent mother hardly can be approached in impersonal terms (1946, pp. 129–30).

Second, attitudes toward concerns and commitments play a large part in someone's character, and these sometimes are highly relevant to what she or he ought to do. This is generally not true in cases of the sort on which ethical theorists have tended to dwell, such as that of the temptation to steal a great amount of money. This should be qualified: Nuance can be important even in cases of this general sort, and if we look closely, we might see that there are many different ways in which not to steal the money, that the differences matter, and that which of these options are available to us may depend on who we are. Be that as it may, what is typically most important in such cases can be dealt with even by a theory that slights the importance of character. Something like this can be argued also of public policy decisions, such as whether increased funding should go to medical research or to student aid. There is, again, a qualification. Someone who is a major political figure, making a series of such decisions, may have to look for a balance or a continuity among the decisions. A snapshot view may work badly for the choices of such a person. However, the major examples of cases for which the snapshot view works badly are those within a series of decisions that someone makes in the context of personal involvement with a group, a political or social cause, a family, or with other individuals. Here, where someone is coming from may be highly relevant to what she or he should do.

Third, if we want to get a sense of the factors that play large parts in whether someone actually does what is morally right, the sensitivity, concern, and commitments that have a crucial relationship to character must be taken very seriously. No major thinker has ever denied that there are factors above and beyond understanding and acceptance of an ethical theory that play a role in actual moral conduct. But there has been a tendency to slide over such factors or to think of them in terms of something that either happens or fails to happen at the actual moment of moral decision: Either Bloggs comes up with, or fails to come up with, a good will on that occasion. Much of my argument has been that what is involved is much more complicated and less a matter of a moment than such accounts suggest. This is very relevant to the practical concerns to be addressed in appendix B. If a society wishes to educate its members to be morally virtuous, it must take care not to overintellectualize the process or to ignore factors such as sensitivity.

Finally, if someone asks, "Why should I be moral?" (a favorite question of philosophers) it is natural in the reply to focus on values associated with morality. The question itself can make clear sense as a request for assurance of rewards. Yet to ask it seriously, in a personal rather than a philosophical context, is a bad sign. It shows a shallow or wavering commitment both to the general ideal of morality and to the considerations that have weight in moral judgment. In the extreme case, if someone, offered a chance to torture and kill some children for a large fee, asks "Why should I be moral?" that person is already a monster.

Recent answers to the question have tended to stress either the likelihood that one cannot permanently conceal a lack of genuine allegiance to what morality demands, along with the resulting deterioration of relationships with other people, or to stress, more generally, the fact that in the long run (as rewards and punishments fall out) immorality is a poor bet against the odds. There is a lot of truth to these responses, and what they suggest is that, at least for the great majority of the members of reasonably affluent and moderately just societies, the path of (at least moderately) virtuous conduct is actually the path of least resistance. In such societies, conspicuous immorality can usually be regarded as maladroit; indeed, many of the people who follow this path are the types who in school never quite caught on. Then, of course, there are the more clever types, the kinds of people implicated in financial scandals, whose immorality might have been limited to specific opportunities and in any case was never intended to be conspicuous. These people, as I have been suggesting, can plausibly be regarded as having had shallow moral commitments even before they took the plunge into outright immorality. Thus, the question that most needs to be answered is, "What values are associated with moral commitments that are not shallow?" When we see the answer to this, we can see why it is advantageous to become the kind of person for whom "Why should I be moral?" would never raise a genuine issue.

The main point is this. To be committed strongly to moral conduct is not merely to have different goals from some other people or to be different in one's willingness on special occasions to suspend pursuit of ordinary goals. It is to be a different person from what one would have been if one had not been strongly committed. This is linked with a set of values many of which are internal to having a certain kind of character.

First and foremost, we should remind ourselves of the argument in chapter 6 that a good life must be a meaningful one and that this, in turn, presupposes a strong character. To be committed strongly to moral conduct is thereby to have a strong as well as good character. Among other things, this is a unifying factor in a life. It means that one always can know the person one is in a way in which the person whose commitment to virtuous conduct is wavering or shallow does not. Second, it means that one generally is in a position to be satisfied with an important element of one's life, one's conduct; as we have seen, one's assessment of one's life is crucial to happiness. This does not mean that a strongly moral person must be happy; other elements in her or his life may go badly wrong. But it does mean that in one crucial area the moral person has what is required for happiness, and it is likely (unless she or he is very good at self-deception) that the shallow, opportunistic person will lack this. To the extent that happiness is important to the value of a life, this is an inducement to genuine moral commitment.

Such inducements usually are both appreciated and taken seriously only after they have been earned. It would be wrong to suggest that people develop the character they do in large part because of calculations of self-interest. Nevertheless, a large part of the place of character in ethics is in making possible a clearer and more realistic sense of the values of virtue. Most philosophers have in their everyday lives something of this sense, although usually it does not benefit from the clear light of an adequate philosophical account. Ethical philosophy can provide adequate accounts of the moral choices and values in people's lives only if the crucial role of character is recognized and examined.

Note

1. This is an appropriate place to say where this book stands in relation to some ethical theories and where my own position is. My fundamental orientation is consequentialist, in that in my view the guiding ideal of an ethics should be that of maximizing the value in the universe (present and future): To put it more crudely, the point of ethics is to bring about good consequences (see Kupperman 1983; also essays in *Mind* 1980 and in *American Philosophical Quarterly* 1981). The consequentialism I endorse is different in a number of ways from well-known forms. First, it is not the form of consequentialism known as utilitarianism, in that arguments have been given against the view that value should be equated with what an individual finds satisfying or would satisfy what an individual wants. Nor is the utilitarian assumption acceptable that the value in the world at any given time is simply the sum of individual values. Both with regard to the values in the world and with regard to the values in a life, a holistic view seems far more plausible than an additive one. Finally, the direct forms of consequentialism are, as many writers have pointed out, both severely counterintuitive and also counterproductive. To aim for best consequences is not necessarily the best way of reaching them; an act which does produce the best consequences available need not be considered by us, reflectively and retrospectively, the right thing to do, even if the agent was motivated entirely by concern for goodness of consequences. To say that the point of ethics is to bring about good consequences is to posit this as a strong constraint on theory at a high level and not necessarily to posit it as a guiding law in every specific, concrete decision. It is to deny that there can be pointless virtues or harmless vices.

This consequentialism will seem to many philosophers to be highly qualified or watered down. This is not the place for an argument that its implications are significant. It should be noted, though, that theories can be developed and modified in various ways and can incorporate (usually not at the highest level of theory) parts of other theories. As J. S. Mill showed in *On Liberty*, consequentialism can incorporate concern for rights; and it clearly can incorporate, in much the same way, a Kantianlike respect for persons and for personal autonomy. Personal autonomy, indeed, is (in my view) both a means to various ends and part of important ends. It should be clear also that to endorse one theory is not necessarily to reject others entirely or to hold that they are in some sense incorrect. Ethical theories are ways of making sense of ethics and of life; even a theory that has some serious flaws can make very good sense of a great deal. There is more than one good ethical theory.

My argument in chapter 4 was that neither Kantians nor utilitarians have done justice to the importance of character, but that there is more room in utilitarianism for recognition of the importance of character in moral decision. The argument of chapter 6, though, is designed to show, among other things, that the distinctively utilitarian account of value is unacceptable and that Kant's account of values (such as it is) also is impoverished.

The point to insist on is that, although my theoretical orientation is consequentialist, none of the arguments in this book rest on consequentialist assumptions. In this respect, the book is intended to be evenhanded and to be useful to a philosopher of any general theoretical or antitheoretical persuasion. The arguments of the book do, of course, have implications for theory. These include the claim that any theory needs to supply a way of understanding continuous patterns of decision and should abandon or modify what I have called a snapshot view. The arguments leave room for a variety of theoretical responses, including, for example, a quasi-Kantian theory that allows for forms of ethical urgency other than duty.

APPENDIX A

Moral Psychology

An important element of many ethical philosophies has been a moral psychology, that is, a set of assumptions or claims about human nature or the variety of human psychologies and, in particular, about the causal factors related to virtue and vice. The specifically normative positions of philosophers such as Plato, Aristotle, and Confucius are very closely linked to empirical claims of this sort. Hume's writing on ethics is consistently a mixture of psychology and philosophy, and something like this is true also of more recent philosophers such as Nietzsche and Sartre. In addition, there are major figures who are not normally classified as philosophers but who, if moral psychology is a genuine subject, may be great moral psychologists. The duc de la Rochefoucauld and Michel Montaigne would appear on such a list. Many would add the names of novelists such as Dostoevsky and Henry James.

To many educated twentieth-century readers this smacks of antiquarian nonsense. As late as Hume's time, psychology was not a science; and perhaps when Nietzsche was alive, it was still not much of one. But now there is rigorous experimental work on human psychology, much of it using statistical methods. What excuse is there for using literature, philosophy, or personal experience (or the social branch of folk psychology) to arrive at psychological judgments, when there is real knowledge to be had? This point can be made about some of the remarks on the psychology of character to be found in this book. It also can be made in relation to any claims about the education of character that do not rest on rigorous experiment.

My reply is not simple. Part of it is that there is, indeed, some very useful scientific work on the psychology of character—referred to elsewhere in this book. It is disappointing that there is not more and that there is so little scientific evidence that can be brought to bear on the major questions related to development of character. If we ask, ''Why is there not more?'' the answer is neither simple nor neat. Let me outline what seem to be the major factors. One of them, which I will discuss last, points toward the worth of much in the older, unscientific tradition of moral psychology.

A first point is that any scientific study of the psychology of character is most revealing if it focuses not on what people say, but on what they do. Furthermore what a person does in commonplace situations may be much less indicative of character than what she or he does when severely tempted or pressed. A striking example of a useful investigation of character was the Abscam Experiment performed by the FBI, who, when looking into the characters of several congressmen, offered them substantial bribes under conditions in which they might well believe that there were minimal risks. One presumes that most or all of the subjects ordinarily talked virtuously, knew very well how to appeal to moral principles, and did not shoplift or steal money from their neighbours. Nevertheless, after some of them accepted the bribes, the investigation was widely held to have revealed something important about their characters.

The closest psychological experiments to this were those performed by Stanley Milgram: Subjects were pressured rather than tempted in order to get them to do things that almost certainly would go against the moral code they normally professed. The results were extremely revealing; although, as I will suggest later, there is room for doubt about exactly what they revealed. One reason why such experiments are not performed more often is that there are strong ethical objections to what can be argued to be, in effect, a procedure of corrupting people to see how easily they can be corrupted. Milgram has argued strenuously that in the event his experiments were not harmful to subjects and often were beneficial (1974, pp. 193–202). But the controversy remains. With the current increase of litigiousness in America, also, it is hard to see how a psychologist who followed in Milgram's footsteps could now expect to avoid expensive lawsuits.

If we avoid risky and possibly unethical surveys of actual behavior under pressure, the major (and simplest) alternative that remains is to ask people questions about what they would do or think should be done in various hypothetical situations. This, in fact, is the primary thrust of the investigations into moral education of Lawrence Kohlberg (1981) and his school. Such research is not valueless: it can be a good test of ethical sophistication *if* one assumes that the questions mirror a reasonable set of ethical distinctions. But the questionnaire method cannot distinguish among (1) what someone's character genuinely is, (2) what someone is pretending his or her character is, and the intermediate case of (3) what someone thinks incorrectly his or her character is. The only way of distinguishing among these is, again, to put subjects under pressure or to present temptations, and then surreptitiously to observe how they actually behave. Because of the ethical objections against major pressures or temptations, minor temptations may be used. Alan Waterman, summarizing research of this sort, reports that the results of research on the connection between scores on Kohlbergian tests of moral development and actual moral behavior "are mixed, on balance favoring cognitive development theory" (1988, p. 289). Anyone but an utter cynic would expect a result like this; even if there is a great deal of hypocrisy in the world, it would be surprising if it were the norm. But it is hardly a strong result, and one can wonder what the results would have been if different temptations had been used or, for that matter, if different standards of ethical sophistication had been used.

There is a growing literature of small temptations. Yuchtman-Yaar and Rahav begin their "Resisting Small Temptations in Everyday Transactions" by making the point that "a major methodological difficulty inherent in the study of moral behavior derives from the typically clandestine nature of unethical acts" (1986, p. 23). They quite prudently decide that the identification of moral judgments is more easily obtained in the gray area of informal deviance. Their method is to have bus drivers in Tel Aviv give too much change—the temptations amounting to as much as 25 percent of a bus fare—to passengers, and then see if the passengers (having made eye contact with the change) are honest enough to return the money. This experiment is not without merit, but it leaves room to wonder about the connections between people's behavior in response to very small temptations of this sort and the way they might behave when significantly tempted. Anyone who has ever gone to the trouble of returning a penny or two of excess change, and then felt like a complete fool afterward because the person reimbursed clearly felt that his or her time was being wasted, might wonder about the role of nonmoral factors in someone's decision. Might it matter if, when you got too much in change, there were four or five people behind you who were trying to get on the bus? It is imaginable that someone might not bother negotiating repayment of a very small amount of money who would be entirely honest if the amount were much larger.

A second point has special force in relation to empirical studies of moral education. Moral development can involve many twists and turns: It is conceivable that someone who was habitually honest as a child could be easily tempted as an adult and that irregular behavior as a child might lead in the direction of solid and reliable virtue in adult life. Something that takes root in a child might bear fruit only many years later. The only way in which these connections can be mapped is by longitudinal studies, by following a group of subjects from early childhood to maturity—and, indeed, onward perhaps until middle age, because many moral crises enter people's lives only in their middle years. If we put together our two points thusfar, what this requires ideally of psychological research is that psychologists spy on people when they are young children and then continue to spy on them when they are adults.

Close scrutiny would be especially required for a study of willed change of character. Is Hume right in suggesting that we cannot change our characters substantially at will? This cannot be assessed adequately unless we can distinguish cases in which someone is making a genuine effort to be a different sort of person from those in which someone merely says that it would be nice. Detailed observation over periods of time would be required to make this distinction.

Something less than spying might have some use in other kinds of investigation as long as it was rigorous and longitudinal. Psychologists are in a position to recognize this. As Shirley L. Jessor has remarked, "Understanding moral development requires, I think, a much greater commitment to a longitudinal strategy so that the course of development of an attitude, a process, or a person's lifestyle may be traced, and thereby understood" (Jessor in DePalma and Foley 1975, p. 179). This still seems to me a good comment on what is lacking in the empirical literature in this field. There have been some longitudinal studies of personality reported on in Brim and Kagan (1980) and also West and Graziano (1989). None of these, however, concern willed change of character, and altogether there has not been as much longitudinal research as an ethicist would want. There are obvious practical reasons why this should be so. Psychologists are under the same pressures as other researchers to obtain relatively quick results. To the extent that funding is crucial to research, longitudinal studies are at a severe disadvantage. It also is true, of course, that adults (unless they are in frequent trouble with the law or are institutionalized) are often difficult to track, which may be one reason why "with the exception of the antisocial personality disorder . . . there is a dearth of empirical research regarding the longitudinal course of personality disorders" (Drake and Vaillant 1988, p. 44). Some of the difficulties are reflected in Kenneth Gergen's remark that "because of the immense demands placed on the researcher" systematic longitudinal studies of individuals are "indeed rare"; he also points out the complication "that developmental trajectories over the life span are highly variable" (Gergen 1982, pp. 150, 161). There also is the fact that adults, unlike children in school, are in a position to resist personality tests and often do. Adult transformations are irregular in timing, and those undergoing them "rarely assemble in groups, making testing difficult" (Stewart, Franz, and Layton 1988, pp. 41–42).

The psychologists who remark on this last go on to suggest that this increases the appeal, compared to available alternatives, of psychological study of personal documents, such as diaries and letters. The case seems reasonable, but it is important to point out how psychological method is highlighted by such a shift. When we have grasped this, we are in a better position to appreciate the value of the older tradition of moral psychology.

When a psychologist analyzes a diary or a series of letters—or what a person says in the psychologist's office—two important variables are what the psychologist treats as significant, and the categories within which what is significant will be represented. The worth of the psychological analysis will depend heavily on these variables. A psychologist who fails to be struck by what is, in fact, important or whose categories are impoverished or irrelevant cannot produce a useful analysis. Conversely, a psychologist who has a good sense of what should seem salient and whose categorial schemes are rich and flexible can produce highly useful work.

The obvious question is, "Why cannot someone who is not a professional psychologist, such as the duc de la Rochefoucauld or leading contributors to the fund of moral psychology that Aristotle drew upon, also have a good sense of what is salient and deploy rich and flexible categories, thus producing highly useful psychological analyses of people's lives?" The lay observer may have the disadvantage of being an interested party in some of the life stories (of friends, rivals, family members, etc.) that she or he knows best, and this is one of many reasons why some accounts and analyses will have to be discounted. On the other hand, the lay observer in many cases has the great advantage of intimate acquaintance with psychological subjects that is continued over long periods of time and under circumstances in which the subjects are not always on guard in the way they express their attitudes and feelings. Someone like La Rochefoucauld or David Hume, both perceptive and reasonably dispassionate, thus can see people not merely as they would like to be seen but as they reveal themselves in a variety of settings.

Such a person, thus, has great advantages over even the most subtle and perceptive professional psychologist, who is likely to have extended professional contact with subjects only when they know they are being looked at by a psychologist (and, therefore, will be unusually concerned with the kind of image they are projecting). Of course, the professional psychologist, like anyone else, can get to know people in nonprofessional settings. But is there any reason to think that her or his observations will be more acute, or more soundly based, than those of the duc de la Rochefoucauld?

The importance of rich and flexible categories must be stressed. Ordinary language philosophers, such as J. L. Austin, have helped us realize how extraordinarily rich and flexible the categories of a natural language such as English are; Austin's (1958) discussion of the subtle differences among "pretending," "feigning," "acting as if," "imitating," "affecting to be," "shamming," and "posing as" is a classic in this way. This suggests that a command of nuances of language is not a minor qualification of someone who wishes to produce rich and subtle accounts of human behavior. At the opposite extreme, one would have to place psychological questionnaires that require yes or no or multiple-choice responses rather than essay answers. Here, the psychologist, however subtle and precise in language she or he may be in ordinary life, is forced to rely on a small number of categorial pigeonholes within which answers can be dropped. There is usually the possibility that a response that straddled categories or that invoked new ones would be a better psychological representation than the response that is elicited by the questionnaire.

Questionnaires reflect the theories and assumptions of the psychologists who devise them. This is an appropriate point to comment both on one distinction in recent psychological theory and results that this distinction bears upon. The distinction rests on the psychological interpretation of personality, which as I remarked in chapter 1 is given a technical meaning by psychologists that is much closer in fact to the ordinary meaning of character than to that of personality. Mark Snyder says, "As a psychological concept, personality refers to regularities and consistencies in the behavior of individuals in the course of their lives. It refers to regularities and consistencies across contexts . . . over time . . . and between behavioral domains" (1983, p. 497). Snyder goes on to distinguish among two main types of people: those who "typically manifest the regularities and consistencies of personality in their social behavior" and those who do not and are "relatively situational" (p. 498). The second group relies on "high self-monitoring"; the first group is "low self-monitoring." The suggestion is that low self-monitoring people (who correspond perhaps, roughly and with qualifications I will suggest, to the people I would refer to as having strong characters) "display considerable temporal stability in their behavior" (p. 499). Snyder goes on to make a suggestion which supports roughly the same claim (reported in chap. 6) as made by Nietzsche, that people "create for themselves social worlds well-suited" to their propensities; a difference is that Nietzsche's suggestion is made in respect to people of character, whereas Snyder's is made in respect both to high self-monitoring and low self-monitoring individuals (p. 507).

Snyder's basic distinction is between behavior's being determined by personality and its being determined by situation; David S. Funder, in another article in the same special-topic issue of the *Journal of Personality*, traces the recent debate in the psychological literature between psychologists who emphasize situations as the determinant (situationists) and those who emphasize personality (personologists). Over a period of time, Funder reports, "a consensus seems to have evolved that the behavior of individuals is *both* coherently patterned across time and situations, *and* discriminatively sensitive to the differences between situations," (1983, p. 347). Funder goes on to argue for a claim that he takes to be widely accepted by personologists and to be widely rejected by situationists, namely, that reports by professional or lay observers of people's behavior in natural settings sometimes can be taken as useful evidence. "The human observer," Funder says, "is clearly a flawed instrument for evaluating behavior, and his or her assessments cannot always be taken at face value. But this is not to say that they are useless" (p. 350).

This summary judgment seems to me to be entirely reasonable, and it, of course, leads to the conclusion that there is a place in psychology (at least as providing starting points for investigation and perhaps in some cases more of a place than this) for the older tradition of moral psychology. My respect for the work of Funder and of Snyder, however, is compatible with some unease at the situation-determined/personality-determined distinction which is entrenched in this branch of psychology and which they both accept. The distinction seems too simple. Consider the following cases. Suppose that Smith would normally (i.e., if other people had not been involved in the way in which they are) have been inclined to do Y in situation S. However she does X.

Case 1   Smith does X because doing Y (as she was inclined to) would have badly hurt Jones's feelings.

Case 2   Smith does X as a compromise with Jones, who had an interest in the outcome: X is intermediate between Y (which Smith continues to think would have been intrinsically preferable) and Z (which Jones preferred).

Case 3   Smith does X because Jones and the rest of the gang expect X or perhaps because Jones is a psychologist who says, ''The experiment demands X.''

In all these cases, Smith's behavior could be considered responsive to the situation; yet from an ethical (and one would think a psychological) point of view, there is a great difference between Case 3 and the other two. It must be admitted that, in practice, there sometimes may be difficulties in arriving at a firm sense of whether what happened is more like Case 2 than like Case 3. All the same, there is a great difference between Case 3, which represents weak character (or, as Kierkegaard would have said, no self), and cases in which someone who has a strong character retains a clear sense of her or his own ideals, although behaving in a flexible way in order to maintain a friendship or family, social, or political harmony.

My suggestion, thus, is that a central distinction in current social psychology is simple in a way that blurs interesting and important possibilities. This categorial impoverishment reinforces the impression that even the best research work on the psychology of character tends to be sculpture done with blunt instruments. All the same, whatever the practical difficulties might be and whatever conceptual complexities might be required, there may seem no reason *on principle* why claims made within the older tradition of moral psychology could not be tested in an acceptable way by contemporary psychologists. Or is there? Let me suggest a useful test case. Maxim 182 of La Rochefoucauld runs as follows: "Vices have a place in the composition of virtues just as poisons in that of medicines: prudence blends and tempers them, utilizing them against the ills of life" (1665, p. 57). This maxim seems to me to contain a mixture of important psychological and ethical truth. Could the former be tested?

We need first to explicate what the ethical and psychological ingredients are. The maxim is only slightly more extreme than many texts in the older tradition of moral psychology in compressing a complicated set of insights into a small space. We should beware of treating such a text as merely a set of messages or as a container (rather like a fortune cookie) from which these messages could be taken. In some cases, the meaning of the text can be understood only in terms of an ordered sequence of normal reader responses, some of them determinate, some to a degree indeterminate, and some running contrary to previous ones. Some texts can be understood not so much as self-contained messages as guides to the perception of behavior or situations.

Maxim 182 presupposes an ethical view very different from a simple Kantianism: Actions which fit the same broad description can be such that one is virtuous and another is wrong. The contours of what is virtuous will be irregular in relation to our broad descriptive categories. Thus, it is often not possible to determine what is right merely by following some general rule or principle. This is a view of ethics that some people find counterintuitive, but it is implicit in Aristotle's discussion of the mean and in Confucian ethics.

The maxim makes a further claim. Not only is the contour of what is virtuous irregular in relation to our broad descriptive categories, but also it is irregular in relation to our habits, impulses, and ongoing attitudes. There will not be a neat and comfortable fit between the path of what is virtuous and the unreflective dispositions of a moderately virtuous person: Even if they coincide in the great majority of cases, they will not coincide in every case. The assertion of lack of fit is both ethical and psychological. It is ethical, in that it claims that the virtuous is more complicated than many might want it to be. It is psychological, in that it posits a limit in the ability of unreflective human dispositions to mirror this complexity.

Any ethics which does not rely simply on general rules and principles is likely to ask whether a fit between a person's unreflective dispositions and what is virtuous is humanly possible. Aristotle does not directly answer this question; but I take some elements of his discussion of the mean, such as the advice to aim a little in the direction of the extreme that is less appealing to us (as a way of compensating for possible bias), to suggest an answer of no (Bk. I, chap. 9, 1109b, p. 50). Confucius is quoted, in a famous passage, as claiming that finally at the age of seventy he could follow the desires of his heart and yet be virtuous (II.4, p. 88). The reader of this passage is meant to be struck, of course, by the fact that Confucius, who worked very hard at self-perfection, did not reach this point until he was seventy.

Whatever the truth of Confucius's claim, it is plausible—if one believes that virtue is not simply a matter of following appropriate general rules—to say that virtually no one will have a perfect fit between unreflective dispositions and what is virtuous. What this means in practice is that habits, impulses, or attitudes normally manifested in virtuous action and which, therefore, might be thought of as virtuous, can lead in some cases plausibly and naturally to actions which are the reverse of virtuous. Smith's honesty, which has made her highly reliable in situations in which many of us might be tempted to equivocate, sometimes leads her to say or do things that cause serious and permanent harm to others. Jones's strength of mind, which leads him to take charge admirably of situations in which something needs to be done and the rest of us are just standing around, sometimes leads to unwarranted interference in other people's lives. And so on. The converse also is true. Qualities which in many settings may seem allied to vices can be conducive to virtue. Winston's stubbornness and desire to dominate, which in some situations lead to obstinate bullying, can make him an admirable foe of tyranny.

Part of the thought of the maxim, then, is that intelligent people who can arrive at a dispassionate sense of their temperaments and motives as well as of when they are at their best and their worst can also, to some degree, shape and guide the ways they respond to situations, thus creating in some cases virtuous responses out of ingredients that could be allied to vice. Instances in which this is done—along with cases in which what is normally virtuous is vicious or vice versa—can be presumed to provide the data on which the maxim is based. The duc de La Rochefoucauld must have seen such cases and distilled what he saw in them in Maxim 182; the responsive reader will think of similar cases that she or he has seen and will get the point accordingly. Such cases not only will provide the supporting data, but also will make possible the resonance of the maxim, in that the responsive reader now is prepared for such cases and more likely to notice them.

This means not only that one is prepared to notice a lack of fit between unreflective dispositions and virtue in others, but also to notice it in oneself. The remedy is self-scrutiny and reflectiveness. Jones can ask, "Is it really appropriate for me to take charge of Bloggs's life at this point? Might my normal take-charge attitude be getting out of hand?" Smith can wonder whether telling Bloggs the truth about X would be seriously damaging. Perhaps her tendency to tell the truth come what may should be tempered or admit of exceptions? What this calls for is, in one respect, a process of reflection about the real-life cases that intersect with one's dispositions. (Is this a form of high self-monitoring?) In another respect, it is a process of self-refinement—as Confucius says, "filing, chiseling" (I.15, p. 87). This process, it should be noted, does not require anything like a heightened sweetness or soulfulness. Rather something like shrewdness is crucial. Prudence, as La Rochefoucauld says, tempers the ingredients of our psychological life.

What can a modern psychologist make of the psychological element of the maxim? Clearly, there is an empirical component, but it is formulated in relation to an ethical component, so that any test would have to begin with what amounted to a formulation of what were the right decisions in some difficult cases. Scholars who try to deal with values when pursuing a value-free methodology sometimes can finesse their difficulties by talking about what such and such a group of people would agree on. John Rawls is the most notable contemporary philosopher who pursues this strategy, and it is available also to psychologists. But as the examination of Rawls's theory in chapter 5 indicates, a result can be a lowest-common-denominator set of values. La Rochefoucauld emphatically is pursuing ethical insights that are not of this sort. There is no clear way in which a psychologist could reconstitute in terms of a group agreement the ethical side of La Rochefoucauld's dictum of lack of fit. The best the psychologist could do, it seems to me, is to validate (1) the existence of cases in which someone who is widely judged to be virtuous acts in a way that *some* intelligent observers think is wrong and in a way that is correlated with personal qualities that these same observers think generally admirable and (2) also validate the existence of cases in which qualities widely thought to be allied to vice contribute to behavior that *some* intelligent observers think is admirable. These would be small results in comparison with the richness and complexity of what La Rochefoucauld has to say.

All of this can be taken as a defense and endorsement of the older tradition of moral psychology. What of such sources as novels and plays? Many readers may feel torn. On the one hand, educated people often *feel* that they have learned something important from reading, say, a Dostoevsky novel. On the other hand, they usually cannot say what it is; if they try, what emerges is usually something very trite. Furthermore, imaginative fiction must be taken as the very paradigm of the unscientific, so how can psychology of any value be gathered from it?

A plausible answer has been suggested by Ira Newman (1984). A central point is that depictions in novels and plays can be taken as modeling aspects of reality. A model brings out detail and relevant connections, enabling us better to focus on the reality it models. This accounts for the way in which novels and plays often allow us to perceive events and connections in the real world that we otherwise might not have taken in, so that people sometimes murmur that life imitates art. A novelist or playwright can look like a great moral psychologist, if she or he gets us to see fundamental connections—either in the psychology of remarkable people or in everyday life—that we otherwise would not have grasped. Conversely, of course, a novelist or playwright can be a poor moral psychologist, pointing toward connections that are not there or that everyone knows about and that consequently seem trite.

It is characteristic of the older tradition of moral psychology, indeed, that although (as I have been suggesting) its results at best can be as useful and important as those of scientific psychology, its methods of validation are nonexistent, so that poor results can be passed off as good. This places a burden on the reader, who must perform some of the validation that in scientific work would be part of what is provided; of course, the reader's validation itself is hardly likely to meet scientific standards. On the other hand, it has to be said that relatively few scientific investigations of moral psychology in recent years have seemed as interesting and important as the results that are found throughout the work of La Rochefoucauld, Hume, and Nietzsche.

One investigation that does meet this standard is Stanley Milgram's (1974) of obedience. At the very least, his experiments together with their replication in various countries prove that most people have weak characters. The basic experiment involves a subject who thinks that he or she has volunteered for a study of the effects of punishment on learning. He is instructed to administer (what appear to be) electric shocks of increasing severity to a learner (who appears to be another subject, but is an actor) if the latter makes errors related to a list of word pairs. As the "shocks" increase in intensity, the responses of the "learner" evolve from verbal complaint to a demand to be released from the experiment. "At 285 volts his response can only be described as an agonized scream," (p. 4). This impels the subject to quit, but "the experimenter, a legitimate authority to whom the subject feels some commitment, enjoins him to continue." Milgram interprets this in relation to the inability to "make a clear break with authority." Roughly two-thirds of the subjects continued to the maximum of 450 volts. Milgram comments, "It is the extreme willingness of adults to go to almost any length on the command of an authority that constitutes the chief finding of the study." He draws a connection, which others also have drawn, with the central thesis of Hannah Arendt's *Eichmann in Jerusalem* (1963). Here is scientific demonstration of, among other things, what Arendt calls the "banality of evil."

It cannot be denied that Milgram's work also points toward the validity of a situationist approach to the conduct of at least two-thirds of the population. Is the result, though, entirely a matter of obedience to authority? Roger Brown suggests that the fact of a single subject at any time in the Milgram experiments was crucial; he seems to think that a majority of groups would rebel. In this view, conformity is a crucial factor. If groups were subjects, and if rebellion of a recalcitrant group took place, then conformity would be on the side of rebellion (1986, pp. 17, 36). Let me suggest also that the smoothness of the apparent experimental routine that Milgram's subjects were placed in is an important factor. It is this which assimilates Milgram's success to that of sexual seducers and confidence men, even though neither of these groups customarily rely on what would normally be termed authority. In all three cases, though, part of the art is to make the subject feel that the normal, expected thing is to go along, to match the rhythm of the situation, and that to refuse would be awkward, indeed gauche. The world of Milgram may have interesting links with the worlds of Pierre Choderlos de Laclos's *Les Liaisons dangereuses* and Herman Melville's *The Confidence-Man* as well as with what can be observed in contemporary political seduction, in which smoothness can be a vital factor. There is ample evidence that people are "slightly anxious, confused, and overwhelmed on first encountering a novel situation'' and that these ''feelings of uncertainty of the social rules interfere with altruistic behavior'' (Argyle, Furnham, and Graham, 1981, p. 48). All of this is arguably true of Milgram's subjects. He himself remarks, ''Underlying all social occasions is a situational etiquette that plays a part in regulating behavior. In order to break off the experiment, the subject must breach the implicit set of understandings that are part of the social occasion'' (1974, p. 149). At this point in the commentary, hierarchy, which Milgram in my view slightly overemphasizes as a factor, recedes, and the anxiety to do the socially right thing becomes central. One is reminded of Leo Tolstoy's insistence in some of his later writing that to do what is morally right is sometimes so disruptive of social rhythms as to be acutely embarrassing.

It would be very useful to have more scientific work on character that is as important and well-supported as that of Milgram. In the meantime, the moral psychologies of such figures as Aristotle, Confucius, and La Rochefoucauld would appear to be as good as any we have.

APPENDIX B

Education of Character

What follows will be an account of moral education congruent with the analysis of character that this book provides. I had at one point intended a book-length treatment of moral education, which is of the greatest importance both for families and polities, but was discouraged by the scarcity of scientific evidence of what works, or fails to work. The reasons for this scarcity were explored in appendix A. This is not to say that there is not some good evidence, of various sorts, but it falls short of the detailed scientific evidence that many people would like to see on this subject. Such evidence could only be the result of very long-term longitudinal studies of actual behavior as well as thought, studies conducted by researchers who used subtle and flexible categorial schemes and whose ethical categories were more sophisticated than those of the simple Kantianism and even more-simple moral relativism that have been dominant in this field, at least in the United States. There is one work of some distinction (although it does not have all of these desiderata), William G. Perry, Jr.'s study of the college years (1970). In the absence of more, recommendations about moral education, including the ones that follow, can merely have the force of suggestions.

There are strong philosophical grounds already, though, for thinking that some existing schemes of moral education are badly conceived. That of Kohlberg is built around the notion that becoming virtuous is rather like becoming good at mathematics, except that there is a different subject matter and a different progression of intellectual skills. This is a view which no major ethical philosopher, including Kant, has held: When I refer to it as a simple Kantianism, part of what this means is that it is far simpler than Kant's Kantianism. The American values-clarification school is very different from Kohlberg's in many respects, but they share an insistence on ignoring the fact that students are in the process of growing into persons of certain sorts as well as acquiring various skills. To treat a student's preferences at a certain stage as basic, incorrigible data is, in effect, to regard the student as incapable of growth. Such an assumption may well promote the result it assumes.

Let us assume that the primary purpose of moral education is to encourage students to develop strong and good characters. When the problem is put in this way, factors emerge that tend to be ignored by many moral educationists. One is, of course, that the educator's goal goes far beyond skill acquisition; it has to do with the kind of person the student eventually is. A second is that it would be wrong, and probably futile as well, to work at this with a detailed blueprint of the results aimed for. In chapter 6, it was argued that there are many different ways in which to have a very good life. No doubt, all people of good character will agree in finding torture, rape, and sadistic acts generally repugnant; indeed, there will be considerable agreement about the core of social morality. But there are enough moral issues and other matters not at the core to which a person's character is relevant that it can be expected that good characters also will be considerably different from one another. Besides this, there is a contradiction in terms in the idea of a teacher, or anyone else, pressuring or instructing someone to have a strong character. Education of character should stimulate reflection and suggest possible directions; once beyond the core of social morality that is taught to very small children, it should not dictate answers.

A third factor is closely related to the analysis in the first part of this book. A character represents a unification through time of a person's tendencies. Someone who lacks a sense of how various parts of her or his life are connected cannot have much of a character and certainly cannot have a strong character. Thus, educating students to have a firmer awareness of connections through time in their lives, although it might seem more akin to the cognitive than the moral, will be an important part of education of character.

We can take a closer look at these factors in the context of various stages of moral education. Because this is intended to be exploratory and suggestive rather than definitive, we can work within a rough distinction among three stages. The first involves students who are acquiring the rudiments of what it is to have a good and strong character, but who are not ready for any sophisticated moral reflection. The second involves students who are beginning to be ready, and who, in some cases, are beginning to adopt independent perspectives. The third involves students who are in a position to make, or to adjust, crucial decisions of who they are. Very roughly, these stages correspond to primary school, secondary school, and college, although there is bound to be some overlap between stages.

The first stage is the only one that should center on dogmatic instruction of central moral norms. The central norms should be presented as assuredly correct; this does not mean, of course, that teachers need be heavy-handed, should refuse to take questions seriously, or refuse to regard what is taught as subject to reflective thought. There are three reasons why a dogmatic stance is appropriate at this stage. One is that it is absurd to suppose that very young children generally are in a position to understand, and to weigh reflectively, justifications for considering, say, murder and theft to be wrong. A second is that any liberal society can and must distinguish between, on the one hand, a set of moral questions on which it can be presumed decent members of the society will agree, agreement on which is essential to the security and well-being of members of the society and, on the other hand, a set of moral questions about which reasonable people can disagree (such as, say, those of the rightness of capital punishment and, I would argue, abortion). Among the former I would include questions of murder, theft, torture, rape, racism, and sexism. I have argued elsewhere that answers to these questions are as well-settled as most issues in the sciences (Kupperman 1983). Even though ethical counterparts of flat earth believers exist, there is no reason why their children cannot be told flatly in school that racism and sexism are wrong.

It cannot be too strongly emphasized that not only can we distinguish between ethical norms about which we can be dogmatic and those about which we cannot, but also that any society must agree on a class of the former. We need to be able to assume that the great majority of the people around us have absorbed (however imperfectly) the idea that murder, theft, and various forms of brutality are wrong. Otherwise daily life is too nasty and insecure. If we wait for reflective consent before instilling these norms, in many cases we will wait too long. A primary school also can be regarded as a kind of society, with its own limits of tolerance: theft, brutality, and (I would argue) racism and sexism cannot be allowed without great resulting damage. Thus, a school has its own internal reasons for instilling basic moral norms.

A third reason why early dogmatism is appropriate is that moral reflection at a more advanced age takes place against the background of habits, attitudes, and categories that already have been formed. To suppose that there can be effective moral reflection without a first stage in which categories are learned and habits and attitudes are formed is as naive in its way as to suppose that secondary-school mathematics can be taught effectively to girls and boys who have never learned number concepts or (perhaps a better analogy) to suppose that we can explore the limits of our obligations to other people with a student who has never heard that anyone else has rights. Ways of seeing the world in which murder, theft, and needless suffering are salient should be part of what early education conveys. The best way of conveying them is by instilling central moral norms.

This is to begin to instill sensitivity to those features of actions that constitute violations of central moral norms. Early education should promote sensitivity of a more general sort: to the feelings—especially the sufferings—of others. This prepares the way for two kinds of reflection that become important at later stages of moral education. One is on the reasons why violations of central moral norms are, indeed, wrong. The sufferings of victims play an important part on any plausible explanation of this. The other kind of reflection is that which is appropriate in difficult cases. When it is not clear that established moral rules interpreted in a straightforward way give us the best answer to the problem at hand, we must be prepared to give due weight to all relevant factors. There is no mechanical substitute for sensitivity in this; there is no routine of picking out salient elements that is guaranteed to work in the absence of our being struck by them or their registering on us in a way that moves us toward taking them seriously. Not all relevant factors will concern suffering or for that matter happiness or joy; the discussion in chapter 6 has indicated the complexity of values that may have to be considered. But insensitivity to suffering is a leading cause of immoral choice. Also, it can be argued, if a student is to become sensitive to others' lives, the easiest thing to become aware of and to empathize with is suffering. It is an easy first step in the education of sympathetic sensibility.

Thusfar I have pointed to two essential elementary steps in the education of character: instilling central moral norms and promoting sensitivity to the feelings—especially the suffering—of others. A third essential step is to begin to familiarize students with the ways in which a life, such as the student's own, is unified through time. It should be said that this, like the previous two suggestions, is hardly novel and, indeed, corresponds to traditional informal instruction in the early years. It has been commonplace to ask a girl or a boy, "What do you want to be when you grow up?" just as it has been commonplace to point out how miserable Jack looks after he has been knocked down ("And how would you feel?") and to tell students that they must not steal. A look at the lives of older students, though, suggests that there may be more failure nowadays in the integration-of-life dimension of education of character than in the other dimensions. A series of looks at how a student's choices may affect her or his life next month or next year rather than merely at some mythic time twenty or thirty years hence can promote integration of character. So, also, can instilling a sense of how many projects and pursuits are, so to speak, long hauls. This would help to counteract the charm of the persuasive image in popular culture of easy victories, of quick fixes, and of magical combinations of circumstances that enable unprepared people to win what they want. That this popular image is related to moral choice is suggested by the finding of Mischel and Gilligan (1964) that when subjects were offered a choice between a small immediate reward and a delayed larger one, those who chose the latter were significantly less likely to cheat. Moral education should dampen expectations of quick and assured successes. In connection with this, even very young children should be given a sense of the possible dignity of failure and enabled to realize that failure is often not final—often it is merely a difficult stage in a long process of achievement.

This can be strengthened at the second stage of moral education by a closer look at life structures. Biographies and novels are ideal vehicles for this aspect of the education of character. The popularity of Plutarch's *Lives* in an earlier era is a good indication that this recommendation, too, is not novel. It would be too much to suggest that, in all of this, the aim is to develop in students what Miguel de Unamuno (1913) called "the tragic sense of life." But it is important for students to realize that not all stories have happy endings, that when they do have happy endings these are often either flawed or greatly delayed from the point of view of the participants, and that what are often taken to be happy endings (e.g., a competitive or career success or a wedding) normally are not endings at all, but lead on to further successes and failures that may well be based on what went before. It is especially important, against the grain of popular culture, to promote a sense of the texture and detail of the lives that ensue from certain kinds of choice. The examples need not be remote: Attention to what comes two years, five years, and ten years after teenage pregnancy may have a beneficial impact on some students.

My suggestion here can be summed up by saying that in the second stage of education of character, students should be exposed to longitudinal close looks at the reality of human lives, including lives like theirs. This can be accomplished in the study of literature and history and does not require any special units of moral education; indeed, if literature and history are treated as containing some depth and reality rather than in terms of plot summaries and names and dates, moral education would be an inescapable part of what they convey. To suppose that moral education must be conducted as a totally separate enterprise from the rest of education would be to trivialize moral education, making it seem like a matter of taste or of arcane intuitions.

Indeed, there are ways in which any field in a student's education, taught and evaluated properly, can contribute to education of character. The account of character developed in this book leads to the view that character requires connections through time and that part of what good character requires is the ability to take on and maintain responsibility. There are a number of ways in which good education, even in scientific subjects and, indeed, even physical education, can strengthen this process. Any experience that a student has of disciplining herself or himself over a period of time in order to reach a difficult goal contributes to strengthening of character. A prime motivating force in strengthening character is a student's pride, or anticipated pride, in accomplishment; this, in turn, requires that what is accomplished not be too easy or too quick but require genuine, sustained effort. There has to be a real possibility of failure for success to be meaningful. A great many teachers who care about their students try, because they care, to protect them from failure. One can applaud the roots of this impulse and still believe that it does the great majority of students no favor. It is true that any careful teacher will structure challenges so that every student can attain some ultimate success, but this does not mean that success should be easy or that there cannot be failure on the way to success. It is also important that success, when it is genuine and hard-won, be adequately recognized. In many American schools, the only way a girl or boy can gain respect is by being a good athlete (athletics being the one area of school life in which no one worries about elitism) or by being viewed by other students as an amusing goof-off. This can be especially demoralizing for bright students, and the damage to them can be more than academic: Without respect, it is difficult to maintain pride, and without pride of accomplishment, there is likely to be inadequate development of character.

This is merely to suggest some ways in which good education at the secondary level, even if it is not directed specifically toward education of character, does further character development, and in which mediocre education retards character development. What about programs that are specifically oriented toward character development? Two things are possible (at least for some groups of students) at the secondary level that would be overambitious for very young children. One is an exploration of explanations for the rules at the core of morality that were instilled in the first stage. The other is examination of difficult cases that are not readily solved by such rules and of controversial areas of morality.

There are two extremes to be avoided in such discussions. One is that of dogmatism or of the excessive influence of students by their teachers. I defended dogmatism at the first stage of moral instruction, both because of the social importance of the core of morality and because this core represents what can be termed established knowledge, about which by and large reasonable people do not disagree. Also, there is no reasonable alternative way of beginning the moral education of very young children. Students at the second stage of instruction, though, can be presumed to have grasped the starting points and to be more capable of reflective analysis. Dogmatism seems inappropriate in teaching them. Any attempt to influence their views of difficult cases or controversial areas of morality might well backfire; in any case, it undermines the ultimate project of educating them to think for themselves about moral questions.

The other extreme to be avoided is that of automatic deference to feelings and first reactions. Here, as elsewhere in education, one must guard against turning out students who are great experts on what they feel but know little about critical thinking or about the world. It is possible, without destroying their self-confidence or inhibiting their willingness to express views, to press students to think further and to justify or revise their first responses. A teacher who keeps her or his own views largely or entirely out of play can do this without its becoming an adversarial proceeding. This is an important part of educating students to think about morality.

One striking feature of philosophical ethics is the greater degree of

congruence in basic moral recommendations than in theoretical explanations. Advocates of highly divergent theories are nearly unanimous in
holding that we can derive from the correct theory claims that torture,
rape, murder, and theft are wrong. There is some analogy with the way in
which controversies among scientists are much less likely to concern
whether certain familiar, everyday phenomena occur than the interpretation of these phenomena or whether certain not-at-all-familiar phenomena occur. Thus, there is more than one story to be told about why murder
or the infliction of needless suffering is wrong: One can focus on general
principles in the light of the golden rule, the basic rights of individuals, or
the undesirability of suffering and the desirability of various states of
being and perhaps of life itself. We need not assume that if one of these
stories is true, there can be no truth in any of the others. The best ethical
theory might include, as secondary structures within itself, what look
like rival theories. In any event, it would be best if students look at more
than one explanation and are led to see that more than one has some force
and plausibility. This will prepare them better to be able to entertain
multiple perspectives on the same problem or phenomenon, which for
reasons shortly to be explained is a goal of advanced education of
character.

Practical considerations are bound to influence the choice of which
controversial moral questions are discussed. The issue of abortion may be
far more touchy than that of capital punishment or of what (if anything)
constitutes a just war. One reason for thinking it important that students at
the second stage take up *some* controversial moral question is this. Any
subject, including morality, runs the risk of seeming dull if it looks as if
all questions are settled. Such a perception heightens a student's sense of
passivity, of being a receptacle into which knowledge is supposed to be
poured. Passive students easily become passive citizens who lack critical
skills of thinking for themselves. The alternative should not be seen as
that of turning out active, emotive, and opinionated citizens who lack
critical skills of thinking beyond their first responses. Students are likely
to have strong views on some controversial moral questions; they have a
right to these views and should not be discouraged from expressing them,
but this is compatible with getting them to see that first responses are not
necessarily the best responses, that any response has points of vulnerability, and that critical reflection sometimes can lead to a more
tenable position. The central point is that it can be both true with regard to
a particular moral issue that there is no answer on which all reasonable

people must agree and also false that any opinion (however unconsidered) is as good as any other.

Something like this is the key realization in William Perry's (1970) scheme of an advanced stage of intellectual and ethical development. One needs to insert a qualification: However much enlightened historians or moralists may disagree on certain (usually rather complicated) issues, there is an answer on which all reasonable people must agree to such questions as "What was the date of Columbus's first voyage?" or "Is torture generally wrong?" Nevertheless, someone who has strong moral views about, say, abortion or capital punishment, must recognize that there are people on the other side who are neither fools, depraved, or careless thinkers. This does not mean that one cannot claim to have the correct answer, but one cannot claim to have a luminously correct answer.

Why is it important that an advanced stage of education of character convey the sense that there are multiple perspectives that reasonable people can bring to bear on moral questions? There are, of course, social and political advantages in pluralistic societies in promoting a degree of tolerance and understanding of opposed viewpoints. Such tolerance and understanding will create the possibility of patient political discourse as well as reduce the risks of factionalism. These are, however, extrinsic advantages of introducing multiple perspectives into education of character. The intrinsic advantage is as follows. As I have already pointed out, a genuinely good character must be strong, especially in being resistant to temptations and pressures. (This is one reason why responses to questionnaires are not good indicators of character.) My argument now is that this strength is promoted by exposure to multiple perspectives and by being able to think critically about them.

In order to see this, we need to move away from a view of character that is simple, plausible, and fundamentally wrong. This view is based on two important truths: Much about us has been formed by the time we are adolescents (and, indeed, cannot be changed by us at will) and our moral conduct normally is heavily determined by our habits and temperament. Given these truths, one might readily conclude that character is very largely a matter of habits and temperament; that it is almost entirely determined by the time someone reaches adolescence (or, at the latest, by the time someone reaches higher education); and that what I have analyzed as the first stage of education of character is the only one that matters. These conclusions, though, are all grossly oversimple.

We can see through this view only when we realize that a normal pattern of correct moral choice need not amount to genuine good character. People who have good habits and weak character may well behave badly in unusual situations to which their habits are not readily applicable or when they are tempted or pressed in unusual ways. One can come to this realization by reading the Myth of Er in Plato's *Republic*, Hannah Arendt's *Eichmann in Jerusalem* (1963), or Stanley Milgram. If someone who has been a pillar of the community is offered a chance to indulge in highly prestigious acts of tyranny or is pressed to administer highly painful (and possibly lethal) electric shocks in a psychological experiment, we regard these as very good tests of character. If the pillar of the community fails the test, we are inclined strongly to doubt that he or she had been genuinely virtuous. This suggests that there is much more to genuinely good character than merely good habits and an engaging temperament. Indeed, as Plato remarks about the man who chooses to become a tyrant, "His virtue was a matter of habit only, and he had no philosophy" (*Republic*, st. 619, vol. 1, p. 877). The aspects of character that are developed or modified during adolescence or later may not play an obvious and dramatic part in everyday life, but they are important.

How do we guard against poor moral choices brought on by great temptation or pressure, by disorientation in an unusual situation, or by the way in which someone who would like to do the socially right thing is swept along by the expectations of others? There is, of course, no infallible system of moral instruction. But this does not mean that some systems are not worse than others. Someone whose moral education ended with the first stage, who has absorbed traditional moral rules and rudiments of sensitivity, is usually in a poor position to resist temptation or pressure. The question "Why should I follow these moral rules?" naturally suggests itself, and the person who has "habits but not philosophy" may not think of a good answer. The risk is intensified if the question arises in the midst of changed circumstances. It may seem that the morality one learned as a child was appropriate for what then seemed the normal world, before the X political party established a dictatorship or before one began to make decisions in the world of high finance: That was then, and this is now. It is, in part, because of such limitations that Confucius remarks, "The 'honest villager' spoils true virtue" (XVII.13, p. 213).

Some investigation of why the core of traditional morality makes sense can help to innoculate students against this moral collapse. This investigation can begin at a secondary level, but it is best pursued in a university-level study of ethical theory. More fundamentally, though, a student who has a strong sense of self accompanied by a willingness to take responsibility for her or his actions is less vulnerable to moral collapse, especially if the student has a highly articulated sense of the values that are important to her or his life. As Gabriele Taylor points out in her study of integrity, "A person can have self-respect, or a sense of her own value, only if she believes some form of life is worth living, and believes that by and large she is capable of leading such a life" (1985, p. 131). Students should be led, both at the second and third stages of moral education, to ask themselves what the most important values available to them are. Their thinking should go beyond a set of first responses: For example, if money and prestige are what is desired, the texture of the life made possible by money and prestige should be explored, their relationship to such larger goals as happiness should be queried, and the possible role of factors other than money and prestige should also be examined.

None of these educational strategies offer assured protection to the student who is weak-minded in the sense of having other people's expectations and interpretations easily overwhelm his or her own. A student who is used to dealing with, and perhaps arguing against, other perspectives may be better prepared not to be overwhelmed; in this way, the higher developmental stages in the scheme of William G. Perry, Jr., correspond to strengthening of character. Traditional liberal education, thus, has a moral value. As Edmund Pellegrino puts it, "The liberal arts are those that make a man free from capture by other men's opinions, judgments, and values—the arts that free us from mindless conviction and groundless beliefs, that enable us to locate ourselves in relationship to the most important issues in life" (1981, p. 3).

Another way of preparing students for challenges to their character is the strategy of preparing them, as far as possible, for the specific kinds of cases in which these challenges are likely to arise. This is part of what is accomplished by applied ethics courses in relation to business, engineering, law, or medicine. The business person or doctor may often have to make decisions in what qualify as difficult cases (gray areas) in relation to the core of traditional morality and sometimes may be under pressure to break rules under circumstances that are so different from ordinary life that it may be difficult to remember that the rules apply. In both kinds of case, it is highly useful to know in advance what one is getting into. This can counteract the tendency of disorientation to put people at their worst.

Someone who knows how to think within multiple perspectives but has a strong sense of her or his own values and is prepared for the most likely sorts of unusual case that will present moral challenges will be better able to function as a sophisticated moral agent of strong character. To be such a person, in the modern world, is like being an experienced traveler. One will be able to appreciate and not be put off balance by unusual situations or new perspectives without surrendering one's integrity.

All of this must be taken as a sketchy and a partial treatment of education of character. There is no reason to suppose that the third stage represents the end of education. Some challenges to character are likely to arise only for adult graduates, and people learn from, and strengthen their characters in response to, such challenges. Adult life also typically centers on commitments of various kinds that are freely entered into. These usually demand increased sensitivity to the needs of others (such as co-workers, marriage partners, and children), and they also typically demand compromises which can range from the highly reasonable to the highly unreasonable. These can provide much of the subject matter for another stage of moral education, as can a growing awareness of how one's behavior and frame of mind can be affected by different circumstances. My concern in this appendix, however, has been with education of character within the traditional structures of education, which center on interaction between teachers and students. In some sense, all education of character, if it is at all effective, is self-education. But I will not attempt to deal here with the self-education that should continue throughout adult life.

BIBLIOGRAPHY

Arendt, Hannah (1958). *The Human Condition*. Chicago: University of Chicago Press.

———— (1963). *Eichmann in Jerusalem*. New York: Viking Press.

Argyle, Michael (1987). *The Psychology of Happiness*. London: Methuen.

Argyle, Michael, Adrian Furnham, and Jean Ann Graham (1981). *Social Situations*. Cambridge: Cambridge University Press.

Aristotle (fourth century B.C./1962). *Nicomachean Ethics*. Trans. Martin Ostwald. Indianapolis: Bobbs-Merrill.

Austin, J. L. (1958). "Pretending." *Proceedings of the Aristotelian Society* (*supp.*) 32: 261–78.

Baier, Annette (1979). "Hume on Heaps and Bundles." *American Philosophical Quarterly* 16: 285–95.

Bennett, Jonathan (1974). "The Conscience of Huckleberry Finn." *Philosophy* 49: 123–34.

Brim, Orville G., Jr., and Jerome Kagan (1980). *Constancy and Change in Human Development*. Cambridge, Mass: Harvard University Press.

Brown, Roger (1986). *Social Psychology*. 2nd ed. New York: Free Press.

Camus, Albert (1942/1955). *The Myth of Sisyphus*. Trans. Justin O'Brien. New York: Random House, Vintage Books.

Cantor, Nancy (1990). "From Thought to Behavior: 'Having' and 'Doing' in the Study of Personality and Cognition." *American Psychologist* 45: 735–50.

Chisholm, Roderick (1976). *Person and Object*. London: Allen & Unwin.

Confucius (ca. 500 B.C./1938). *The Analects*. Trans. Arthur Waley. New York: Random House, Vintage Books.

Csikszentmihalyi, Mihaly (1990). *Flow*. New York: Harper & Row.

Dennett, Daniel (1985). *Elbow Room: The Varieties of Free Will Worth Wanting*. Cambridge, Mass.: MIT Press.

DePalma, David J., and Jeanne M. Foley (1975). *Moral Development: Current Theory and Research*. Hillsdale, N.J.: Earlbaum.

Doctrine of the Mean (third or second century B.C./1870). In *The Chinese Classics*. Vol. 1. Trans. James Legge. New York: Hurst.

Donagan, Alan (1977). *The Theory of Morality*. Chicago: University of Chicago Press.

Drake, Robert E., and George E. Vaillant (1988). "Introduction: Longitudinal Views of Personality Disorder." *Journal of Personality Disorders* 2: 44–48.

Erikson, Erik (1968). *Identity, Youth, and Crisis*. New York: Norton.

Fingarette, Herbert (1988). *Heavy Drinking: The Myth of Alcoholism as a Disease*. Berkeley and Los Angeles: University of California Press.

Foot, Philippa (1978). *Virtues and Vices*. Berkeley and Los Angeles: University of California Press.

Frankfurt, Harry (1976). "Identification and Externality." In Amelie Rorty, *The Identities of Persons*. Berkeley and Los Angeles: University of California Press.

——— (1987). "Identification and Wholeheartedness." In *Responsibility, Character, and the Emotions*, ed. Ferdinand Schoeman. Cambridge: Cambridge University Press.

Funder, David S. (1983). "The 'Consistency' Controversy and the Accuracy of Personality Judgments." *Journal of Personality* 51: 346–59.

Gergen, Kenneth J. (1982). *Toward Transformation in Social Knowledge*. New York: Springer-Verlag.

Glover, Jonathan (1988). *I. The Philosophy and Psychology of Personal Identity*. London: Allen Lane.

Goldsmith, H. Hill, et al. (1987). "Roundtable: What Is Temperament? Four Approaches." *Child Development* 58: 505–29.

Griffin, James (1986). *Well-Being*. Oxford: Clarendon Press.

Halfron, Mark S. (1989). *Integrity*. Philadelphia: Temple University Press.

Hare, R. M. (1963). *Freedom and Reason*. Oxford: Clarendon Press.

——— (1964). "The Promising Game." *Revue internationale de philosophie* 70: 398–412.

——— (1976). "Ethical Theory and Utilitarianism." In *Contemporary British Philosophy*, 4 ser., ed. H. D. Lewis. London: Allen & Unwin.

——— (1981). *Moral Thinking*. Oxford: Clarendon Press.

Harman, Gilbert (1975). "Moral Relativism Defended." *Philosophical Review* 84: 3–22.

Hartshorne, Hugh, M. A. May, and F. K. Shuttleworth (1930). *Studies in the Organization of Character*. New York: Macmillan.

Held, Virginia (1984). *Rights and Goods*. New York: Free Press.

Herman, Barbara (1985). "The Practice of Moral Judgment." *Journal of Philosophy* 82: 414–36.

Higgins, E. Tory (1987). "Self-Discrepancy Theory." *Psychological Review* 94: 319–40.

Hume, David (1739/1978). *A Treatise of Human Nature*. 2nd ed. Ed. L. A. Selby-Bigge, rev. P. H. Nidditch. Oxford: Clarendon Press.

————— (1742). "The Sceptic." In *Essays,* ed. Eugene Miller. Indianapolis: Liberty Fund, Liberty Classics.

Hunt, Lester H. (1987). "Generosity and the Diversity of Virtues." In *The Virtues,* ed. Robert B. Kruschwitz and Robert C. Roberts. Belmont, Calif.: Wadsworth.

Jacobs, Jonathan A. (1989). *Virtue and Self-Knowledge.* Englewood Cliffs, N.J.: Prentice-Hall.

Kant, Immanuel (1781/1985). *Critique of Pure Reason.* Trans. Norman Kemp Smith. New York: St. Martin's Press.

————— (1785/1959). *Foundations of the Metaphysics of Morals.* Trans. Lewis White Beck. Indianapolis: Bobbs-Merrill.

————— (1788/1898). *Critique of Practical Reason.* Trans. Thomas Abbott. London: Longmans, Green.

————— (1797/1964). *Metaphysical Principles of Virtue.* Trans. James Ellington. Indianapolis: Bobbs-Merrill.

Kekes, John (1990). *Facing Evil.* Princeton, N.J.: Princeton University Press.

Kierkegaard, Søren (1846/1960). *Concluding Unscientific Postscript.* Trans. David F. Swenson and Walter Lowrie. Princeton, N.J.: Princeton University Press.

————— (1849/1968). *The Sickness Unto Death.* Trans. Walter Lowrie. Princeton, N.J.: Princeton University Press.

Kohlberg, Lawrence (1981). *The Philosophy of Moral Development: Moral Stages and the Idea of Justice.* San Francisco: Harper & Row.

Kohut, Heinz (1977). *The Restoration of Self.* New York: International Universities Press.

Kovesi, Julius (1967). *Moral Notions.* London: Routledge & Kegan Paul.

Kupperman, Joel (1983). *The Foundations of Morality.* London: Allen & Unwin.

————— (1984–1985). "Character and Self-Knowledge." *Proceedings of the Aristotelian Society* 85: 219–38.

————— (1988). "Character and Ethical Theory." *Midwest Studies in Philosophy* 13: 115–25.

La Rochefoucauld, François, duc de (1665/1959). *Maxims.* Trans. L. W. Tancock. Baltimore: Penguin Books.

Locke, John (1690/1841). *An Essay Concerning Human Understanding.* 29th ed. London: Thomas Tegg.

Lomasky, Loren (1987). *Persons, Rights, and the Moral Community.* New York: Oxford University Press.

McDowell, John (1979). "Virtue and Reason." *Monist* 62: 331–50.

————— (1985). "Values and Secondary Qualities." In *Morality and Objectivity,* ed. Ted Honderich. London: Routledge & Kegan Paul.

MacIntyre, Alasdair (1978). *After Virtue.* Notre Dame. Ind.: University of Notre Dame Press.

———— (1988). *Whose Justice? Which Rationality?* London: Duckworth.

Madell, Geoffrey (1981). *The Identity of the Self.* Edinburgh: Edinburgh University Press.

Malcolm, Norman (1958). *Ludwig Wittgenstein: A Memoir.* London: Oxford University Press.

Meyers, Diana (1987). "Personal Autonomy and the Paradox of Feminine Socialization." *Journal of Philosophy* 84: 619–28.

Milgram, Stanley (1974). *Obedience to Authority.* London: Tavistock.

Mill, John Stuart (1838/1962). "Bentham." In *Utilitarianism,* ed. Mary Warnock. New York: New American Library.

———— (1859/1978). *On Liberty.* Ed. Elizabeth Rapaport. Indianapolis: Hackett Books.

———— (1861/1979). *Utilitarianism.* Ed. George Sher. Indianapolis: Hackett Books.

Mischel, W., and Carol Gilligan (1964). "Delay of Gratification. Motivation for the Prohibited Gratification, and Response to Temptation." *Journal of Abnormal and Social Psychology* 69: 411–17.

Moore, G. E. (1903). *Principia Ethica.* Cambridge: Cambridge University Press.

Nakone, Chie (1970). *Japanese Society.* Berkeley and Los Angeles: University of California Press.

Nishida, Kitaro (1911/1990). *An Inquiry into the Good.* Trans. Masao Abe and Christopher Ives. New Haven, Conn.: Yale University Press.

Newman, Ira (1984). "Fiction and Discovery." Ph.D. diss., University of Connecticut.

Nietzsche, Friedrich (1883–1891/1978). *Thus Spake Zarathustra.* Trans. Walter Kaufmann. New York: Penguin Books.

———— (1886/1966). *Beyond Good and Evil.* Trans. Walter Kaufmann. New York: Random House, Vintage Books.

Norton, David L. (1976). *Personal Destinies.* Princeton, N.J.: Princeton University Press.

O'Flaherty, Wendy (1980). *Karma and Rebirth in Classical Indian Traditions.* Berkeley and Los Angeles: University of California Press.

Parfit, Derek (1984). *Reasons and Persons.* Oxford: Clarendon Press.

Paton, H. J. (1953–1954). "An Alleged Right to Lie, a Problem in Kantian Ethics." *Kant Studien* 45: 190–203.

Pellegrino, Edmund (1981). "The Clinical Arts and the Art of the Word." *The Pharos of Alpha Omega Alpha* 44: 2–8.

Perry, John (1975). *Personal Identity.* Berkeley and Los Angeles: University of California Press.

Perry, William G., Jr. (1970). *Forms of Intellectual and Ethical Development in the College Years: A Scheme.* New York: Holt, Rinehart and Winston.

Pincoffs, Edmund L. (1986). *Quandaries and Virtues*. Lawrence: University Press of Kansas.

Plato (fourth century B.C./1937). *Philebus*. Trans. Benjamin Jowett. New York: Random House.

———— (1937). *Republic*. Trans. Benjamin Jowett. New York: Random House.

The Questions of King Milinda. (1963). Trans. T. W. Rhys Davids. New York: Dover Books.

Quinton, Anthony (1982). *Thoughts and Thinkers*. New York: Holmes & Meier.

Rawls, John (1971). *A Theory of Justice*. Cambridge, Mass.: Harvard University Press.

———— (1988). "The Priority of Right and Ideas of the Good." *Philosophy and Public Affairs* 17: 251–76.

Rorty, Amelie (1976). *The Identities of Persons*. Berkeley and Los Angeles: University of California Press.

Rorty, Amelie, and David Wong (forthcoming). "Aspects of Identity and Agency." In *Identity, Character and Morality*, ed. Amelie Rorty and Owen Flanagan. Cambridge, Mass: MIT Press.

Rushton, J. Philippe (1982). "Altruism and Society: A Social Learning Perspective." *Ethics* 92: 425–46.

Ryle, Gilbert (1949). *The Concept of Mind*. New York: Barnes & Noble.

Sankara (n.d.) *The Vedanta Sutras of Badarayana with Commentary by Sankara*. Vol. 1. Trans. G. Thibaut. New York: Dover Books.

Sartre, Jean-Paul (1943). *Being and Nothingness*. Trans. Hazel Barnes. New York: Philosophical Library.

———— (1946/1955). "Existentialism Is a Humanism." In *The Age of Analysis*, ed. Morton White. New York: New American Library, Mentor Books.

Sherman, Nancy (1985). "Character, Planning, and Choice in Aristotle." *Review of Metaphysics* 39: 83–106.

———— (1989). *The Fabric of Character: Aristotle's Theory of Virtue*. Oxford: Clarendon Press.

Shoemaker, Sydney (1975). "Personal Identity and Memory." In John Perry, *Personal Identity*. Berkeley and Los Angeles: University of California Press.

Smart, J. J. C., and Bernard Williams (1973). *Utilitarianism For and Against*. Cambridge: Cambridge University Press.

Snyder, Mark (1983). "The Influence of Individuals on Situations: Implications for Understanding the Links Between Personality and Social Behavior." *Journal of Personality* 51: 497–516.

Sommers, Christina Hoff (1986). "Filial Morality." *Journal of Philosophy* 83: 439–56.

Stewart, Abigail J., Carol Franz, and Lynne Layton (1988). "The Changing Self:

Using Personal Documents to Study Lives." *Journal of Personality* 56: 41–74.

Stitsworth, Michael H. (1989). "Personality Changes Associated with a Sojourn in Japan." *Journal of Social Psychology* 129: 213–24.

Strawson, P. F. (1961). "Social Morality and Individual Ideals." *Philosophy* 36: 1–17.

Taylor, Charles (1976). "Responsibility for Self." In Amelie Rorty, *The Identities of Persons*. Berkeley and Los Angeles: University of California Press.

Taylor, Gabriele (1985). *Pride, Shame, and Guilt: Emotions of Self-Assessment.* Oxford: Clarendon Press.

Unamuno, Miguel de (1913/1962). *The Tragic Sense of Life*. London: Fontana Books.

The Upanishads (1971). Trans. J. Mascaro. Harmondsworth, Eng.: Penguin Books.

Waley, Arthur (1950). *The Poetry and Career of Li Po*. London: Allen & Unwin.

Walker, A. D. M. (1989). "Virtue and Character." *Philosophy* 64: 349–62.

Wallace, James D. (1978). *Virtues and Vices*. Ithaca, N.Y.: Cornell University Press.

——— (1988). *Moral Relevance and Moral Conflict*. Ithaca, N.Y.: Cornell University Press.

Warner, Richard (1987). *Freedom, Enjoyment, and Happiness*. Ithaca, N.Y.: Cornell University Press.

Waterman, Alan S. (1988). "On the Use of Psychological Theory and Research in the Process of Ethical Inquiry." *Psychological Bulletin* 103: 283–98.

West, Stephen G., and William G. Graziano (1989). "Long-Term Stability and Change in Personality: An Introduction." *Journal of Personality* 57: 175–93.

Williams, Bernard (1976). "Persons, Character and Morality." In Amelie Rorty, *The Identities of Persons*. Berkeley and Los Angeles: University of California Press.

——— (1985). *Ethics and the Limits of Philosophy*. London: Fontana Books.

Yuchtman-Yaar, Ephraim, and Gloria Rahav (1986). "Resisting Small Temptations in Everyday Transactions." *Journal of Social Psychology* 126: 23–30.

Zimbardo, Philip G. (1973). "On the Ethics of Intervention in Human Psychological Research: With Special Reference to the Stanford Prison Experiment." *Cognition* 2: 243–56.

INDEX

191